Canadian Boundaries

CANADIAN BOUNDARIES

The Foreign Treaties And Other Instruments That Defined Our Realm

Peter W Noonan

MAGISTRALIS

Ottawa, Canada

Cataloguing in Publication Data for this book can be obtained from:

Library and Archives Canada
395 Wellington Street
Ottawa, ON K1A 0N4
CANADA

ISBN 978-0-9683534-5-5 (hardback).

Published by Magistralis, Ottawa, Canada

DEDICATION

For Vilayvanh

Contents

DETAILED TABLE OF CONTENTS

THE SOUTHERN BOUNDARY 1763-1871 — Page 87

INTRODUCTION

A vintage aphorism states that good fences make good neighbours. The same may be said about adjacent countries – good borders make good neighbours.[1] That, at least, has been the historical experience of Canada over the last two centuries. But the existence of friendly relations with our neighbouring countries has not been fortuitous. The need to establish firm and acceptable boundaries took a great deal of diplomatic imagination over the course of Canadian history, and there were times when border disputes threatened the maintenance of peaceful relations. One academic observer has remarked: "Basically, disputes over territory are human problems. Boundaries derive their significance primarily from the fact that they divide people, not because they divide land."[2] On the whole however, the creation of Canada within the framework of international law occurred largely through diplomacy rather than war. This book seeks to survey the diplomatic history that led us to the present day international boundaries of Canada.

The focus of the following chapters is on the development of Canada's boundaries within the framework of international law and the community of nations. Much of that development occurred during the colonial era, with boundaries that were initially vague or undetermined, and which only gradually became fixed as exploration yielded new information about the vast territories that today make up the modern Canadian state. Canadians had little influence over the decisions taken in the far-off capitals of Europe during what became the formative years of the Canadian territorial entity. In fact it was not until the negotiation of the Treaty of Washington in 1870-71 that a senior Canadian political figure, in the form of Prime Minister Sir John A. Macdonald, was actually included in an imperial delegation that negotiated North American issues. Hence the bulk of diplomatic efforts that led to modern Canada as we now know it took place during the colonial period by decision-makers in the far-off capitals of Europe, and by their diplomatic representatives.

The formation of international borders is an element of a larger process of establishing the territorial authority of a state that marries two concepts, the legal concept of sovereignty, and the geographical concept of territory. Boundaries require the existence of multiple state entities. The concept of a fixed external border was essentially unknown to the Roman Empire, although vague external boundaries existed in the empire in the form of marshlands, or boundary zones.[3] It took the development of the community of multiple sovereign states to create a requirement for fixed boundaries between them.

Sovereignty is an essential legal concept within this process. Legal philosophers have given us expansive descriptions of what sovereignty entails. Professor John Austin, a legal philosopher whose work on legal positivism was particularly influential in the field of jurisprudence in the nineteenth and early twentieth centuries, when Canada's boundaries were being fixed, said this about the locus of sovereignty in a society:

> In order that a given society may form a society political and independent, . . . two distinguishing marks . . . must unite. The generality of the given society must be in the habit of obedience to a determinate and common superior: whilst that determinate person, or determinate body of persons must not be habitually obedient to a determinate person or body. It is the union of that positive, with this negative mark, which renders that certain superior sovereign or supreme, and which renders that given society (including that certain superior) a society political and independent.[4]

The existence of this legal entity, a supreme authority, within a defined geographical area gives rise to a sovereign political entity. Why is that important? It is important because the framework of international law since the end of the Thirty Years War in Europe in 1648 requires the recognition of the existence of separate states that possess exclusive supremacy over their own territories, and whose borders should not be interfered with by any other state. Although the treaties that established the Peace of Westphalia, at the conclusion of the Thirty Years War, did not actually articulate these principles they developed within international law in the aftermath of the Westphalian treaties, and so we refer to this seminal event as the creation of the Westphalian Order, which has governed the relations between independent states from that time to the present.

The effect of the Westphalian Order has been to establish the state as the principal actor in international law, and to legitimize the state as the only acceptable interlocutor in international relations. Canada's admission to the international community of states occurred through an evolutionary process between the time that Canada separately signed the Treaty of Versailles in 1919, ending hostilities with Germany, and the enactment of the Statute of Westminster, 1931, by the Imperial Parliament. However, a separate status for what were then called British dominions was conceded by Great Britain as early as the Imperial Conference in 1926, and was further elaborated upon at the Commonwealth Conference in 1930. The Statute of Westminster, 1931, gave formal *de jure* validity to an evolutionary process and since the passage of that statute Canada has exercised all of the rights and privileges of a sovereign state within the framework of international law.

In the context of international treaties relating to territorial sovereignty, we can identify three main diplomatic periods. In the first period, which might be called the Age of Exploration and Conquest, extending from the reigns of Isabel of Castile and Ferdinand of Aragon to the conclusion, in 1763, of the Seven Years War, monarchs generally enjoyed absolute power within their domains, or at least the widest possible ambit of personal discretion. During this period the state, and all of its property, was constituted as a personal possession of the monarchs. Countries, and the populations that were under the control of a particular monarch, were often traded in treaties of peace as if they were mere chattels. This phenomenon was particularly acute in Europe but North America was not immune, and some territories (e.g., Nova Scotia, Cape Breton Island, Florida, and the Louisiana Territory) were traded several times between monarchs without any consideration for the views of the people that lived in those territories. Toward the end of this period however, the position of monarchs began giving way to the concept of the nation-state as the Westphalian Order rose to prominence in international relations.

The second era in diplomatic relations we may call the Age of the Nation-State and it began around the end of the Seven Years War and encompassed the historical periods of the Age of Enlightenment, the Industrial Revolution, and the Modern Era up to the creation of the United Nations in 1946. During that period the Westphalian conception of the state as a national entity, rather than merely an emanation of a monarch, fully flowered and the state became the dominant actor within international law regardless of the outward form of the government possessed by each state. The trading of countries and peoples fell into disfavour and much more credence was given to the wishes of the inhabitants of a territory, at least with respect to those populations that were identified as meeting the norms of European civilization (it was another story altogether for the indigenous inhabitants of territories that were colonized by Europe). The concept of a state as a defined territory that embodied the common language, culture, religion, and an integrated economy for a particular area gained ground and became predominant in the concept of international relations.

The third era of diplomatic relations began with the founding of the United Nations in 1946, and can perhaps best be described as the Multilateral Era. It has been characterized by multi-state approaches to international problems. In this era, large multilateral treaty regimes have been established for the management of the common property of mankind, such as the oceans, the seabeds, international airspace, and the outer space adjacent to Earth. Additionally, there has also been the creation of new transnational structures reflecting a pooling of national sovereignty, such as the creation of the European Community and structures to regulate the world-wide economy.

Recently, there has been growing criticism of the Westphalian Order. Some critics have suggested that the state is of diminishing importance in international relations. The renewed importance of human rights within the community of nations, and the economic linkages created by globalization, have served to reduce the over-riding emphasis on the state in international law. There have also been some attempts to focus on people rather than states as subjects of international law. A concept described as the Responsibility to Protect has been fostered as a means of allowing the community of nations to intervene in the domestic affairs of one of its members where humanitarian violations that are repulsive to the international community are occurring within a state, with the connivance or default of its rulers. An International Criminal Court has been created to bring to justice state leaders who have violated the norms of international conduct. There has been some resistance to such developments however, and it is by no means certain that the trajectory of international law will move substantially away from a focus on the state as the primary subject of international law. Despite some diminution of exclusive state sovereignty in an era of closer economic, political, and social relations, the position of the state as the prime actor in international relations seems secure for some time yet.

Philosophical objections to the Westphalian Order have been largely confined to western countries and the growing economic and political importance of countries in Asia, Latin America, and Africa, all of which have tended to support the Westphalian Order, suggests that the concept of the sovereign state will retain its vitality long into the twentieth-first century, and perhaps beyond. Even some western nations have been reconsidering the degrees to which interdependence and globalization have benefited their societies and in some countries populist and overtly nationalist approaches toward international relations have lately been coming into greater prominence.

I turn now from the international context to the domestic. A word is required about the process of establishing domestic sovereignty within Canada. Although the focus of this book is on Canada as an internationally defined and recognized territorial state within the community of nations there is also a domestic aspect to territorial sovereignty that is important. When the early explorers from Europe first ventured onto Canada's shores our land was not empty. For thousands of years the indigenous population of Canada had inhabited this land, although for the most part not in the settled manner of the peoples of the Old World. They nevertheless occupied the territory of Canada, at least nomadically, and therefore possessed ancient rights associated with it.

During the period in which France ruled Canada little consideration was given to the rights of the aboriginal inhabitants of New France because France did not then recognize the inherent rights of non-Christian peoples to the lands that they occupied. Under the French regime, rights accrued to aboriginal peoples only when they converted to Christianity and sought and obtained the status of a French subject. However, despite the fact that the French regime did not recognize the inherent rights of the indigenous inhabitants the colonial authorities were realistic about their precarious hold on Canadian territory and they sought to maintain peaceful relations with their aboriginal neighbours by entering into alliances with them. After the fall of the French regime in 1760, the British established control over Canada and brought with them from 1763 onward the English conceptions of public law.

Under the British legal structure, the rights of indigenous inhabitants to the lands which they occupied were recognized and the practice of the British authorities was to negotiate and obtain surrenders to the Crown of aboriginal lands from the indigenous inhabitants through the negotiation of treaties. Thus, a system of treaty negotiation was established and that was reinforced by the strictures of the Royal Proclamation of 1763, which prohibited individual British subjects from obtaining transfers of land from the First Nation communities. The surrender of land through the negotiation of treaties with the aboriginal inhabitants of Canada was, and is, an exclusive prerogative of the Crown.

The system of aboriginal treaty negotiation proceeded throughout the British colonial period in the eighteenth and nineteenth centuries and has continued under Canadian jurisdiction following Confederation in 1867 unto the present day. In this, Canada may be distinguished from other states that emerged from the British Empire. In the United States the process of negotiating treaties was continued after independence but subsequent to the American Civil War the process of treaty negotiation was abandoned, and the terms under which Indian lands were taken were made the subject of Executive Orders. In Australia, little consideration was given to the aborigines, the original inhabitants of Australia, whose rights were often overlooked (until recent times) during the process of state formation. In New Zealand the Crown did negotiate a treaty with the Maori Nation but it has only been in the modern era that a significant effort has been made to fully adhere to the spirit and terms of that treaty. Only Canada has consistently maintained the process of negotiating treaties with multiple First Nations as part of its internal development of sovereignty.

Unfortunately, Canada's history with respect to its adherence to those historic treaties with the indigenous population has also left much to be desired, and the effort to right historic wrongs done to First Nations and the aboriginal community in general remains an important policy objective for the Federal Government in the present era. There is much work left to be done in this important area of public policy. Nevertheless, the existence of a treaty with the indigenous peoples, or the lack of one, does not impair in any way the existence or recognition of Canada's sovereign boundaries from the perspective of international law. The process of negotiating treaties with the indigenous nations is a matter of domestic rather than international law. As a consequence, the process of negotiating and implementing internal treaties with indigenous nations falls outside of the scope of this book.

Finally, in quoting from historical treaties, I have taken the liberty in some cases of changing the spelling of some of the words found in the text in order to conform to modern spelling conventions. I have done that where I considered that the modern spelling of a word would render the meaning of the quotation clearer to the reader.

ENDNOTES

[1] I will use the words "borders" and "boundaries" interchangeably in this book, while acknowledging that the correct legal nomenclature in Canada is "international boundaries".

[2] Norman Hill, *Claims to Territory in International Law and Relations,* Oxford University Press, New York, 1945, page 31.

[3] Hill, page 23.

[4] John Austin, Extract from *The Province of Jurisprudence Determined* in Lord Lloyd of Hampstead, *Introduction to Jurisprudence,* Third Edition, London, Stevens & Sons, 1972, at page 221.

1.

TERRITORIAL AND POLITICAL SOVEREIGNTY

Territorial Sovereignty

In the ancient world there was less need of fixed boundaries because transportation and communication were localized, and there was little movement of populations. In Greece, and in the Roman Empire, there were border areas, or border marshes, but no real territorial boundaries as we know them today. The reality of ambiguous boundaries also carried over into the early medieval period.[1] However, as transportation and communications improved over time the establishment of fixed boundaries between politically sovereign communities became necessary in order to manage the movement of people.

During the medieval period the role of Kings predominated and the people of Europe and the geographical territories in which they lived were traded back and forth with little regard for their ethnicity, languages, or the customs of the people concerned. Much was made of property rights, and the rights of inheritance vested in royal families. Marriages between royal families were often contracted with the purpose of bringing new territories under the sway of a particular monarch. Furthermore, since the state and the monarch were one and the same, any conflict that arose over land became a personal dispute between separate monarchs. In the absence of international adjudication claims to territory were usually dealt with by force.

The Age of Exploration and Conquest brought new territories

abroad into the European ambit and at first the mediating influence of the Holy See assisted in managing the conflicts over territory that inevitably arose between European monarchs. In the case of so-called pagan territories the Popes held that they had temporal authority to award the newly discovered lands to various Christian kings.[2] However, some kingdoms were reluctant to recognize papal authority in such matters and the Reformation hastened the decline of papal authority over temporal matters. International law began to flourish and new scholarly authorities such as Hugo Grotius, and Emmerich de Vattel, were critical of the theory of the papacy's temporal authority. In addition, initial conceptions of monarchical ownership of lands in the New World based on a first discovery, and a first claim to new territories, began to give way to the concept of occupation as a necessary corollary to a discovery claim in order to establish the legitimacy of a claim.

A claim to have occupied territory required that the land not be taken by any others, and that it was therefore *terra nullius,* meaning that the land belonged to no one. In order to obtain a valid sovereign title to *terra nullius* it came to be seen that the claimant country had to discover and annex the territory, and then to settle it with people from its own territories.[3] This was not possible where the territory was subject to the recognized sovereignty of another state that was part of the international community.

However, it was possible to occupy territory that was not subject to the sovereignty of a state recognized by the international community even though it was occupied by indigenous peoples who governed themselves under tribal laws. Under British common law, though not under the French common law, the tribal groups that lived in a territory to which a claim of sovereignty was made continued to maintain a claim to the land of that territory which could only be extinguished by a treaty of cession. Nevertheless, the presence of indigenous peoples living within tribal organizations on lands claimed by the British Crown did not negate British sovereignty arising through occupation and settlement vis-a-vis other states within the community of nations.

Occupation was clearly established by the construction of settlements, or forts, on the lands in question. However, lesser forms of occupation eventually came to be accepted in international law to be effective for the purpose of establishing sovereignty. For example, in the Eastern Greenland Case, in 1933, the Permanent Court of International Justice held that Denmark had established its sovereignty over the entire island of Greenland to the exclusion of Norwegian claims in eastern Greenland despite the fact that there were no Danish settlements in the eastern part of the island, and that Danish jurisdiction had essentially been limited to legislative enactments purporting to extend over the entire island. The court held that those Danish actions alone were sufficient to express "an intention and will to exercise such sovereignty and the manifestations of state activity."[4]

Occupation thus became generally accepted in international law as the primary means of effecting a valid claim to *terra nullius,* as the nineteenth and twentieth centuries progressed. It was adopted by the Congress of Berlin (1884-85) in connection with European claims to territory in Africa, and it has subsequently been regarded as a general principle of international law with respect to territorial claims.

Cession is also an important basis of asserting a sovereign claim to territory. In a cession one state will transfer all of its sovereign title, rights, and interests in a defined territory to another state by treaty. A cession can be of various types. There is, firstly, the sale of territory from one state to another. Two good examples within North America are the purchase of the Louisiana Territory by the United States from France in 1803 for approximately 15 million US dollars, and the purchase by the United States of Russian America (Alaska) in 1867 for approximately 7.2 million US dollars.[5]

An exchange of territory also constitutes a cession of territory. An exchange may be used to rationalize the boundary between two states. An example of a North American exchange is the Anglo-American Convention of 1818 in which Great Britain ceded that portion of Rupert's Land lying below the 49th parallel of latitude to the United States in exchange for the cession by the United States of that part of the Louisiana Purchase (Missouri Territory) that lay above the 49th parallel of latitude.

Gifts of territory are a form of cession that occur when one state voluntarily transfers part of its territory to another state. In North America two examples of a transfer by gift are the transfers of Horseshoe Reef from Great Britain (on behalf of Canada) to the United States in 1850, and the transfer from the United States to Canada in 1925 of two-and-one-half acres of US water territory in the Lake of the Woods that were completely surrounded by Canadian waters.

Forced cessions occur when a more powerful state threatens another state, or actually conquers the territory of another state, and insists upon a transfer of territory to the aggressor as one of the conditions of peace. In that way a conquest is transformed into a cession, albeit forced. In Canada's history the prime example of this type of cession is the conquest of New France by Great Britain in 1760. The conquest was effected by the Capitulations signed by the victorious British army commander with Governor General Vaudreuil at Montreal in September 1760, following the defeats suffered by the Franco-Canadian army. Subsequently, the King of France ceded all of Canada and what remained of Acadia to Great Britain by the Treaty of Paris, 1763, thus transforming the British military conquest into a forced cession of French territory.

The conquest of territory is itself a third method of establishing sovereignty. It involves the military subjugation of a territory with the intention of ruling it. The fall of New France to British arms in 1759-60 was an example of sovereignty by conquest. In the Capitulations signed by the Governor General, the Marquis de

Vaudreuil, and the British commander, General Jeffrey Amherst, in 1760, the surrendering French colonial government attempted to secure the right of Canadians to remain neutral in the ongoing conflict between France and Great Britain but the formal document maintained that "They become subjects of the King [of Great Britain]," an acknowledgement of the transfer of sovereignty by conquest.[6] However, where, as in the case of Canada, the conquered territory is later formally ceded to the conqueror by the former Sovereign the conquest is transformed into a transfer of sovereignty by cession, and the acquisition of the territory is subsequently considered to have been acquired by cession.

Modern international law is averse to conquest as a means of obtaining sovereignty over territory and in some recent cases, such as the Iraq-Kuwait war of 1990-91, the international community has intervened through the United Nations to prohibit such a conquest. On other occasions, members of the community of nations have dissuaded a threatened conquest through diplomacy or a show of force.[7]

Another, less common means of asserting a claim to territory is the principle of contiguity or propinquity by which a state that which borders upon *terra nullius*, may claim it on the basis of attraction. This principle has underlain the Sector Principle that was originally articulated by Canadians but subsequently adopted by other polar claimants as a means of asserting sovereignty over land lying principally within the Arctic and Antarctic regions. The Sector Principle asserts sovereignty over *terra nullius* lands lying within an area defined by the meridians of longitude reaching the North or South poles from the coastline of the territory possessed by the claimant state. Canada has flirted with the Sector Principle as a basis for its sovereignty over the Arctic Archipelago, and possibly even the permanently frozen polar sea, but in recent years it seems to have resiled from any overt sovereignty claims in the Arctic based on the Sector Principle.[8] Claims to sovereignty based on contiguity or propinquity have not always been accepted by scholarly authorities, or by the community of nations, and it is a weaker basis for the assertion of sovereignty than any of the other recognized principles.

Prescription is another basis in international law for asserting a valid title. It is based on an actual and public occupation of territory where that occupation has been uninterrupted for a substantial period of time. The principle recognizes that a long and continuous exercise of sovereignty undisturbed by any other state ought to be sufficient to establish a sovereign title. The length of time required to establish prescriptive sovereignty is, however, undefined. Certainly a possession since time immemorial would be sufficient to establish prescription but a much lesser period may also suffice. This basis of asserting sovereignty is available when no other principle applies. It can have application in the case of certain remote uninhabited territories where the sovereignty of a particular state has long been asserted without challenge by any other state.

Accretion is the extension of the land territory of a state that results from the action of water, whether riverine or oceanic. In the case of a riverine extension, if the river is a boundary between states the gradual shifting of the course of the river will alter the placement of the boundary. However, a sudden change in the course of a river (a process defined in law as an avulsion) will not shift the boundary between the states. Rather, the boundary will follow the median point of the former riverbed. Where accretion involves oceanic action, the extension of the surface area will belong to the state which owns the coastline and it is irrelevant whether that accretion is gradual or sudden.

Arbitration is a process whereby two states that are uncertain of the boundary between them, and which have engaged in a dispute concerning the location of that boundary, may submit their cause to an impartial panel who will determine the boundary, or adjudicate the dispute over the boundary, and provide the parties with a binding award that will settle the definition of sovereignty with respect to the particular location at issue. The process is entirely voluntary and no state may be compelled to submit to arbitration. The arbitrators charged with resolving a dispute will apply the principles of international law to arrive at a solution but where the parties so wish the arbitrators may be empowered to act as a type of *amiable compositeur*, and to decide the case on the basis of natural equity, as opposed to law, by following the principle of *ex aequo et bono*.[9] There has been a long history of the use of arbitration to define the boundaries between Canada and the United States of America tracing back to the determination of the St. Croix River boundary in the eighteenth century.

Arbitration can occur through the creation of an arbitral panel by the state parties themselves or the state parties can avail themselves of the offices of the Permanent Court of Arbitration at the Hague, which was established pursuant to the Convention for the Pacific Settlement of International Disputes in 1899. Cases may also be brought before the International Court of Justice at the Hague, which is an arm of the United Nations. The International Court of Justice may sit *en banc* or in a chamber of three or five judges. The Court applies international law but it can be authorized to act, in effect, as an *amiable compositeur* applying the principles of natural equity pursuant to the maxim *ex aequo et bono*. The Gulf of Maine Case between Canada and the United States was adjudicated by a Chamber of the Court.

Political Sovereignty

The principal actors within international law consist of sovereign states. As a working definition a sovereign state may be defined as a political community whose members habitually obey a superior authority within that political community that is not subservient to any external authority. Generally, in order for a population to habitually obey a superior authority that authority must have control of a territory in which the population that habitually obeys it can reside.[10]

In Canada, the identification of the superior authority to whom the population showed habitual obedience has changed over the passage of time. During the early years of the country following European settlement the primary government of the country was the Kingdom of France, and the sovereignty of France, which was based on the doctrine of the absolute right of kings, was vested solely in the King of France and Navarre. During the first four reigns following the initial French settlement in 1608, the sovereignty of Canada was held by the King of France and Navarre absolutely.

Following the conquest, and the cession of Canada to Great Britain by France in the Treaty of Paris, 1763, the sovereignty over Canada was vested in the King in the Parliament of Great Britain (from 1801 the United Kingdom of Great Britain and Ireland) and was initially exercised by the King of Great Britain in Council, in an exercise of the Royal Prerogative. The King was advised by his Ministers, who were able to command the confidence of the House of Commons but the Crown was afforded a great discretion by the Royal Prerogative in the government of any ceded colony in which no legislature had been established. Thus, important constitutional measures were taken by the King in Council without any reference to the British Parliament, a prime example being the issuance of the Royal Proclamation, 1763.

However, under the public law of Great Britain, once the Crown has granted a representative legislature to a colony the King-in-Council may no longer legislate for that colony through an exercise of the Royal Prerogative. Afterwards, it was necessary for a colonial legislature, or the Parliament of Great Britain, to legislate for that colony. Thus, following the grant of representative legislatures to Lower Canada and Upper Canada in 1791, only the Imperial Parliament (consisting of the House of Commons, the House of Lords and the King) could exercise sovereign powers of governance over those colonies (as the colonial legislatures could only exercise legislation over matters that were wholly of a local nature). This ultimate sovereign authority remained with the King (or Queen) in the Parliament of the United Kingdom even after Confederation in 1867.

It was only in 1926 that the Balfour Declaration, emerging from the Imperial Conference of 1926, determined as a matter of imperial relations that each of the British dominions (including Canada and Newfoundland) would thereafter be held to be equal to the United Kingdom under the Crown. Thereafter, the Governors General of the dominions acted solely on the advice of their dominion governments, in their capacity as the personal representative of the Sovereign within the dominion, and they no longer possessed a formal connection to the Imperial Government. That substantive change marked the internal independence of the British dominions (Canada, Australia, South Africa, New Zealand and Newfoundland) within the Empire/British Commonwealth although it did not confer external sovereignty on the dominions as sovereign states within the community of nations.

Internationally recognized independence was ultimately made available to the dominions by the enactment of the Statute of Westminster, 1931, and both Canada and South Africa took early advantage of the new status available on them by ascending to the status of juridically independent sovereign states within the international community of nations. (Australia and New Zealand deferred this last step to the following decade, and Newfoundland never ascended to international sovereignty because it surrendered its status as a dominion and reverted to the status of a colony in 1934, in the depths of the Great Depression.) Therefore, from 1931, the sovereignty of Canada was exclusively its own, and was and continues to be vested in the Queen (or King) in the Parliament of Canada together with the Queen (or King) in the Legislatures of the Provinces.[11]

As a final step in Canada's evolution, the patriation of the Constitution of Canada from the United Kingdom occurred in 1982 (involving the removal of the Parliament of the United Kingdom from the process of amending the Canadian constitution). However, that was a matter of constitutional process reform rather than a declaration of sovereignty since the sovereignty of Canada had by then been well established in international law prior to the patriation of the constitution in 1982.

It is the combination of these two features, the existence of a political sovereign (the Queen in the Parliament of Canada, with the Queen in the Legislatures of the Provinces, all acting on the constitutional advice of elected Ministers) together with the existence of an internationally recognized geographical territory controlled by the political sovereign of Canada that creates the sovereign territorial state of Canada, and confers upon Canada its entitlement to membership in the international community of nations for the purposes of international law.

ENDNOTES

[1] Hill, p. 23.

[2] Hill, p. 145-46.

[3] T. J. Lawrence, *The Principles of International Law*, D. C. Heath & Co., Boston, 1910, p. 153.

[4] Quoted in Hill, pp. 148-49.

[5] The purchase of Rupert's Land and the North-Western Territory by Canada from the Hudson Bay Company for 300,000 pounds sterling in 1869 would have qualified as a cession if Canada had been an independent state. Since Canada was not an independent state in 1869 the transaction was effected as a transfer from territories under the Crown of Great Britain (Rupert's Land and the North-Western Territory) to another territory under the Crown of Great Britain (the Dominion of Canada).

[6] Maurice Ollivier, Q.C., *British North America Acts and Selected Statutes, 1967-1962*, Roger Duhamel, Queen's Printer and Controller of Stationary, Ottawa, 1962, p. 12.

[7] Such was the case in the lead up to the 1981 independence of Belize from the United Kingdom. The community of nations dissuaded Guatemala from pursuing its territorial claims against when that country through diplomacy at the United Nations. The United Kingdom also dispatched an aircraft carrier battle group to the Caribbean Sea in 1977 as a warning to Guatemala [J. R. Hill (ed.), *The Oxford Illustrated History of the Royal Navy*, Oxford University Press, Oxford (UK) 1995, pp. 393-95.].

[8] Byers, *International Law*, p. 117, fn. 105.

[9] Hill, p. 206.

[10] Very exceptionally a sovereign subject of international law may exist without territory. This can occur during wartime when a legitimate government has been divested of its territory by a contested conquest and maintains its right to a restoration of its rule upon the conclusion of hostilities. Several governments in exile with no territory to rule were maintained in London during World War Two. There are also examples of entities that have been recognized by some states of the international community as a sovereign, or quasi-sovereign, subject of international law despite the loss of all of its territory e.g. the Sovereign Military Order of Malta.

[11] Although the Sovereign Queen or King of Canada is a single person and the Crown is deemed to be indivisible for domestic purposes, the Sovereign acts in different capacities in exercising the powers of the Federal Government or of a provincial government. Thus, when acting for a particular government the expression 'the Queen in Right of Canada' is used to denote an action undertaken by the Crown in a federal capacity. Similarly, the expression (for example) 'the Queen in Right of Nova Scotia',

will be used to express an action taken by the Crown in a provincial capacity.

2.

THE AGE OF EXPLORATION AND CONQUEST

Introduction

Originally claims to territory were, in effect, the claims of a personal monarch. In the history of diplomacy the Age of Exploration and Conquest represented a period of history in which the dominant principle of state organization held that European monarchs were absolutely sovereign in their own realms. In many realms there was no parliament to constrain the impulses of the monarch. All public property in what we now refer to as a state was actually held as the personal property of the monarch. As such, the transfer of territory from one monarch to another was effected through the application of the laws of property and inheritance, conquest, or the cession of territory. European monarchs frequently warred with one another to expand their control over territory, or entered into convenient marriages that expanded the territorial reach of their realms. After consolidating their gains they ultimately passed their territorial properties through the laws of inheritance to their heirs. Thus, all disputes with respect to territory were in the nature of personal disputes between monarchs.[1]

With the discovery of the New World the concepts of property law and the laws of inheritance were inadequate to establish the legitimacy of claims to territories beyond the seas. Accordingly, new types of claims were made on the basis of first discovery.[2] However, even in this early period the mere fact of discovery could be inadequate to sustain a claim, as when explorers acting in the name of a particular King or Queen merely coasted along the shores of lands that they spied from the sea. Consequently, most kingdoms developed a ritualized approach for their claims to lands in the New World. That resulted in a symbolic process to establish the legitimacy of a claim on behalf of a particular monarch. Although practices varied, the core elements of the symbolic procedure entailed the landing from a ship of an official party with authority to make a claim on behalf of a particular monarch, the placing or hoisting of a flag representing the monarchical realm, and the firing of a gun salute followed by a declaration that the discovered lands were taken in the name of the King or Queen of the kingdom which had sent out the expedition. In many cases a physical monument of the act of claiming the territory was erected at the site of the ceremony. Such monuments often consisted of a cross, or pole, upon which the royal arms of the monarch would be affixed, as well as a written form of the declaration of the claim.[3] In most situations it was impossible for the early explorers to define the limits of the claims that they made, which led to many later extravagant claims to territory in the New World by European monarchs.

During the Age of Exploration and Conquest the only international constraint upon monarchs was the temporal authority of the Pope, although the Protestant Reformation eventually limited the reach of the Pope's temporal authority over European monarchs. During the period in which the initial discoveries were made, however, the Holy See attempted to regulate territorial claims in the newly discovered lands. The papacy held that it had authority to allow European monarchs the right to claim lands that were uninhabited, or inhabited only by non-Christian peoples in the New World, as an aspect of the Pope's temporal authority. Papal authority was actually exercised in a number of edicts that together constituted the Papal Bulls of Donation, the most prominent of which is the Papal Bull *Inter Caetera*, issued by Pope Alexander VI in 1493.

The Papal Bulls of Donation

In the Vatican legal practice of the 15th century binding legal instruments issued by the Holy See consisted of Briefs or Bulls, the latter being the most formal of the public decrees issued by the Pope. The Bulls of Donation were issued by Pope Alexander VI in 1493, following the first receipt of the news of the discoveries in the New World by Christopher Columbus. The first of the papal bulls was entitled *Inter Caetera*, and was dated May 3, 1493, whereby the Pope recognized the rights of the monarchs of Spanish Castile, Leon, Aragon, Granada, and Sicily (i.e., King Ferdinand and Queen Isabella) to claim the lands newly discovered by Columbus, although the rights of Portugal were protected by a statement that "no right conferred upon any Christian Prince is hereby to be understood as withdrawn or to be withdrawn."[4] That vague formulation was, however, found to be unsatisfactory by the Portuguese. Representations made to the papacy resulted in the issuance of a third bull, as a replacement, which was also entitled *Inter Caetera*, and which was dated May 4, 1493[5]. That bull granted to Castile, Leon, Aragon, Granada and Sicily sovereign rights in the lands lying west of a line drawn between the North Pole and the South Pole 100 leagues west and south of the Azores and Cape Verde Islands.[6] It is this latter bull that created moral and legal restrictions respecting territorial claims as between the two Iberian states.

A fourth papal bull, *Dudum Siquidem* was issued later in 1493, which further reinforced the preeminent position of Spanish claims in the New World by conferring on the Spanish monarchs the right to acquire any islands or major land forms encountered by the Spanish in their explorations of the ocean toward the west that lay east and south of India. This bull caused additional concern in Portugal as it further restricted the scope for the acquisition of territories in the New World by Portugal.

Inter Caetera

May 4, 1493

Alexander, bishop, servant of the servants of God, to the illustrious sovereigns, our very dear son in Christ, Ferdinand, king, and our very dear daughter in Christ, Isabella, queen of Castile, Leon, Aragon, Sicily, and Granada, health and apostolic benediction. Among other works well pleasing to the Divine Majesty and cherished of our heart, this assuredly ranks highest, that in our times especially the Catholic faith and the Christian religion be exalted and be everywhere increased and spread, that the health of souls be cared for and that barbarous nations be overthrown and brought to the faith itself. Wherefore inasmuch as by the favour of divine clemency, we, though of insufficient merits, have been called to this Holy See of Peter, recognizing that as true Catholic kings and princes, such as we have known you always to be, and as your illustrious deeds already known to almost the whole world declare, you not only eagerly desire but with every effort, zeal, and diligence, without regard to hardships, expenses, dangers, with the shedding even of your blood, are labouring to that end; recognizing also that you have long since dedicated to this purpose your whole soul and all your endeavours—as witnessed in these times with so much glory to the Divine Name in your recovery of the kingdom of Granada from the yoke of the Saracens—we therefore are rightly led, and hold it as our duty, to grant you even of our own accord and in your favour those things whereby with effort each day more hearty you may be enabled for the honour of God himself and the spread of the Christian rule to carry forward your holy and praiseworthy purpose so pleasing to immortal God.

We have indeed learned that you, who for a long time had intended to seek out and discover certain islands and mainlands remote and unknown and not hitherto discovered by others, to the end that you might bring to the worship of our Redeemer and the profession of the Catholic faith their residents and inhabitants, having been up to the present time greatly engaged in the siege and recovery of the kingdom itself of Granada were unable to accomplish this holy and praiseworthy purpose; but the said kingdom having at length been regained, as was pleasing to the Lord, you, with the wish to fulfill your desire, chose our beloved son, Christopher Columbus, a man assuredly worthy and of the highest recommendations and fitted for so great an undertaking, whom you furnished with ships and men equipped for like designs, not without the greatest hardships, dangers, and expenses, to make diligent quest for these remote and unknown mainlands and islands through the sea, where hitherto no one had sailed; and they at length, with divine aid and with the utmost diligence sailing in the ocean sea, discovered certain very remote islands and even mainlands that hitherto had not been discovered by others; wherein dwell very many peoples living in peace, and, as reported, going unclothed, and not eating flesh. Moreover, as your aforesaid envoys are of opinion, these very peoples living in the said islands and countries believe in one God, the Creator in heaven, and seem sufficiently disposed to embrace the Catholic faith and be trained in good morals.

And it is hoped that, were they instructed, the name of the Saviour, our Lord Jesus Christ, would easily be introduced into the said countries and islands. Also, on one of the chief of these aforesaid islands the said Christopher has already caused to be put together and built a fortress fairly equipped, wherein he has stationed as garrison certain Christians, companions of his, who are to make search for other remote and unknown islands and mainlands. In the islands and countries already discovered are found gold, spices, and very many other precious things of divers kinds and qualities.

Wherefore, as becomes Catholic kings and princes, after earnest consideration of all matters, especially of the rise and spread of the Catholic faith, as was the fashion of your ancestors, kings of renowned memory, you have purposed with the favour of divine clemency to bring under your sway the said mainlands and islands with their residents and inhabitants and to bring them to the Catholic faith. Hence, heartily commending in the Lord this your holy and praiseworthy purpose, and desirous that it be duly accomplished, and that the name of our Saviour be carried into those regions, we exhort you very earnestly in the Lord and by your reception of holy baptism, whereby you are bound to our apostolic commands, and by the bowels of the mercy of our Lord Jesus Christ, enjoin strictly, that inasmuch as with eager zeal for the true faith you design to equip and despatch this expedition, you purpose also, as is your duty, to lead the peoples dwelling in those islands and countries to embrace the Christian religion; nor at any time let dangers or hardships deter you therefrom, with the stout hope and trust in your hearts that Almighty God will further your undertakings.

And, in order that you may enter upon so great an undertaking with greater readiness and heartiness endowed with the benefit of our apostolic favour, we, of our own accord, not at your instance nor the request of anyone else in your regard, but of our own sole largess and certain knowledge and out of the fullness of our apostolic power, by the authority of Almighty God conferred upon us in blessed Peter and of the vicarship of Jesus Christ, which we hold on earth, do by tenor of these presents, should any of said islands have been found by your envoys and captains, give, grant, and assign to you and your heirs and successors, kings of Castile and Leon, forever, together with all their dominions, cities, camps, places, and villages, and all rights, jurisdictions, and appurtenances, all islands and mainlands found and to be found, discovered and to be discovered towards the west and south, by drawing and establishing a line from the Arctic pole, namely the north, to the Antarctic pole, namely the south, no matter whether the said mainlands and islands are found and to be found in the direction of India or towards any other quarter, the said line to be distant one hundred leagues towards the west and south from any of the islands commonly known as the Azores and Cape Verde.

With this proviso however that none of the islands and mainlands, found and to be found, discovered and to be discovered, beyond that said line towards the west and south, be in the actual possession of any Christian king or prince up to the birthday of our Lord Jesus Christ just past from which the present year one thousand four hundred and ninety-three begins. And we make, appoint, and depute you and your said heirs and successors lords of them with full and free power, authority, and jurisdiction of every kind; with this proviso however, that by this our gift, grant, and assignment no right acquired by any Christian prince, who may be in actual possession of said islands and mainlands prior to the said birthday of our Lord Jesus Christ, is hereby to be understood to be withdrawn or taken away.

Moreover we command you in virtue of holy obedience that, employing all due diligence in the premises, as you also promise—nor do we doubt your compliance therein in accordance with your loyalty and royal greatness of spirit—you should appoint to the aforesaid mainlands and islands worthy, God-fearing, learned, skilled, and experienced men, in order to instruct the aforesaid inhabitants and residents in the Catholic faith and train them in good morals. Furthermore, under penalty of excommunication late sententie to be incurred ipso facto, should anyone thus contravene, we strictly forbid all persons of whatsoever rank, even imperial and royal, or of whatsoever estate, degree, order, or condition, to dare, without your special permit or that of your aforesaid heirs and successors, to go for the purpose of trade or any other reason to the islands or mainlands, found and to be found, discovered and to be discovered, towards the west and south, by drawing and establishing a line from the Arctic pole to the Antarctic pole, no matter whether the mainlands and islands, found and to be found, lie in the direction of India or toward any other quarter whatsoever, the said line to be distant one hundred leagues towards the west and south, as is aforesaid, from any of the islands commonly known as the Azores and Cape Verde; apostolic constitutions and ordinances and other decrees whatsoever to the contrary notwithstanding.

We trust in Him from whom empires and governments and all good things proceed, that, should you, with the Lord's guidance, pursue this holy and praiseworthy undertaking, in a short while your hardships and endeavours will attain the most felicitous result, to the happiness and glory of all Christendom. But inasmuch as it would be difficult to have these present letters sent to all places where desirable, we wish, and with similar accord and knowledge do decree, that to copies of them, signed by the hand of a public notary commissioned therefor, and sealed with the seal of any ecclesiastical officer or ecclesiastical court, the same respect is to be shown in court and outside as well as anywhere else as would be given to these presents should they thus be exhibited or shown. Let no one, therefore, infringe, or with rash boldness contravene, this our recommendation, exhortation, requisition, gift, grant, assignment, constitution, deputation, decree, mandate, prohibition, and will. Should anyone presume to attempt this, be it known to him that he will incur the wrath of Almighty God and of the blessed apostles Peter and Paul. Given at Rome, at St. Peter's, in the year of the incarnation of our Lord one thousand four hundred and ninety-three, the fourth of May, and the first year of our pontificate.

Gratis by order of our most holy lord, the pope.

June. For the referendary,

For J. Bufolinus,A. de Mucciarellis.A. Santoseverino.

Podocatharus.[7]

The *Inter Caetera* was supplemented later that same year by the issuance on September 26, 1493 of an extension bull, the *Dudum Siquidem*, which offered Isabella and Ferdinand the right to discover lands in the ocean near by India, lying to the south and west, or east, of that land.

Dudum Siquidem

September 26, 1493[8]

ALEXANDER, Bishop, Servant of the Servants of God, to the illustrious sovereigns, his very dear son in Christ Ferdinand, the king, and to his very dear daughter in Christ, Isabella, the queen of Castile, Leon, Aragon and Granada—Health and apostolic benediction.

Whereas, a while ago, we, of our mere will, certain knowledge and in the fulness of our apostolic power, gave, conceded and assigned, in perpetuity, to you and your heirs and successors, the kings of Castile and Leon, all and singular the islands and mainlands discovered or to be discovered, towards the west and south, which were not under the actual temporal dominion of some Christian master; with these we invest you and your heirs and successors aforesaid; and we have constituted and appointed you as lords of those regions, with full, free and entire power, authority and jurisdiction, as set forth more fully in our letters drawn up for that purpose; the purport of which letters we ordain to be held as completely expressed as if they were recited in these present letters, word for word.

Since, moreover, it may happen that your emissaries, captains, or vassals, when sailing towards the west and south, may turn towards the eastern regions and find islands and mainlands which are, or were, to that quarter pertaining; wishing to follow up our gracious favours to you by similar favours, we, of our will, knowledge and fulness of apostolic power, equally extend and enlarge, with apostolic authority, by the tenor of these presents, in everything and in all respects, the same as if in the aforesaid letters full and express mention had been made of them, the donation, concession, assignment and letters aforesaid, with all and singular the clauses contained in the same letters, to apply to all and singular the islands and mainlands found and to be found, discovered and to be discovered, which in sailing or journeying in this manner towards the west or south may be, or shall be, or shall appear, whether they actually are in western or in southern and eastern regions or in India.

Granting to you and to your heirs and successors aforesaid, the full and free faculty of taking and perpetually holding, freely of your own authority, by yourselves or by another or others, bodily possession of the aforesaid islands and lands, and also of defending them against all persons who may obstruct; and most strictly prohibiting all persons soever, even of any dignity soever, or status, rank, order, or condition, under penalty of excommunication (latse sententiae) which transgressors by the very act will incur, from presuming to go, or send, to the said part, to navigate, fish, or seek out islands or mainlands, under any pretext, without the special and express license of you and your aforesaid heirs.

Notwithstanding constitutions and apostolic ordinances and any donations, concessions, faculties and assignments, made by ourselves or our predecessors to all persons whomsoever; to kings or princes, to persons of royal houses (infantibus), or any other persons, to regular orders and to military orders, for the aforesaid regions, seas, islands and lands or for any part of them, without regard to the causes of the grant, even if for objects of piety, or of religion, or of redeeming captives or to other causes of the most urgent nature, and with clauses of whatever kind, even derogations of derogations the strongest most efficacious and unusual, and containing judgments, censures and penalties of any kind which have not come into effect by means of actual and real possession, even supposing that, at some time, those to whom donations and concessions of this nature have been made or their emissaries may have sailed there.

Moreover, holding that the tenor of those letters are sufficiently expressed and inserted in these presents, we revoke them altogether by similar will, knowledge and apostolic power and we will them to be held as never made, in so far as they refer to lands and islands not actually in possession, and so we have decreed notwithstanding everything in the aforesaid letters and all other things to the contrary.

Given at St. Peter's at Rome in the year of our Lord 1493, on Sept. 25th, and in the second year of our pontificate.

Consequences of the Papal Bulls of Donation

Scholars have debated whether the intention of Pope Alexander VI in *Inter Caetera* was to actually confer title on newly discovered lands in the New World upon the Spanish monarchs, or merely to confer upon them the right to legitimately claim such territories through discovery. The consensus view among scholars is that the latter was intended.[9] Nevertheless, the imprimatur of papal authority in *Inter Caetera* conferred a perceived advantage upon the Spanish kingdoms, as opposed to Portugal, in the race to acquire new territories in the New World. Actually, *Inter Caetera* merely reflected the fact of the Spanish discoveries in the New World, while preserving the Portuguese discoveries in the east. With *Dudum Siquidem* the position of Spain was further enhanced and the latter bull has been viewed as conferring a preferred position upon Spain for the exploitation of territories lying in the Pacific Ocean, particularly the Philippine Islands.

The disadvantages incurred by Portugal encouraged its monarch, King John II, to threaten war but also to seek to enter into negotiations with the Spanish kingdoms. The Spanish monarchs, Ferdinand II of Aragon, and Isabella I of Castile, agreed to negotiate, perhaps realizing that, as a practical matter, the Pope's bulls could do little to prevent competition with Portugal for new territories.

The result of the negotiations between the Spanish kingdoms and Portugal was the Treaty of Tordesillas, signed on June 7, 1494, by which the Iberian powers agreed to move the demarcation line set out by the Pope in *Inter Caetera* 270 leagues further to the west so that the demarcation line between Spain and Portugal in the New World would be established 370 leagues beyond the westernmost point of the Cape Verde Islands in the Atlantic Ocean.[10] The new demarcation line, established at approximately 46 degrees, 37 minutes west of Greenwich, enabled Spain to subsequently claim all of the non-Christian lands lying to the west of the demarcation line while Portugal could lay claim to all lands lying to the east of the said line. The westward movement of the line established by Pope Alexander VI was later validated by Pope Julius II in 1506.[11] The line drawn by *Inter Caetera* and as amended by the Treaty of Tordsedillas, left all but the most easterly part of South America (now a part of Brazil) to Spain, and thus denied Portugal access to the bulk of the New World. However, that was not understood to be so in the 15th century. At that time, due to the uncertainties in global measurement, and the poor understanding of the geography of the Americas, it was thought that the demarcation line also crossed over Nova Scotia, thus allotting the island of Newfoundland to Portugal.[12]

In the years following the issuance of the Bulls of Donation the monarchs of both Spain and Portugal largely adhered to it without any further contest. In the result, most of South America was colonized by Spain, and only the eastern part of continent fell within the ambit of the Portuguese, which became Portuguese-speaking Brazil. The two Iberian powers continued to rely on the papal bulls long afterwards to strengthen their claims on territories in the Americas, as did their successor states in Latin America.[13]

The implications for Canada of the papal Bulls of Donation are harder to discern. Spain made no effort to obtain sovereignty over any territory in eastern North America that now constitutes Canada. While the Portuguese did make some half-hearted claims to Canadian territory based on the results of Portuguese explorations around the island of Newfoundland, and the Labrador coast,[14] the Portuguese were unable to compete effectively for territory in North America with France and Great Britain.

However, the papal bulls remained an authority that was relied upon by Spain for its acquisition of western South America, Central America, and the west coast of North America, including the Pacific Coast of what is now British Columbia, prior to the expulsion of the Spanish settlements on Vancouver Island by the British in the late eighteenth century. The Spanish claims were later transferred to the United States and formed the basis of that country's claim to the Oregon Country. Spanish claims on the west coast of Canada can be traced to the papal Bulls of Donation which provided a framework for the acquisition of territory by Spain in what is now British Columbia, and was a basis for the subsequent American claim.

Despite the reliance, if often only in name, by Spain and Portugal on the Bulls of Donation they did not acquire any larger degree of adherence by other European powers. Neither Catholic France, Protestant England, or the Netherlands, allowed it to constrain their own efforts to secure territories in the New World, which they increasingly based upon the concept of discovery and occupation.[15] According to one scholar a document in the Vatican archives (*De Canadia et Nova "Francia*) presented an argument (promoted by France) that *Inter Caetera* was never intended to apply to the lands discovered by France in North America because *Inter Caetera* applied by its terms only to discoveries made by Spanish-flagged vessels.[16]

Prior to the seventeenth century, in the eastern half of North America, large claims were made by explorers on behalf of their European monarchs. Chief among the early claimants in Canada was the French explorer Jacques Cartier, who explored the Labrador coast and the Gulf of St. Lawrence in 1534, and later, in 1535, explored inland on the St. Lawrence River as far west as the location of modern day Montreal. Before leaving the country to return to France Cartier erected a cross on the Gaspé coast with a shield displaying the fleur-de-lys and a testament to the King of France, thus signifying the claim of France to the lands within the present day province of Quebec. His action caused much consternation to the aboriginal population, who were aware that the erection of such a monument represented a significant act of claim by the Europeans and they protested against it.[17] Similar claims to Newfoundland were made on behalf of England by John Cabot based on his early explorations of that country.[18] Subsequently, Sir Humphrey Gilbert made a formal territorial claim to the island of Newfoundland on behalf of England in 1583.

Extravagant claims to eventual Canadian territory by France and England in the 16th century did not, however, represent a definitive acquisition of sovereignty. Until the 17th century, there were no permanent European settlements within the territory that eventually became Canada, although there were frequent seasonal visits by fishers. Without actual occupation it was impossible for the European monarchs to enforce the claims made on their behalf to territories in the New World. In practical terms the concept of prior sovereign rights based on discovery was insufficient to establish sovereignty. Eventually, discovery was seen to be nothing more than an inchoate title that could be made manifest only by the actual occupation of the discovered territories.[19] In Canada, the era of actual occupation began with the establishment of the first permanent settlement at Quebec in 1608.

ENDNOTES

[1] Hill, page 143

[2] At this juncture in history scant regard was paid by the European monarchs to the existing rights of the indigenous inhabitants in the lands of the New World. European laws did not extend protections to the non-Christian inhabitants of the New World, although of course the inhabitants were seen by the Christian Church as potential converts to the Christian faith.

[3] Hill, page 149

[4] Quoted in: Bailey W. Diffie and George D. Winius, *Foundations of the Portuguese Empire, 1415-1580,* University of Minnesota Press, 1978 at page 173.

[5] A second bull, issued the next day and known as *Eximiae devotionis,* dealt with Africa and Guinea, and is unrelated to the Americas.

[6] The Pope apparently did not choose the demarcation line arbitrarily. Samuel Edward Dawson (see note 8 below) states that Christopher Columbus had reported that the magnetic variation on his compass had changed from an easterly orientation to a westerly orientation at about 100 leagues west of the Azores. Thus, there was a scientific basis for the demarcation line chosen by Pope Alexander VI (Dawson, pages 491-493).

[7] Wikisource, *Inter Caetera*, [https://en.wikisource.org/wiki/Inter_Caetera] (accessed February 22, 2018).

[8] Samuel Edward Dawson, *The Lines of Demarcation of Pope Alexander VI and the Treaty of Tordesillas A.D. 1493 and 1494*, in From the Transactions of the Royal Society of Canada, Second Series – 1899-1900, vol V, Section II, page 465 at pages 539-40.

[9] Dawson, at page 477: "Whatever be their form, the true nature of these Bulls is an award and not a donation; for they are all drawn subject to a right by discovery ... upon condition that no other Christian king or prince has actual possession..."

[10] Diffie & Winius, page 174

[11] Dawson, at page 495.

[12] Dawson, at page 522.

[13] Hill, pages 145-46. Professor Hill states that Venezuela relied upon the papal bull in 1876 in a territorial dispute with Great Britain over the boundaries of British Guiana.

[14] Labrador is named for Portugese explorer João Fernandes Lavrador, who explored the Labrador coast between 1498 and 1500.

[15] Hill, page 145.

[16] Dawson, at page 495. The same argument could be applied to the discoveries relating to Newfoundland by John Cabot.

[17] Craig Brown, ed. *The Illustrated History of Canada,* Lester and Orpen Dennys, Toronto, 1987, at page 74.

[18] Brown, page 20-21.

[19] Hill, page 146.

3.

BRITAIN AND FRANCE CONTEST FOR SUPREMACY IN AMERICA

Introduction

With the arrival of the seventeenth century in 1601, the European kingdoms began to go beyond the mere exploration of the New World to occupy territory as a means of bolstering their territorial claims. This period coincided with the growing power and rivalry between France and Great Britain. During this century France would rise to dominance on the European continent while in Britain a more coordinated government would emerge for the whole island following the accession to the thrones of both Scotland and England by the House of Stuart.

In Canada, Samuel de Champlain helped to found a French colony on the Bay of Fundy in 1604, which lasted three years before its abandonment in 1607 but afterwards he led a project to establish a permanent settlement inland along the St. Lawrence River, at what is today Quebec City, in 1608. Although it was an arduous task to maintain the small colony along the St. Lawrence Champlain succeeded by allying the colony with the local aboriginals in their internecine warfare, and by establishing a successful fur trade, particularly the trade in beaver pelts. The small colony was placed under the administration of the Compagnie des Cent-Associés, a company organized by the government in Paris, which consisted of traders and members of the nobility.

South of Canada, along the Atlantic littoral, the British were likewise establishing colonies in New England and at other places further south along the coast. Other European powers, such as the Dutch, were also busy establishing New World colonies along the Atlantic coast. During the seventeenth century the colonies established by European kingdoms in North America remained small and isolated. There were no fixed territorial boundaries as such and it is probably best to think of the European colonies more like spheres of influence rather than as defined countries for most of the seventeenth century. Only in the late seventeenth century did colonial boundaries (such as that of Acadia along the Kennebec river) begin to take form.

The prevalence of conflict on the European continent meant that soon the newly established colonies of the European kingdoms would be drawn into the conflicts of their far-off parent countries. As the seventeenth century wore on the sovereignty over newly established colonies would be traded back and forth by European powers. The sovereignty over the territories that would eventually make up present-day Canada were not immune to this phenomenon, and a long-lasting and titanic competition to possess eastern North America would ensue between France and Great Britain, reaching its culmination in the middle of the eighteenth century.

The Treaty of Susa, 1629

Between 1627 and 1629 the first of the colonial struggles between France and Great Britain in North America took place as part of the Anglo-French War. That war was a subsidiary conflict within the Thirty Years War, which would not be resolved until the Peace of Westphalia in 1648. The Anglo-French War was largely a naval conflict precipitated by English fears of the growing power of the French navy. England and Scotland allied with the Huguenots, who were French Protestants opposed to the Catholic central government in Paris, and a siege of La Rochelle, a Huguenot stronghold in coastal France, was the main European focal point of the conflict.

In North America, Champlain had risen to the position of Governor of the colony of Quebec, although the colony remained a small outpost with a precarious existence. During the Anglo-French war a Scottish expedition led by David Kirke and his brothers, operating under letters of marques, attacked the French possessions in Canada and seized Acadia (Port Royal, St. John, and Penobscot) in 1628. In the same year Sir William Alexander established a British colony at the now-vacated Port Royal. The Kirke brothers prevented the resupply of Quebec by the Compagnie des Cent-Associés in 1628, and thereby forced Champlain to surrender Quebec in 1629, in order to avoid starvation. However, Champlain's surrender took place some three months after the Treaty of Susa had ended the Anglo-French War.

Treaty of Susa

April 24, 1629

Treaty of Peace and Confederacy between Louis XIII, King of France, and Charles I King of England, made at Susa 24 April, 1629.

I The two Kings shall agree to renew the ancient alliances between the two crowns, and to preserve them inviolably, together with a safe and free commerce. And with regard to the said commerce, if there be anything to be added or taken away, that shall be done by the mutual consent and liking both parties, according as it shall be judged proper,

II And for as much as it would be difficult to make restitution on both sides, the divers prizes that have been taken, and seizures made during the war, the two crowns have agreed, that none shall be made, nor shall any reprisal be granted by sea, or in any other manner, or anything that has passed between the two Kings and their subjects during this last war,

III As to what concerns the articles and contract of marriage between the said king and queen of Great Britain, they shall be confirmed bona fide.

IV And as to what concerns the Queen's house, if there be anything to be added or taken away, that shall be done by the mutual consent of both sides, according as it shall be judged most proper for the service of the said Queen.

V All the ancient alliances, as well of the one as of the other crown, shall remain in their vigour, without any alteration made by the present Treaty.

VI The two Kings being by this Treaty replaced in their former friendship, affection and correspondence, shall respectively employ themselves, in giving assistance to their allies and friends, according as the situation of affairs, and the advantage of the public good shall require an permit; the whole on design to procure the entire quiet of Christendom, for which the ambassadors of both crowns shall be furnished with propositions and overtures.

VIII And for as much as there are several ships out at sea, with letters of Mark, and power to fight the enemy, who cannot hear of this piece so early, nor receive orders to desist from all hostilities; it shall be agreed by this article, that what ever happens for the space of two months after this agreement is made, shall not derogate from, nor hinder this peace, nor the goodwill of those two crowns; on condition however, that what is taken in the space of those two months, after the signing of this treaty shall be restored on both sides.

IX The two Kings shall sign the present articles the 24th of this present month of April, which shall be consigned in the meantime, by their command, into the hands of the Sieurs, the ambassadors of Venice, George Zorzi and Lewis Contarini, residing at their courts, in order to have them reciprocally delivered to the said two Kings on a set date, as soon as each of them shall have known from *the other that they have the said articles in their hands. And from the day of signing all acts of hostility, as well by sea as by land, shall cease, and the proclamations necessary for that effect shall be made the 20th day of May in both their kingdoms. And on the first day of June next, the two Kings shall order their ambassadors, the one to be at Calais, and the other at Dover, to go over at the same time, the one to England, and the other to France.*

Done at Susa the 24th day of April, 1629.

Consequences of the Treaty of Susa

By the terms of the Treaty of Susa the capture of Quebec by the Kirke brothers was unraveled and French sovereignty over New France was restored. That was necessary because the capture of Quebec occurred after the peace had been declared by the terms of the treaty. However, Acadia was considered to be in a different situation and the Scots and English argued that France had abandoned Acadia before the British took possession and thus they should be allowed to retain it. To that France would not agree. Protracted negotiations ensued between 1630 and 1632, during a period in which the position of King Charles I in England steadily weakened as he attempted to rule without Parliament in the years leading up to the English Civil War. Finally, it was agreed by King Charles that both Acadia and Quebec would be restored to French sovereignty. That was a blow to the fortunes of Sir William Alexander, who held British Crown patents for Nova Scotia but the blow was ameliorated by raising him into the peerage as a Viscount, and providing him with a comfortable sinecure.[1]

The Treaty of Saint Germain-en-Laye, 1632

Following the Treaty of Susa, the ambassadors of both France and England proceeded to negotiate a treaty to restore the lost provinces in North America to France, which resulted in the Treaty of Saint Germain-en-Laye, signed in March 1632. The treaty was subsequently ratified by King Charles I of England and Scotland in April 1632. Following the execution and ratification of the Treaty of St. Gemain-en-Laye the territories of Quebec and Acadia were restored to the sovereignty of France in the summer of 1632.

Treaty of Saint Germain-en-Laye (Extracts)

March 29, 1632

Treaty between Louis XIII King of France, and Charles I King of Great Britain, for the restitution of new France, Acadia and Canada, and the ships and merchandises taken on both sides.

. . . .

III on the part of his Majesty of Great Britain, the said Lord Ambassador, by virtue of the power granted to him, which shall be inserted at the end of these presents, hath promised, and doth promise, for and in the name of his said Majesty, render and restore to his most Christian Majesty all the places possessed in New France, Acadia and Canada, by the subjects of his Majesty of Great Britain, and cause them to depart from those places. And for that effect the said Lord Ambassador Shall presently, upon passing and signing these presents, deliver to the commissioners of the most Christian King, in good form, the power of which he hath received from his Majesty of Great Britain, for the restitution of the said places, together with the orders of his said Majesty to such as command in Port Royal, Port Québec and Cape Breton, to give up the said places and Fort, and deliver them into the hands of those whom it shall please his most Christian Majesty to appoint, in eight days after the said orders shall have been notified to those who do command, or shall command in the said places; the said space of eight days being given them to remove, in the meantime, out of the said places and Fort, their arms, baggage, merchandises, gold, silver, utensils, and in general everything that belongs to them: to whom, and to all who live in the said places, is granted the space of three weeks after the expiration of the said eight days, for entering [during the said time, or sooner if possible] into their ships, with their arms, ammunition, baggage, gold, silver, utensils, merchandises, furs, and in general everything belonging to them, in order to depart thence into England, without any longer stay in the said countries.

Consequences of the Treaty of Saint Germain-en-Laye

The Treaty of St Germain-en-Laye restored all of the French colonies in North America to the sovereignty of France. Although the treaty also made an effort to make the dispossessed French colonists whole, the small colony at Quebec suffered an economic set back as a result of the Anglo-French War and it took some time to restore its fortunes. Despite the economic challenges an influx of settlers under the auspices of the Compagnie des Cent-Associés continued to expand the population base of the colony and its permanent infrastructure also continued to develop. The dream of Samuel de Champlain to create a settled French colony centred on the banks of the St. Lawrence river eventually became a reality and New France was eventually taken out of the control of the Compagnie des Cent-Associés and made a royal colony under the control of the government of King Louis XIV in Paris, in 1663. Canada would subsequently grow from the seeds of the small French colony planted by Champlain at Quebec.

The Treaty of Breda, 1667

The Second Anglo-Dutch War (1665-67) was fought between Great Britain against Holland and its allies, including France. A number of causes led to the war but commercial competition between the two powers was one of the primary causes of the war. Previously, during a period of hostilities between France and Commonwealth England in the 1650's, the French colony of Acadia, always lying exposed to the possibility of an English assault, was captured in 1654 by British colonial forces operating from New England.[2]

Financial pressures in Great Britain quickly created an impossible situation for King Charles II who was compelled to enter into peace negotiations at Breda, in the Netherlands with both Holland and France. The English position was further undermined by a successful Dutch naval attack on England while negotiations to restore the peace were underway. Peace between Great Britain and Holland was signed on July 31, 1667, while on July 21, 1667 the British and French entered into a peace treaty by which Acadia was restored to the sovereignty of France.

Treaty of Breda (Extracts)

July 21, 1667

I. There shall be a universal peace, and perpetual, true and sincere friendship between the Most Serene and Most Potent King of Great Britain and the Most Serene and Most Potent Christian King, and their heirs and successors, and also between their kingdoms, states and subjects, and this peace shall be preserved and respected so sincerely and inviolably that each shall promote the profit, honour, and advantage of the other; and on all sides neighbourly confidence and secure cultivation of peace and friendship shall be renewed and flourish.

....

X. Moreover the said lord King of Great Britain shall restore to the said lord the Most Christian King, or to those who shall receiver for that purpose his powers duly passed under the great seal of France, the country which is called Acadia, situated in North America, which the said lord the Most Christian King formerly possessed; and for this purpose immediately upon the ratification of this treaty the said lord King of Great Britain, shall deliver or order to be delivered to the said lord the Most Christian King, or to his ministers empowered therefor, all acts and orders, properly drawn up, which shall be necessary to the said restitution.

XI. If however any of the inhabitants of that country called Acadia shall prefer to be subject in future to the rule of the Most Serene King of Great Britain, they shall be at liberty to depart within the space of one year, to be reckoned from the day of the restitution of that country; they shall be at liberty to sell, alienate, or otherwise, as shall seem good to them, freely dispose of their lands, field, slaves, and all their goods, movable and immovable; and whoever shall have contracted with them for the same shall be held to fulfill such contracts by the authority of the Most Serene Christian King. But if they shall prefer to carry away with them their money, household furnishings, utensils, slaves, and all their movables, they may do so freely without any hindrance or molestation whatsoever.

Consequences of the Treaty of Breda

Acadia was restored to the sovereignty of France although the physical restoration of French authority did actually not occur until 1670. One of the problems of the Treaty of Breda was that it did not articulate a defined boundary for Acadia, and the uncertainty that resulted from that failure would continue to cause frictions between France and Great Britain in the New World.[3]

The most significant result of the Second Anglo-Dutch War was the capture and retention of New Netherlands by Great Britain. Renamed New York, it established the dominance of Great Britain along the Atlantic littoral and brought the English possessions in North America into an increased proximity to New France by removing The Netherlands from the frontiers of New France. Thus, the Treaty of Breda established the final relative positions of the British and French empires in North America before the great contest for dominance in the New World that would occupy those two powers throughout the eighteenth century.

Treaty of Ryswick, 1697

War between the European kingdoms broke out again in the late

1690's in what was known in Europe as the War of the League of Augsburg and in North America as King William's War. In that conflict, which involved the French, English, and their allied aboriginal first nations there was a multiplicity of devastating raids in Acadia, Newfoundland, and New England. However, neither side was strong enough in North America to conquer the territorial possessions of the other kingdom. Although the population of New France was far below the population of the British colonies to the south New France was able to maintain its territorial integrity. In part, that was due to the greater geographical cohesiveness of the French territories in contrast to the more widely dispersed British colonies of New England. By comparison, the British colonies were strung out all along the Atlantic littoral and could not easily combine their forces. The French colonies also had a higher proportion of male inhabitants with a military background, which was very useful to the colonial authorities for the purposes of colonial defense.

Although the population of New France and Acadia had remained small until the government of King Louis XIV assumed the actual administration of the territories in 1663, thereafter a substantial population growth ensued, although the overall population growth of the French possessions never approached the comparatively massive immigration from Europe that was occurring in the English colonies. The colonial authorities in New France therefore made a much greater effort to maintain friendly relations and military alliances with the aboriginal populations within its territories.

Treaty of Ryswick (Extracts)

September 20, 1697

I. That there be an universal perpetual peace, and a true and sincere friendship, between the most serene and mighty prince William III King of Great Britain, and the most serene and mighty Prince Louis XIV the most Christian King, their heirs and successors, and between the kingdoms, states and subjects of both; and that the same be so sincerely and inviolably observed and, that the one shall promote the interests, honour, and advantage of the other, and that on both sides and faithful neighbourhood, and true observation of peace and friendship, may daily flourish and increase.

. . . .

VII. The most Christian King shall restore to the said King of Great Britain, all countries, islands, forts and colonies, wheresoever situated, which the English did possess before the declaration of this present war. And in like manner the King of Great Britain shall restore to the most Christian King, all countries, islands, forts and colonies, wheresoever situated, which the French did possess before the said declaration of war. And this restitution shall be made on both sides, within the space of six months, or sooner, if it can be done. And to that end, immediately after the ratification of this treaty, each of the said King shall deliver, or cause to be delivered to the other, or to commissioners authorized in his name for that purpose, all acts of concession, instruments, and necessary orders, duly made and in proper form; so that they may have their effect.

VIII. Commissioners shall be appointed on both sides, to examine and determine the rates and pretensions which either of the said King's hath to the places situated in Hudson's Bay; but the possession of those places which were taken by the French, during the peace that preceded the present war, and were retaken by the English during this war, shall be left to the French, by virtue of the foregoing article. The capitulation made by the English on 5 September, 1696, shall be observed, according to its form and tenor; the merchandises therein mentioned shall be restored; the governor of the Fort taken there shall be set at liberty, if it be not already done; the differences arisen concerning the execution of the said capitulation, and the value of the goods there lost, shall be adjudged and determined by the said commissioners, who immediately after the ratification of the present treaty, shall be invested with sufficient authority for settling the limits and confines of the lands to be restored on either side, by virtue of the foregoing article, and likewise for exchanging of lands, as may conduce to the mutual interest and advantage of both Kings.

And to this end the commissioners, so appointed, shall, within the space of three months from the time of the ratification of the present treaty, meet in the city of London, and within six months, to be reckoned from their first meeting, shall determine all differences and disputes which may arise concerning this matter; after which, the articles the said commissioners shall agree to, shall be ratified by both Kings, and shall have the same force and vigour, as if they were inserted word for word in the present treaty.

Consequences of the Treaty of Ryswick

In the Treaty of Ryswick of 1697, which ended the war, it was agreed that the former boundaries of territory in North America would be restored under the principle of *status quo ante bellum*. This treaty gave credence to the claim of France that the boundary of Acadia extended as far south as the Kennebec River.

The territorial consequences of the Treaty of Ryswick in North America were minor. There was, however, one significant area of change with respect to territorial claims. During King William's War, for the first time, Hudson Bay became an active theater of war. The economic penetration of that region had been undertaken by the Hudson's Bay Company in the late seventeenth century under a royal charter granted by King Charles II of England in 1670. The penetration of Hudson's Bay by the English fur trading firm conflicted with French claims to the same territory, the French having earlier reached the shores of Hudson Bay by land. Consequently, a series of raids and naval battles both preceded and continued during King William's War, in which the Canadian naval commander, Pierre Le Moyne d'Iberville, played an important role. The French Canadians successfully took control of most of the outposts established by the Hudson's Bay Company. Unfortunately for the proprietors of the Hudson's Bay Company, most of the outposts taken by the French were taken prior to the outbreak of formal hostilities and, as a result, the application of the *status quo ante bellum* rule meant that the Hudson's Bay Company could not recover those outposts from the French. Thus the colonial government of New France was able to thwart the penetration of the Hudson Bay region by the English, and the extension of the sovereignty of France into the Hudson Bay region was the only real territorial consequence of King William's War. Nevertheless, New France's control of Hudson's Bay remained tenuous and the conflict between the two empires would shortly be resumed as the seventeenth century passed into history and the eighteenth century arrived.

The Treaty of Utrecht, 1713

After the Treaty of Ryswick the European monarchs turned their attention to the question of who would inherit the throne of Spain after the death of King Charles II, who was the last of his line of a branch of the Hapsburg royal house to hold the throne of Spain. There were three prominent claimants to the Spanish throne including a member of the French royal family, as well as members of the Austrian Hapsburg line. In the early eighteenth century Spain wielded a vast empire both in Europe and abroad and thus possession of the Spanish throne by a member of either the French or Austrian royal families would have upset the balance of power in Europe to a substantial degree. Following the death of King Charles II in 1700, a general conflict broke out in the following year after King Louis XIV of France accepted the accession of his grandson to the Spanish throne under the terms of the will of Charles II. The resulting War of the Spanish Succession (also known in North America as Queen Anne's War) brought within it most of the major powers in Europe, and resulted in a war in North America as well. Although King Louis XIV was ultimately successful in establishing a branch of his royal house on the throne of Spain, the cost to France with respect to its North American possessions was substantial.

Treaty of Utrecht (Extracts)

March 31st and April 11th 1713

Whereas it has pleased Almighty God, for the glory of his name, and for the universal welfare, so to direct the minds of Kings for the healing, now in his own time, the miseries of the wasted world, that they are disposed towards one another with a mutual desire of making peace: be it therefore known to all and singular whom it may concern, that under this divine guidance, the most serene and most potent Princess and Lady Anne, by the grace of God, Queen of Great Britain, France, and Ireland, and the most serene and most potent Prince and Lord Louis XIV, by the grace of God, the most Christian King, consulting as well the advantage of their subjects, as providing [as far as mortals are able to do] for the perpetual tranquility of the whole Christian world, have resolved at last to put an end to the war, which was unhappily kindled, and has been obstinately carried on above these 10 years, being both cruel and destructive, by reason of the frequency of battles, and the effusion of Christian blood.

. . . .

I. That there be a universal perpetual peace, and a true and sincere friendship, between the most serene and most potent Princess Anne, Queen of Great Britain, and the most serene and most potent Prince Louis XIV, the most Christian King, and their heirs and successors, as also the kingdoms, states, and subjects of both, as well without as within Europe; and that the same be so sincerely and inviolably preserved and cultivated, that the one to promote the interest, honour, and advantage of the other, and that a faithful neighbourhood on all sides, and a secure cultivating of peace and friendship, do daily flourish again and increase.

. . . .

X. The said most Christian King shall restore to the kingdom and Queen of Great Britain, to be possessed in full right for ever, the Bay and Straits of Hudson, together with all lands, seas, the seacoast, rivers and places situate in the said Bay and Straits, and which belong thereunto, no tracts of land or of sea being excepted, which are at present possessed by the subjects of France. All which, as well as any buildings there made, in the condition they now are, and likewise all fortresses erected, either before or since the French seized the same, shall within six months from the ratification of the present treaty, or sooner, if possible, be well and truly delivered to the British subjects, having commission from the Queen of Great Britain to demand and receive the same, and entire and undemolished, together with all the cannon and cannonball which are therein, as also with a quantity of powder, if it be there found, in proportion to the cannonball, and with the other provision of war usually belonging to cannon. It is, however, provided, that it may be entirely free for the company of Québec, and all other subjects of the most Christian King whatsoever, to go by land, or by sea, whithersoever they please, out of the lands of the said bay, together with all their goods, merchandises, arms, and effects, of what nature or condition soever, except such things as are above reserved in this article. But it is agreed on both sides, to determine within a year by commissioners to be forthwith named by each party, the limits which are to be fixed between the said Bay of Hudson and the places appertaining to the French; which limits both the British and French subjects shall be wholly forbidden to pass over, or thereby to go to each other by sea or by land. The same commissioners shall also have orders to describe and settle, in like manner, the boundaries between the other British and French colonies in those parts.

XI. The above-mentioned most Christian King shall take care that satisfaction be given, according to the rule of justice and equity to the English company trading to the Bay of Hudson, for all damages and spoil unto their colonies, ships, persons, and goods, by the hostile incursions depredations of the French, in time of peace, an estimate being made thereof by the comissionaries to be named at the requisition of each party. The same commissionaries shall moreover inquire as well into the complaints of the British subjects concerning ships taken by the French in time of peace, as also concerning the damages sustained last year in the island called Montserrat and others, as into those things of which the French subjects complain, relating to the capitulation in the island of Nevis, and the Castle of Gambia also to French ships if perchance any such have been taken by British subjects in time of peace; and in like manner into all disputes of this kind, which shall be found to have arisen between both nations, and which are not yet ended; and due justice shall be done on both sides without delay.

XII. The most Christian King shall take care to have delivered to the Queen of Great Britain, on the same day that the ratifications of this treaty shall be exchanged, solemn and authentic letters, or instruments by virtue whereof it shall appear, that the island of St. Christopher's is to be possessed alone hereafter by British subjects, likewise all Nova Scotia or Acadia, with its ancient boundaries, as also the city of Port Royal, now called Annapolis Royal, and all other things in those parts, which depend on the said lands and islands, together with the dominion, propriety, and possession of the said islands, lands, and places, and all right whatsoever, by treaties, or by any other way obtained, which the most Christian King, the crown of France, or any of the subjects there off, have hitherto, had to the said islands, lands, and places, and the inhabitants of the same, are yielded and made over to the Queen of Great Britain, and to her crown, forever, as the most Christian King doth at present yield and make over all the particulars above said; and that in such ample manner and for that the subjects of the most Christian King shall hereafter be excluded from all kind of fishing in the said seas, bays, and other places on the coast of Nova Scotia, that is to say, on those which lie towards the east, within 30 leagues, beginning from the island commonly called Sable, inclusively, and thence stretching along towards the south west.

XIII the island called Newfoundland, with the adjacent islands, shall from this time forward belong of right wholly to Britain; and to that end the town and fortress of Placentia, and what ever other places in the said Island are in the possession of the French, shall be yielded and given up, within seven months from the exchange of the ratifications of this treaty, or sooner if possible, by the most Christian King, to those who have a commission from the Queen of Great Britain for that purpose. Nor shall the most Christian King, his heirs and successors, or any of their subjects at any time hereafter, lay claim to any right to the said Island and islands, or to any part of it, or them. Moreover, it shall not be lawful for the subjects of France to fortify any place in the said Island of Newfoundland, or to erect any buildings there, besides stages made of boards, and huts necessary and usual for drying of fish; or to resort to the said Island, beyond the time necessary for fishing, and drying of fish. But it shall be allowed to the subjects of France to catch fish, and to dry them on land, in that part only, and in no other besides that, of the said island of Newfoundland, which stretches from the place called Cape Bonavista to the northern point of the said Island, and from thence running down by the Western side, reaches as far as the place called Point Riche. But the island called Cape Breton, as also all others, both in the mouth of the River of St. Lawrence, and in the Gulf of the same name, shall hereafter belong of right to the French, and the most Christian King shall have all manner of liberty to fortify any place or places there.

XIV. It is expressly provided, that in all the said places and colonies to be yielded and restored by the most Christian King, in pursuance of this treaty, the subjects of the said King may have liberty to remove themselves, within a year, to any other place, as they shall think fit, together with all their movable effects. But those who are willing to remain there, and to be subject to the kingdom of Great Britain, are to enjoy the free exercise of their religion, according to the usage of the church of Rome, as far as the laws of Great Britain do allow the same.

XV. The subjects of France inhabiting Canada, and others, shall hereafter give no hindrance or molestation to the five nations or cantons of Indians, subject to the dominion of Great Britain, nor to the other natives of America, who are friends to the same. In like manner the subjects of Great Britain shall behave themselves peaceably towards the Americans who are subjects or friends to France; and on both sides they shall enjoy full liberty of going and coming on account of trade. As also the natives of those countries shall, with the same liberty, resort, as they please, to the British and French colonies, for promoting trade on one side and the other, without any molestation or hindrance, either on the part of the British subjects or of the French. But it is to be exactly and distinctly settled by commissionaries, who are, and who ought to be accounted the subjects and friends of Britain or of France.

Consequences of the Treaty of Utrecht

The territorial losses of France in North America were substantial as a result of Queen Anne's War. France was forced to give up its positions in Hudson Bay and the island of Newfoundland and it lost the portion of Acadia that the British called Nova Scotia.

Through this peace treaty the proprietors of the Hudson's Bay Company succeeded in reversing the losses that they had sustained by virtue of the Treaty of Ryswick. The ouster of the French from Hudson Bay allowed the company to consolidate its position in Rupert's Land and British sovereignty over the Bay was not seriously threatened subsequently.

Although Newfoundland had been claimed by England as early as 1583, by Sir Humphrey Gilbert, the island had remained divided by spheres of influence with the British in the north of the island and the French in the south. Fishers from other countries (Basques from Spain and Portuguese fishers) also ventured seasonally to the island for the purpose of fishing the Grand Banks. The French established the capital of their Newfoundland possessions at Placentia on the Avalon peninsula and they were largely successful in defending it from British attacks. Although France retained the right to dry fish on the Newfoundland coast in the Treaty of Utrecht, France was compelled to surrender its sovereignty in Newfoundland and many of the French settlers departed for Cape Breton island following the transfer of sovereignty to Great Britain.

By far the most important loss of territory involved Nova Scotia, which until then had been part of Acadia. Although as early as 1629 a Scottish settlement was established at Port Royal (now Annapolis Royal) pursuant to a royal charter granted to Sir William Alexander in 1621, France was able to recover the territory in the Treaty of Saint Germain-en-Laye. Although there were subsequent British military successes against Acadia in other wars France had been successful in reestablishing its sovereignty over Acadia throughout the seventeenth century by diplomatic negotiations after the cessation of hostilities . In Queen Anne's War however, Port Royal was taken after a siege in 1710, and renamed Annapolis Royal in honour of the Queen. Afterwards, in the peace negotiations, France was unsuccessful in reasserting its control and Nova Scotia was permanently severed from French Acadia, and the sovereignty over Nova Scotia passed to Great Britain. Although France would make subsequent attempts to recover Nova Scotia in later wars those attempts would not succeed, and Nova Scotia remained British.

To compensate for the loss of Nova Scotia and Newfoundland, France built a new Acadian capital and fortress at Louisbourg on Cape Breton Island. France also declined to transfer any part of Acadia to Great Britain other than Nova Scotia despite British claims that the treaty reference to "Acadia, with its ancient boundaries" entitled Britain to all of Acadia except for Cape Breton Island and Ile St. Jean (today's Prince Edward Island). That dispute would remain a continuing source of conflict between France and Great Britain and both France and Britain would continue to fight for sovereignty over Acadia in the ensuing colonial wars until the Treaty of Paris in 1763.

The Treaty of Aix-la-Chapelle, 1748

The European kingdoms once again went to war between 1740-48 in the War of the Austrian Succession. That war concerned the entitlement of Maria Theresa, the daughter the Holy Roman Emperor Charles VI, to succeed him as sovereign of Austria, Hungary, and Bohemia. The war dragged in most of the European kingdoms including France and Great Britain, which were on opposite sides in the war (Britain was allied with Austria and France with Prussia). However, a formal state of war between France and Great Britain only existed between the years 1744-48.

In North America this war is commonly known as King George's War. Although the main battles were fought in Europe the conflict also occurred in North America, primarily on Ile Royale (Cape Breton Island) and in Nova Scotia. At the outset of the war the French governor in Acadia had authorized privateering against British colonial merchantmen, and had seized the settlement at Canso in Nova Scotia across the narrow strait from Ile Royale. That caused a sensation in Nova Scotia and in New England. New England prepared a militia invasion force and the Royal Navy supplied warships as an escort. The invasion force was predictably of substantial size, given that the fourteen British colonies along the Atlantic coast[4] were populated by more than one million people. Conversely, the French settlements on Ile Royale remained small in comparison, and the fortress at Louisbourg was only manned by a peacetime complement of professional soldiers. After a six-weeks siege, during which the stone fortress was considerably degraded, Louisbourg surrendered to the colonial forces of New England. Elsewhere, however, the military situation had not gone to Britain's advantage, particularly in India where Madras had been lost to the French. Overall the war in Europe and abroad was largely inconclusive on both sides and peace negotiations between Britain and France began in Breda, Holland, in 1746, and culminated with the Treaty of Aix-la-Chapelle in 1748. Under its terms, France restored Madras in India to the British Crown and in return the British restored Louisbourg and Ile Royale to France.

Treaty of Aix-la-Chapelle (Extracts)

October 18, 1748

V. All the conquests, that have been made since the commencement of the war, or which, since the conclusion of the preliminary articles, signed 30 April last, may have been or shall be made, either in Europe, or the East or West Indies, or in any other part of the world whatsoever, being to be restored without exception, in conformity to what was stipulated by the said preliminary articles and by the declarations since signed; the high contracting parties engage to give orders immediately for proceeding to that restitution...

. . . .

IX. In consideration that, notwithstanding the reciprocal engagement taken by the 18th article of the preliminaries, importing, that all the restitution's and cessions should be carried on equally and should be executed at the same time, his most Christian Majesty engages, by the sixth article of the present treaty, to restore within the space of six weeks, or sooner if possible, to be reckoned from the day of the exchange of the ratifications of the present treaty, all the conquests which he has made in the low countries; whereas it is not possible considering the difference of the countries, that what relates to America should be affected within the same time, or even to fix the time of its entire execution; his Britannic Majesty likewise engages on his part to send to his most Christian Majesty, immediately after the exchange of the ratifications of the present treaty, two persons of rank and consideration, who shall remain there as hostages, till there shall be received a certain and authentic account of the restitution of Ile Royale called Cape Breton, and of all the conquests which the arms or subjects of his Britannic Majesty may have made before, or after the signing of the preliminaries, in the East and West Indies.

Their Britannic and most Christian Majesties obliged themselves likewise to cause to be delivered, upon the exchange of the ratifications of the present treaty, the duplicates of the orders addressed to the commissionaries appointed to restore, and receive, respectively, whatever may have been conquered, on either side, in the said East and West Indies, agreeably to the second article of the preliminaries, and to the declarations of the 21st and 31st of May and 8 July last, in regard to what concerns the said conquests in the East and West Indies. Provided nevertheless, that Ile Royale called Cape Breton shall be restored with all the artillery and warlike stores, which shall have been found therein on the day of its surrender, conformably to the inventories, which have been made thereof, and in the condition that the said place was in, on the said day of its surrender...

Consequences of the Treaty of Aix-la-Chapelle

There were no immediate territorial consequences flowing from the Treaty of Aix-la-Chapelle, which essentially resulted in a restoration of the *status quo ante bellum*. However, King George's War underscored the vulnerability of Nova Scotia to an assault from Ile Royale if France chose to maintain a larger military force there. As a result, Great Britain began to make a serious effort to populate Nova Scotia with settlers drawn from Britain and from New England – a policy that would ultimately lead to the expulsion of the existing Acadian population of Nova Scotia as an imperial security threat. France also took steps to protect its Ile Royale colony by repairing the fortress at Louisbourg and by posting a larger garrison there, as well as undertaking the task of building forts along the *de facto* border between Acadia and Nova Scotia in the Isthmus of Chignecto.

In New England, the British Americans were appalled by the restoration to France of the fortress of Louisbourg, which had been taken at considerable cost by the New England militia. To some extent the restoration of Louisbourg was viewed as a betrayal by a remote and disconnected Imperial Government. Undoubtedly this result of the treaty reinforced a growing division between the British Americans in North America and the British in the home islands, which would ultimately lead to the rebellion.

In general, however, the Treaty of Aix-la-Chapelle was merely a way point in the ongoing struggle between France and Great Britain for colonial dominance in North America, a struggle which would soon culminate in the Seven Years War.

The Treaty of Paris 1763

The Seven Years War (also known in Canada as the War of the Conquest, and in America as the French and Indian War) represents the climactic end to the decades-long struggle between Great Britain and France for supremacy in North America. France had expanded into the interior of North America and now controlled a vast expanse of territory stretching from the Gulf of St. Lawrence through the Great Lakes and down the Mississippi river to the French settlement at New Orleans. The interior, called Louisiana, although initially a part of New France, had been separated from New France in the early part of the eighteenth century and was subsequently administered from New Orleans. Despite the great geographical extent of the French territories in North America the French colonies continued to be markedly underpopulated in comparison to the British American colonies along the Atlantic coast. As the British Americans increasingly forged west into the wilderness from their base in the littoral colonies they presented a strategic challenge to French control of the interior. France responded by building forts into the Ohio valley, and expanding the colonial garrison in New France. New artillery and engineering units were also incorporated into an expanded colonial army.

The Seven Years War began in North America with clashes in the Ohio valley. The first blows occurred when a militia expedition from Virginia under the command of a young militia officer, George Washington, clashed with a French force under the command of Ensign Jumonville. Although the French were defeated, and their commander slain, a much larger French force subsequently pursued the victorious Virginians. After taking refuge at the hastily constructed Fort Necessity, Washington was compelled to surrender in order to avoid a massacre. Thereafter, colonial forces from both French Canada and British America began to maneuver in the backwoods, and battles for control of the heartland of eastern North America began in earnest. On the east coast, the British colonial authorities, feeling themselves threatened by the substantial Acadian population of Nova Scotia who sought neutrality in any Anglo-French war as a result of their historic ties to France, began the process of deporting the Acadians to British colonies farther to the south or, in some cases, to Europe. The destruction of the Acadian society in Nova Scotia wrought by this expulsion was virtually complete, and although many of the exiled Acadians would subsequently return to historic Acadia in the future, their farmlands remained lost, and they were forced to resettle in the east into what subsequently became the province of New Brunswick.

Formal declarations of war between France and Great Britain only came to pass in 1756, but from that time onward the war was prosecuted in earnest by both sides in North America. In 1755 the commander of the army in Canada, Baron Jean-Armand Dieskau, was wounded and taken captive. Command of the army then passed to the Marquis de Montcalm, who was sent out from France as a replacement for General Dieskau. Montcalm would retain command of the colonial forces until his death at Quebec in 1759. Throughout the final struggle from 1755 onward until the conquest of the country in 1760, the overall administration of Canada remained in the hands of Governor General, the Marquis de Vaudreuil, a Canadian by birth, and the first Canadian to hold the vice-regal position in Canada.

For the first time the British strategy was to seek to conquer French colonial possessions as the primary objective of a North American war. In previous contests between the two kingdoms Europe had been the main battlefield. Now, using the dominance of the Royal Navy, the British were able to invest and take the fortress of Louisbourg on Ile Royale and to mount multiple assaults on New France. The key battle in the contest was the Battle of the Plains of Abraham before the walls of Quebec City in 1759. There, a British force under General James Wolfe succeeded in scaling the heights upon which Quebec sat and in the short, violent, struggle that followed in the European manner of fighting the British broke the French line and mortally wounded its commander, General de Montcalm (General Wolfe was also fatally wounded in the battle). The city had previously been devastated by artillery fire during a long siege and with the army broken, and the city in ruins, the new army commander, the Chevalier de Levis, decided to evacuate the capital and seek refuge further west in Montreal. Accordingly, the army evacuated Quebec and the city fell to the British.

Over the winter of 1759-60 the army recovered sufficient strength to persuade Levis to attempt to retake the capital at Quebec and, accordingly, the army moved east in the spring of 1760. Near Quebec, at the village of Ste. Foy, the British army met Levis in battle, which resulted in a French victory. Nevertheless, during the winter the British had made repairs to the defenses of Quebec and the British army retreated into the city where Levis put them under siege. With the spring ice breakup in the St. Lawrence River however, the Royal Navy returned bringing fresh reinforcements and supplies to the beleaguered British garrison at Quebec. Faced with a resupplied antagonist, Levis ordered the army to fall back upon Montreal where it now faced the danger of a pincer movement with the British moving one column west from Quebec, and another column north up along the historic invasion route following the Lake Champlain valley and the Richelieu River. Faced with overwhelming military odds, and with no hope of succor from France due to the British Royal Navy's command of the seas, Governor General Vaudreuil bowed to the inevitable and surrendered New France to the British army at Montreal in September 1760.

Thereafter, Canada remained under British military occupation until the European powers decided to resolve their differences through diplomatic negotiations. The resulting Treaty of Paris in 1763 terminated the sovereignty of France throughout eastern North America with the exception of two small islands in the Gulf of St. Lawrence, thus ending the titanic battle for dominance in North America by the two European powers.

The Treaty of Paris was signed by Great Britain, France and Spain (and with Portuguese concurrence). Under its terms French sovereignty over what was New France and Acadia was permanently ceded to Great Britain. Great Britain also received that portion of Louisiana lying east of the Mississippi river.

Due to its importance in the evolution of Canada the Treaty of Paris is set out in full below.

Treaty of Paris

February 10, 1763[5]

The definitive Treaty of Peace and Friendship between his Britannic Majesty, the Most Christian King, and the King of Spain. Concluded at Paris the 10th day of February, 1763. To which the King of Portugal acceded on the same day.

In the Name of the Most Holy and Undivided Trinity, Father, Son, and Holy Ghost. So be it.

Be it known to all those whom it shall, or may, in any manner, belong,

It has pleased the Most High to diffuse the spirit of union and concord among the Princes, whose divisions had spread troubles in the four parts of the world, and to inspire them with the inclination to cause the comforts of peace to succeed to the misfortunes of a long and bloody war, which having arisen between England and France during the reign of the Most Serene and Most Potent Prince, George the Second, by the grace of God, King of Great Britain, of glorious memory, continued under the reign of the Most Serene and Most Potent Prince, George the Third, his successor, and, in its progress, communicated itself to Spain and Portugal: Consequently, the Most Serene and Most Potent Prince, George the Third, by the grace of God, King of Great Britain, France, and Ireland, Duke of Brunswick and Lunenbourg, Arch Treasurer and Elector of the Holy Roman Empire; the Most Serene and Most Potent Prince, Lewis the Fifteenth, by the grace of God, Most Christian King; and the Most Serene and Most Potent Prince, Charles the Third, by the grace of God, King of Spain and of the Indies, after having laid the foundations of peace in the preliminaries signed at Fontainebleau the third of November last; and the Most Serene and Most Potent Prince, Don Joseph the First, by the grace of God, King of Portugal and of the Algarves, after having acceded thereto, determined to complete, without delay, this great and important work. For this purpose, the high contracting parties have named and appointed their respective Ambassadors Extraordinary and Ministers Plenipotentiary, viz. his Sacred Majesty the King of Great Britain, the Most Illustrious and Most Excellent Lord, John Duke and Earl of Bedford, Marquis of Tavistock, c. his Minister of State, Lieutenant General of his Armies, Keeper of his Privy Seal, Knight of the Most Noble Order of the Garter, and his Ambassador Extraordinary and Minister Plenipotentiary to his Most Christian Majesty; his Sacred Majesty the Most Christian King, the Most Illustrious and Most Excellent Lord, Cesar Gabriel de Choiseul, Duke of Praslin, Peer of France, Knight of his Orders, Lieutenant General of his Armies and of the province of Britanny, Counsellor of all his Counsils, and Minister and Secretary of State, and of his Commands and Finances: his Sacred Majesty the Catholic King, the Most Illustrious and Most Excellent Lord, Don Jerome Grimaldi, Marquis de Grimaldi, Knight of the Most Christian King's Orders, Gentleman of his Catholic Majesty's Bedchamber in Employment, and his Ambassador Extraordinary to his Most Christian Majesty; his Sacred Majesty the Most Faithful King, the Most Illustrious and Most Excellent Lord, Martin de Mello and Castro, Knight professed of the Order of Christ, of his Most Faithful Majesty's Council, and his Ambassador and Minister Plenipotentiary to his Most Christian Majesty.

Who, after having duly communicated to each other their full powers, in good form, copies whereof are transcribed at the end of the present treaty of peace, have agreed upon the articles, the tenor of which is as follows:

I. There shall be a Christian, universal, and perpetual peace, as well by sea as by land, and a sincere and constant friendship shall be re established between their Britannic, Most Christian, Catholic, and Most Faithful Majesties, and between their heirs and successors, kingdoms, dominions, provinces, countries, subjects, and vassals, of what quality or condition soever they be, without exception of places or of persons: So that the high contracting parties shall give the greatest attention to maintain between themselves and their said dominions and subjects this reciprocal friendship and correspondence, without permitting, on either side, any kind of hostilities, by sea or by land, to be committed from henceforth, for any cause, or under any pretence whatsoever, and every thing shall be carefully avoided which might hereafter prejudice the union happily reestablished, applying themselves, on the contrary, on every occasion, to procure for each other whatever may contribute to their mutual glory, interests, and advantages, without giving any assistance or protection, directly or indirectly, to those who would cause any prejudice to either of the high contracting parties: there shall be a general oblivion of every thing that may have been done or committed before or since the commencement of the war which is just ended.

II. The treaties of Westphalia of 1648; those of Madrid between the Crowns of Great Britain and Spain of 1661, and 1670; the treaties of peace of Nimeguen of 1678, and 1679; of Ryswick of 1697; those of peace and of commerce of Utrecht of 1713; that of Baden of 1714; the treaty of the triple alliance of the Hague of 1717; that of the quadruple alliance of London of 1718; the treaty of peace of Vienna of 1738; the definitive treaty of Aix la Chapelle of 1748; and that of Madrid, between the Crowns of Great Britain and Spain of 1750: as well as the treaties between the Crowns of Spain and Portugal of the 13th of February, 1668; of the 6th of February, 1715; and of the 12th of February, 1761; and that of the 11th of April, 1713, between France and Portugal with the guaranties of Great Britain, serve as a basis and foundation to the peace, and to the present treaty: and for this purpose they are all renewed and confirmed in the best form, as well as all the general, which subsisted between the high contracting parties before the war, as if they were inserted here word for word, so that they are to be exactly observed, for the future, in their whole tenor, and religiously executed on all sides, in all their points, which shall not be derogated from by the present treaty, notwithstanding all that may have been stipulated to the contrary by any of the high contracting parties: and all the said parties declare, that they will not suffer any privilege, favour, or indulgence to subsist, contrary to the treaties above confirmed, except what shall have been agreed and stipulated by the present treaty.

III. All the prisoners made, on all sides, as well by land as by sea, and the hostages carried away or given during the war, and to this day, shall be restored, without ransom, six weeks, at least, to be computed from the day of the exchange of the ratification of the present treaty, each crown respectively paying the advances which shall have been made for the subsistence and maintenance of their prisoners by the Sovereign of the country where they shall have been detained, according to the attested receipts and estimates and other authentic vouchers which shall be furnished on one side and the other. And securities shall be reciprocally given for the payment of the debts which the prisoners shall have contracted in the countries where they have been detained until their entire liberty. And all the ships of war and merchant vessels Which shall have been taken since the expiration of the terms agreed upon for the cessation of hostilities by sea shall likewise be restored, bona fide, with all their crews and cargoes: and the execution of this article shall be proceeded upon immediately after the exchange of the ratifications of this treaty.

IV. His Most Christian Majesty renounces all pretensions which he has heretofore formed or might have formed to Nova Scotia or Acadia in all its parts, and guaranties the whole of it, and with all its dependencies, to the King of Great Britain: Moreover, his Most Christian Majesty cedes and guaranties to his said Britannic Majesty, in full right, Canada, with all its dependencies, as well as the island of Cape Breton, and all the other islands and coasts in the gulf and river of St. Lawrence, and in general, every thing that depends on the said countries, lands, islands, and coasts, with the sovereignty, property, possession, and all rights acquired by treaty, or otherwise, which the Most Christian King and the Crown of France have had till now over the said countries, lands, islands, places, coasts, and their inhabitants, so that the Most Christian King cedes and makes over the whole to the said King, and to the Crown of Great Britain, and that in the most ample manner and form, without restriction, and without any liberty to depart from the said cession and guaranty under any pretense, or to disturb Great Britain in the possessions above mentioned. His Britannick Majesty, on his side, agrees to grant the liberty of the Catholic religion to the inhabitants of Canada: he will, in consequence, give the most precise and most effectual orders, that his new Roman Catholic subjects may profess the worship of their religion according to the rites of the Romish church, as far as the laws of Great Britain permit. His Britannic Majesty farther agrees, that the French inhabitants, or others who had been subjects of the Most Christian King in Canada, may retire with all safety and freedom wherever they shall think proper, and may sell their estates, provided it be to the subjects of his Britannic Majesty, and bring away their effects as well as their persons, without being restrained in their emigration, under any pretense whatsoever, except that of debts or of criminal prosecutions: The term limited for this emigration shall be fixed to the space of eighteen months, to be computed from the day of the exchange of the ratification of the present treaty.

V. The subjects of France shall have the liberty of fishing and drying on a part of the coasts of the island of Newfoundland, such as it is specified in the XIIIth article of the treaty of Utrecht; which article is renewed and confirmed by the present treaty, (except what relates to the island of Cape Breton, as well as to the other islands and coasts in the mouth and in the gulf of St. Lawrence:) And his Britannic Majesty consents to leave to the subjects of the Most Christian King the liberty of fishing in the gulf of St. Lawrence, on condition that the subjects of France do not exercise the said fishery but at the distance of three leagues from all the coasts belonging to Great Britain, as well those of the continent as those of the islands situated in the said gulf of St. Lawrence. And as to what relates to the fishery on the coasts of the island of Cape Breton, out of the said gulf, the subjects of the Most Christian King shall not be permitted to exercise the said fishery but at the distance of fifteen leagues from the coasts of the island of Cape Breton; and the fishery on the coasts of Nova Scotia or Acadia, and every where else out of the said gulf, shall remain on the foot of former treaties.

VI. The King of Great Britain cedes the islands of St. Pierre and Miquelon, in full right, to his Most Christian Majesty, to serve as a shelter to the French fishermen; and his said Most Christian Majesty engages not to fortify the said islands; to erect no buildings upon them but merely for the conveniency of the fishery; and to keep upon them a guard of fifty men only for the police.

VII. In order to reestablish peace on solid and durable foundations, and to remove for ever all subject of dispute with regard to the limits of the British and French territories on the continent of America; it is agreed, that, for the future, the confines between the dominions of his Britannic Majesty and those of his Most Christian Majesty, in that part of the world, shall be fixed irrevocably by a line drawn along the middle of the River Mississippi, from its source to the river Iberville, and from thence, by a line drawn along the middle of this river, and the lakes

Maurepas and Pontchartrain to the sea; and for this purpose, the Most Christian King cedes in full right, and guaranties to his Britannic Majesty the river and port of the Mobile, and every thing which he possesses, or ought to possess, on the left side of the river Mississippi, except the town of New Orleans and the island in which it is situated, which shall remain to France, provided that the navigation of the river Mississippi shall be equally free, as well to the subjects of Great Britain as to those of France, in its whole breadth and length, from its source to the sea, and expressly that part which is between the said island of New Orleans and the right bank of that river, as well as the passage both in and out of its mouth: It is farther stipulated, that the vessels belonging to the subjects of either nation shall not be stopped, visited, or subjected to the payment of any duty whatsoever. The stipulations inserted in the IVth article, in favour of the inhabitants of Canada shall also take place with regard to the inhabitants of the countries ceded by this article.

VIII. The King of Great Britain shall restore to France the islands of Guadeloupe, of Mariegalante, of Desirade, of Martinico, and of Belleisle; and the fortresses of these islands shall be restored in the same condition they were in when they were conquered by the British arms, provided that his Britannic Majesty's subjects, who shall have settled in the said islands, or those who shall have any commercial affairs to settle there or in other places restored to France by the present treaty, shall have liberty to sell their lands and their estates, to settle their affairs, to recover their debts, and to bring away their effects as well as their persons, on board vessels, which they shall be permitted to send to the said islands and other places restored as above, and which shall serve for this use only, without being restrained on account of their religion, or under any other pretense whatsoever, except that of debts or of criminal prosecutions: and for this purpose, the term of eighteen months is allowed to his Britannic Majesty's subjects, to be computed from the day of the exchange of the ratifications of the present treaty; but, as the liberty granted to his Britannic Majesty's subjects, to bring away their persons and their effects, in vessels of their nation, may be liable to abuses if precautions were not taken to prevent them; it has been expressly agreed between his Britannic Majesty and his Most Christian Majesty, that the number of English vessels which have leave to go to the said islands and places restored to France, shall be limited, as well as the number of tons of each one; that they shall go in ballast; shall set sail at a fixed time; and shall make one voyage only; all the effects belonging to the English being to be embarked at the same time. It has been farther agreed, that his Most Christian Majesty shall cause the necessary passports to be given to the said vessels; that, for the greater security, it shall be allowed to place two French clerks or guards in each of the said vessels, which shall be visited in the landing places and ports of the said islands and places restored to France, and that the merchandise which shall be found herein shall be confiscated.

IX. The Most Christian King cedes and guaranties to his Britannic Majesty, in full right, the islands of Grenada, and the Grenadines, with the same stipulations in favour of the inhabitants of this colony, inserted in the IVth article for those of Canada: And the partition of the islands called neutral, is agreed and fixed, so that those of St. Vincent, Dominica, and Tobago, shall remain in full right to Great Britain, and that of St. Lucia shall be delivered to France, to enjoy the same likewise in full right, and the high contracting parties guaranty the partition so stipulated.

X. His Britannic Majesty shall restore to France the island of Goree in the condition it was in when conquered: and his Most Christian Majesty cedes, in full right, and guaranties to the King of Great Britain the river Senegal, with the forts and factories of St. Lewis, Podor, and Galam, and with all the rights and dependencies of the said river Senegal.

XI. In the East Indies Great Britain shall restore to France, in the condition they are now in, the different factories which that Crown possessed, as well as on the coast of Coromandel and Orixa as on that of Malabar, as also in Bengal, at the beginning of the year 1749. And his Most Christian Majesty renounces all pretension to the acquisitions which he has made on the coast of Coromandel and Orixa since the said beginning of the year 1749. His Most Christian Majesty shall restore, on his side, all that he may have conquered from Great Britain in the East Indies during the present war; and will expressly cause Nattal and Tapanoully, in the island of Sumatra, to be restored; he engages farther, not to erect fortifications, or to keep troops in any part of the dominions of the Subah of Bengal. And in order to preserve future peace on the coast of Coromandel and Orixa, the English and French shall acknowledge Mahomet Ally Khan for lawful Nabob of the Carnatick, and Salabat Jing for lawful Subah of the Decan; and both parties shall renounce all demands and pretensions of satisfaction with which they might charge each other, or their Indian allies, for the depredations or pillage committed on the one side or on the other during the war.

XII. The island of Minorca shall be restored to his Britannic Majesty, as well as Fort St. Philip, in the same condition they were in when conquered by the arms of the Most Christian King; and with the artillery which was there when the said island and the said fort were taken.

XIII. The town and port of Dunkirk shall be put into the state fixed by the last treaty of Aix la Chapelle, and by former treaties. The Cunette shall be destroyed immediately after the exchange of the ratifications of the present treaty, as well as the forts and batteries which defend the entrance on the side of the sea; and provision shall be made at the same time for the wholesomeness of the air, and for the health of the inhabitants, by some other means, to the satisfaction of the King of Great Britain.

XIV. France shall restore all the countries belonging to the Electorate of Hanover, to the Landgrave of Hesse, to the Duke of Brunswick, and to the Count of La Lippe Buckebourg, which are or shall be occupied by his Most Christian Majesty's arms: the fortresses of these different countries shall be restored in the same *condition they were in when conquered by the French arms; and the pieces of artillery, which shall have been carried elsewhere, shall be replaced by the same number, of the same bore, weight and metal.*

XV. In case the stipulations contained in the XIIIth article of the preliminaries should not be competed at the time of the signature of the present treaty, as well with regard to the evacuations to be made by the armies of France of the fortresses of Cleves, Wezel, Guelders, and of all the countries belonging to the King of Prussia, as with regard to the evacuations to be made by the British and French armies of the countries which they occupy in Westphalia, Lower Saxony, on the Lower Rhine, the Upper Rhine, and in all the empire; and to the retreat of the troops into the dominions of their respective Sovereigns: their Britannic and Most Christian Majesties promise to proceed, bona fide, with all the dispatch the case will permit of to the said evacuations, the entire completion whereof they stipulate before the 15th of March next, or sooner if it can be done; and their Britannic and Most Christian Majesties farther engage and promise to each other, not to furnish any succours of any kind to their respective allies who shall continue engaged in the war in Germany.

XVI. The decision of the prizes made in time of peace by the subjects of Great Britain, on the Spaniards, shall be referred to the Courts of Justice of the Admiralty of Great Britain, conformably to the rules established among all nations, so that the validity of the said prizes, between the British and Spanish nations, shall be decided and judged, according to the law of nations, and according to treaties, in the Courts of Justice of the nation who shall have made the capture.

XVII. His Britannic Majesty shall cause to be demolished all the fortifications which his subjects shall have erected in the bay of Honduras, and other places of the territory of Spain in that part of the world, four months after the ratification of the present treaty; and his Catholic Majesty shall not permit his Britannic Majesty's subjects, or their workmen, to be disturbed or molested under any pretence whatsoever in the said places, in their occupation of cutting, loading, and carrying away log-wood; and for this purpose, they may build, without hindrance, and occupy, without interruption, the houses and magazines necessary for them, for their families, and for their effects; and his Catholic Majesty assures to them, by this article, the full enjoyment of those advantages and powers on the Spanish coasts and territories, as above stipulated, immediately after the ratification of the present treaty.

XVIII. His Catholic Majesty desists, as well for himself as for his successors, from all pretension which he may have formed in favour of the Guipuscoans, and other his subjects, to the right of fishing in the neighbourhood of the island of Newfoundland.

XIX. The King of Great Britain shall restore to Spain all the territory which he has conquered in the island of Cuba, with the fortress of the Havana; and this fortress, as well as all the other fortresses of the said island, shall be restored in the same condition they were in when conquered by his Britannic Majesty's arms, provided that his Britannic Majesty's subjects who shall have settled in the said island, restored to Spain by the present treaty, or those who shall have any commercial affairs to settle there, shall have liberty to sell their lands and their estates, to settle their affairs, recover their debts, and to bring away their effects, as well as their persons, on board vessels which they shall be permitted to send to the said island restored as above, and which shall serve for that use only, without being restrained on account of their religion, or under any other pretense whatsoever, except that of debts or of criminal prosecutions: And for this purpose, the term of eighteen months is allowed to his Britannic Majesty's subjects, to be computed from the day of the exchange of the ratifications of the present treaty: but as the liberty granted to his Britannic Majesty's subjects, to bring away their persons and their effects, in vessels of their nation, may be liable to abuses if precautions were not taken to prevent them;

it has been expressly agreed between his Britannic Majesty and his Catholic Majesty, that the number of English vessels which shall have leave to go to the said island restored to Spain shall be limited, as well as the number of tons of each one; that they shall go in ballast; shall set sail at a fixed time; and shall make one voyage only; all the effects belonging to the English being to be embarked at the same time: it has been farther agreed, that his Catholic Majesty shall cause the necessary passports to be given to the said vessels; that for the greater security, it shall be allowed to place two Spanish clerks or guards in each of the said vessels, which shall be visited in the landing places and ports of the said island restored to Spain, and that the merchandise which shall be found therein shall be confiscated.

XX. In consequence of the restitution stipulated in the preceding article, his Catholic Majesty cedes and guaranties, in full right, to his Britannic Majesty, Florida, with Fort St. Augustine, and the Bay of Pensacola, as well as all that Spain possesses on the continent of North America, to the East or to the South East of the river Mississippi. And, in general, every thing that depends on the said countries and lands, with the sovereignty, property, possession, and all rights, acquired by treaties or otherwise, which the Catholic King and the Crown of Spain have had till now over the said countries, lands, places, and their inhabitants; so that the Catholic King cedes and makes over the whole to the said King and to the Crown of Great Britain, and that in the most ample manner and form. His Britannic Majesty agrees, on his side, to grant to the inhabitants of the countries above ceded, the liberty of the Catholic religion; he will, consequently, give the most express and the most effectual orders that his new Roman Catholic subjects may profess the worship of their religion according to the rites of the Romish church, as far as the laws of Great Britain permit. His Britannic Majesty farther agrees, that the Spanish inhabitants, or others who had been subjects of the Catholic King in the said countries, may retire, with all safety and freedom, wherever they think proper; and may sell their estates, provided it be to his Britannic Majesty's subjects, and bring away their effects, as well as their persons without being restrained in their emigration, under any pretence whatsoever, except that of debts, or of criminal prosecutions: the term limited for this emigration being fixed to the space of eighteen months, to be computed from the day of the exchange of the ratifications of the present treaty. It is moreover stipulated, that his Catholic Majesty shall have power to cause all the effects that may belong to him, to be brought away, whether it be artillery or other things.

XXI. The French and Spanish troops shall evacuate all the territories, lands, towns, places, and castles, of his Most faithful Majesty in Europe, without any reserve, which shall have been conquered by the armies of France and Spain, and shall restore them in the same condition they were in when conquered, with the same artillery and ammunition, which were found there: And with regard to the Portuguese Colonies in America, Africa, or in the East Indies, if any change shall have happened there, all things shall be restored on the same footing they were in, and conformably to the preceding treaties which subsisted between the Courts of France, Spain, and Portugal, before the present war.

XXII. All the papers, letters, documents, and archives, which were found in the countries, territories, towns and places that are restored, and those belonging to the countries ceded, shall be, respectively and bona fide, delivered, or furnished at the same time, if possible, that possession is taken, or, at latest, four months after the exchange of the ratifications of the present treaty, in whatever places the said papers or documents may be found.

XXIII. All the countries and territories, which may have been conquered, in whatsoever part of the world, by the arms of their Britannick and Most Faithful Majesties, as well as by those of their Most Christian and Catholic Majesties, which are not included in the present treaty, either under the title of cessions, or under the title of restitutions, shall be restored without difficulty, and without requiring any compensations.

XXIV. As it is necessary to assign a fixed epoch for the restitutions and the evacuations, to be made by each of the high contracting parties, it is agreed, that the British and French troops shall complete, before the 15th of March next, all that shall remain to be executed of the XIIth and XIIIth articles of the preliminaries, signed the 3d day of November last, with regard to the evacuation to be made in the Empire, or elsewhere. The island of Belleisle shall be evacuated six weeks after the exchange of the ratifications of the present treaty, or sooner if it can be done. Guadeloupe, Desirade, Mariegalante Martinico, and St. Lucia, three months after the exchange of the ratifications of the present treaty, or sooner if it can be done. Great Britain shall likewise, at the end of three months after the exchange of the ratifications of the present treaty, or sooner if it can be done, enter into possession of the river and port of the Mobile, and of all that is to form the limits of the territory of Great Britain, on the side of the river Mississippi, as they are specified in the VIIth article. The island of Goree shall be evacuated by Great Britain, three months after the exchange of the ratifications of the present treaty; and the island of Minorca by France, at the same epoch, or sooner if it can be done: And according to the conditions of the VIth article, France shall likewise enter into possession of the islands of St Peter, and of Miquelon, at the end of three months after the exchange of the ratifications of the present treaty. The Factories in the East Indies shall be restored six months after the exchange of the ratifications of the present treaty, or sooner if it can be done. The fortress of the Havana, with all that has been conquered in the island of Cuba, shall be restored three months after the exchange of the ratifications of the present treaty, or sooner if it can be done: And, at the same time, Great Britain shall enter into possession of the country ceded by Spain according to the XXth article. All the places and countries of his most Faithful Majesty, in Europe, shall be restored immediately after the exchange of the ratification of the present treaty: And the Portuguese colonies, which may have been conquered, shall be restored in the space of three months in the West Indies, and of six months in the East Indies, after the exchange of the ratifications of the present treaty, or sooner if it can be done. All the fortresses, the restitution whereof is stipulated above, shall be restored with the artillery and ammunition, which were found there at the time of the conquest. In consequence whereof, the necessary orders shall be sent by each of the high contracting parties, with reciprocal passports for the ships that shall carry them, immediately after the exchange of the ratifications of the present treaty.

XXV. His Britannic Majesty, as Elector of Brunswick Lunenbourg, as well for himself as for his heirs and successors, and all the dominions and possessions of his said Majesty in Germany, are included and guarantied by the present treaty of peace.

XXVI. Their sacred Britannic, Most Christian, Catholic, and Most Faithful Majesties, promise to observe sincerely and bona fide, all the articles contained and settled in the present treaty; and they will not suffer the same to be infringed, directly or indirectly, by their respective subjects; and the said high contracting parties, generally and reciprocally, guaranty to each other all the stipulations of the present treaty.

XXVII. The solemn ratifications of the present treaty, expedited in good and due form, shall be exchanged in this city of Paris, between the high contracting parties, in the space of a month, or sooner if possible, to be computed from the day of the signature of the present treaty.

In witness whereof, we the underwritten their Ambassadors Extraordinary, and Ministers Plenipotentiary, have signed with our hand, in their name, and in virtue of our full powers, have signed the present definitive treaty, and have caused the seal of our arms to be put thereto. Done at Paris the tenth day of February, 1763.

Bedford, C.P.S. Choiseul, Duc de Praslin. El Marq. de Grimaldi.

(L.S.) (L.S.) (LS)

SEPARATE ARTICLES

I. Some of the titles made use of by the contracting powers, either in the full powers, and other acts, during the course of the negotiation, or in the preamble of the present treaty, not being generally acknowledged; it has been agreed, that no prejudice shall ever result therefrom to any of the said contracting parties, and that the titles, taken or omitted on either side, on occasion of the said negotiation, and of the present treaty, shall not be cited or quoted as a precedent.

II. It has been agreed and determined, that the French language made use of in all the copies of the present treaty, shall not become an example which may be alleged, or made a precedent of, or prejudice, in any manner, any of the contracting powers; and that they shall conform themselves, for the future, to what has been observed, and ought to be observed, with regard to, and on the part of powers, who are used, and have a right, to give and to receive copies of like treaties in another language than French; the present treaty having still the same force and effect, as if the aforesaid custom had been therein observed.

III. Though the King of Portugal has not signed the present definitive treaty, their Britannic, Most Christian, and Catholic Majesties, acknowledge, nevertheless, that his Most Faithful Majesty is formally included therein as a contracting party, and as if he had expressly signed the said treaty: Consequently, their Britannic, Most Christian, and Catholic Majesties, respectively and conjointly, promise to his Most Faithful Majesty, in the most express and most binding manner, the execution of all and every the clauses, contained in the said treaty, on his act of accession.

The present Separate Articles shall have the same force as if they were inserted in the treaty.

In witness whereof, We the under-written Ambassadors

Extraordinary, and Ministers Plenipotentiary of their Britannic, Most Christian and Catholic Majesties, have signed the present separate Articles, and have caused the seal of our arms to be put thereto.

Done at Paris, the 10th of February, 1763.

Bedford, C.P.S. Choiseul, Duc El Marq. de

(L.S.) de Praslin. Grimaldi. (L.S.) (L.S.)

Consequences of the Treaty of Paris

The consequences for Canada of the Treaty of Paris, 1763, were profound. The sovereignty of France in both New France and Acadia was extinguished, except for the two small islands of St. Pierre and Miquelon located in the Gulf of St. Lawrence near the island of Newfoundland. The loss of the French colonies to the British, together with the subsequent transfer of western Louisiana to the Spanish, ended the French empire in North America and served as an existential shock to the francophone inhabitants of those territories.

Canada was now part of a large imperial territory – British America, which consisted of 19 territories under British sovereignty (Rupert's Land, Newfoundland, Quebec, Nova Scotia, New Hampshire, Massachusetts, Connecticut, Rhode Island, Pennsylvania, New York, New Jersey, Maryland, Delaware, Virginia, North Carolina, South Carolina, Georgia, East Florida, and West Florida) in addition to an unorganized territory reserved for the aboriginal population under the terms of the Royal Proclamation of 1763. The Mississippi River was the western border of this entity beyond which lay Spanish Louisiana. The northern borders of Spanish Louisiana were considered to fall along the natural watershed divide between the Mississippi-Missouri watershed basin and the Hudson's Bay watershed basin. As such, a portion of territory in what is now southern Saskatchewan and southern Alberta formed part of Louisiana and therefore a colonial border existed between Spain (Louisiana) and Great Britain (Rupert's Land).

For the British Americans in the littoral colonies along the Atlantic coast the removal of France from North America removed an existential threat to the peace and security of British America. However, it also removed an important reason for the political elites to favour a continued political relationship with Great Britain. Now that the threat from the north had disappeared the colonies were less willing to accept political subordination to a far-off government. At the same time, British policy was moving toward greater efforts at cost recovery from the colonies for the security and other services that the Imperial Government did provide to the colonies. The impetus for that policy was motivated by the cost pressures of the Seven Years War. The desire of the Imperial Government to extract greater revenue from the North American portion of the empire clashed with the views of the colonists who were now newly freed from the military threat once posed by France. Relations were further inflamed by the decision of the Imperial Government to deny British-American colonists the opportunity to acquire and exploit new lands west of the Appalachian mountain chain, which was reserved to the aboriginals under the Royal Proclamation of 1763. Thus, the stage was set for a colonial rebellion that would have tremendous effects upon the territorial integrity and eventual territorial sovereignty of Canada.

Treaty of Fontainebleau, 1762 (1764)[6]

The Treaty of Fontainebleau was a secret treaty between France and Spain that provided for the transfer of France's western Louisiana colony to Spain. The eastern portion of Louisiana (i.e., the part east of the Mississippi river) was transferred to Great Britain under the terms of the Treaty of Paris, 1763. The Treaty of Fontainebleau, 1762, was kept secret during the negotiations between France and Great Britain that resulted in the Treaty of Paris, 1763. It was only revealed when the royal government of

France informed its Governor of the transfer of the colony to Spain in 1764. The controversy produced by this treaty among the inhabitants of western Louisiana meant that Spain was unable to firmly establish its sovereignty over the territory until 1769

Treaty of Fontainebleau 1762

November 3, 1762

Louis, by the grace of God, King of France and Navarre, to all to whom these presents shall come, greeting :

Whereas our very dear and well-beloved cousin, the Duke de Choiseul, peer of our realm, knight of our orders and of the golden fleece, lieutenant general of our armies, governor of Touraine, colonel general of the Swiss and Grisons, grandmaster and superintendent general of the posts and relays of France, our Minister and Secretary of State for the Departments of War and Marine and the correspondence with the courts of Madrid and Lisbon, did sign, in our name, with the Marquis de Grimaldi, knight of our orders, gentlemen of the chamber, in exercise of our very dear and well-beloved brother and cousin the Catholic King, and his ambassador extraordinary near us, a preliminary convention, whereby, in order to give to our said brother and cousin a new testimonial of our tender friendship, of the strong interest which we take in satisfying him and promoting the welfare of his crown, and of our sincere desire to strengthen and render indissoluble the bonds which unite the French and Spanish nations, we ceded to him entire and perpetual possession of all the country known under the name of Louisiana, together with New Orleans and the island in which that city stands, which convention had only been signed conditionally and sub sperati by the Marquis de Grimaldi : and whereas our said brother and cousin the Catholic King, animated by the same sentiments towards us which we have evinced on this occasion, has agreed to the said cession, and ratified the conditional acceptation made by his said ambassador extraordinary, which convention and ratification are here inserted, word for word, as follows :

Don Carlos, by the grace of God, King of Castile, of Leon, of Aragon, of the Two Sicilies, of Jerusalem, of Navarre, of Granada, of Toledo, of Valencia, of Gallicia, of Majorca, of Seville, of Sardinia, of Cordova, of Corsica, of Murcia, of Jaen, of the Algarves, of Algesiras, of Gibraltar, of the Canary Islands, of the East and West Indies, and the islands and main land of the ocean ; Archduke of Austria ; Duke of Burgundy, of Brabant and Milan ; Count of Hapsburg, of Flanders, of Tyrol, and of Barcelona ; Lord of Biscay and of Molina, &c.

Whereas, on the third day of the present month, the preliminaries of a peace were signed between the crowns of Spain and France on the one part, and those of England and Portugal on the other, and the Most Christian King, my very dear and well-beloved cousin, purely from the nobleness of his heart, and the love and friendship in which we live, thought proper to dispose that the Marquis de Grimaldi, my ambassador extraordinary near his royal person, and the Duke de Choiseul, his Minister of State, should on the same day sign a convention, by which the crown of France ceded immediately to that of Spain the country known by the name of Louisiana, together with New Orleans and the island in which that city stands, and by which said ambassador agrees to the cession only conditionally sub sperati, as he is not furnished with orders to execute it absolutely ; the tenor of which convention is the following :

The Most Christian King, being firmly resolved to strengthen and perpetuate the bonds of tender amity which unite him to his cousin the Catholic King, proposes in consequence to act with his Catholic Majesty, at all times and in all circumstances, in a perfect uniformity of principle, for the common glory of their house and the reciprocal interests of their kingdoms.

With this view, his Most Christian Majesty, being fully sensible of the sacrifices made by the Catholic King in generously uniting with him for the restoration of peace, desires, on this occasion, to give him a proof of the strong interest which he takes in satisfying him and affording advantages to his crown.

The Most Christian King has accordingly authorized his minister, the Duke de Choiseul, to deliver up to the Marquis de Grimaldi, the ambassador of the Catholic King, in the most authentic form, an act whereby his Most Christian Majesty cedes, in entire possession, purely and simply, without exception, to his Catholic Majesty and his successors, in perpetuity, all the country known under the name of Louisiana, as well as New Orleans and the island in which that place stands.

But, as the Marquis de Grimaldi is not informed with sufficient precision of the intentions of his Catholic Majesty, he has thought proper only to accept the said cession conditionally and sub sperati, until he receives the orders expected by him from the King his master, which, if conformable with the desires of his Most Christian Majesty, as he hopes they will be, will be followed by the authentic act of cession of the said country, stipulating also the measures and the time, to be fixed by common accord, for the evacuation of Louisiana and New Orleans, by the subjects of his Most Christian Majesty, and for the possession of the same by those of his Catholic Majesty.

In testimony whereof, we, the respective ministers, have signed the present preliminary convention, and have affixed to it the seals of our arms.

Done at Fontainebleau, on the third of November, one thousand seven hundred and sixty-two.

The Duke de Choiseul.

The Marquis de Grimaldi.

Therefore, in order to establish between the Spanish and French nations the same spirit of union and friendship which should subsist as they do in the hearts of their sovereigns, I, therefore, take pleasure in accepting, as I do accept, in proper form, the said act of cession, promising also to accept those which may hereafter be judged necessary for carrying it into entire and formal execution, and authorizing the said Marquis de Grimaldi to treat, conclude, and sign them.

In testimony whereof, I have ordered these presents to be drawn up, signed by my hand, sealed with my privy seal, and countersigned by my Councillor of State and chief Secretary of State and War.

Given at San Lorenzo el Real, on the thirteenth of November, seventeen hundred and sixty-two.

The King.

Countersigned : Ricardo Wall.

The said acceptation and ratification having been approved by us, and regarded as a strong evidence of the friendship and good will of our very dear and well-beloved cousin the Catholic King, we renew and confirm by these presents the cession of Louisiana and of New Orleans, with the island in which that city stands, promising immediately to conclude with our said brother and cousin a convention, in which the measures to be taken in concert for executing and consummating this cession to our mutual satisfaction will be fixed by common accord.

In faith whereof, we have caused these presents to be drawn up, which we have signed with our hands, and have affixed to them our secret seal.

Given at Versailles, on the twenty-third day of the month of November, in the year of grace one thousand seven hundred and sixty-two, and of our reign the forty-eighth.

Louis.

By the King : Choiseul, Duke de Praslin.

Consequences of the Treaty of Fontainebleau

Under the Treaty of Fontainebleau the whole of western Louisiana was transferred from the sovereignty of France to the sovereignty of Spain. Since the northern boundary of the Louisiana territory extended as far north as the watershed divide between the Mississippi-Missouri river drainage basin, and the Hudson's Bay drainage basin, a small portion of what later became Canadian territory in the provinces of Saskatchewan and Alberta formed part of this transfer.

An additional consequence of this treaty is that Canada (Rupert's Land) acquired a land border with Spain along the northern edge of Spanish Luisiana.

ENDNOTES

[1] Frances Gardiner Davenport, ed., *European Treaties Bearing on the History of the United States and Its Dependencies to 1648*, Carnegie, Washington, 1817, at page 317.

[2] *Treaty of Breda*, The Canadian Encyclopaedia, http://www.thecanadianencyclopedia.ca/en/article/treaty-of-breda/ [accessed March 2, 2018]

[3] Uncertainty concering the boundaries of Nova Scotia and Acadia resulted from a conflict between the grant made to certain proprietors, principally Sir Thomas Temple, by Oliver Cromwell during the ascendancy of the English Commonwealth government in the 1650's, and the letters patent issued by King Charles II for implementing the return of Acadia pursuant to the Treaty of Breda. The latter document held that Port Royal, St. John's and

Pentagoet (Penobscot) were all within Acadia – a fact strongly disputed by Sir Thomas Temple who held that they were within the boundaries of Nova Scotia. While the King's letters patent prevailed the boundary dispute continued to fester in the succeeding years.

[4] Including Nova Scotia

[5] This version of the treaty is sourced from Yale University, the Avalon Project.

[6] Although the Treaty of Fontainebleau was executed a year prior to the Treaty of Paris, 1763, it remained a secret treaty until its existence was publicized in 1764. Therefore it has been included here subsequent to the Treaty of Paris, 1763.

4.

THE SOUTHERN BOUNDARY

Introduction

With the end of the Seven Years War the long history of Canadian territory being traded back and forth between two European kingdoms came to an end. The vast majority of the geographic territory that would subsequently become modern-day Canada was now under the sovereignty of the United Kingdom of Great Britain. Accordingly, Great Britain took steps to organize the territory of British America to take into account the new possessions that it had acquired from France.

The Royal Proclamation, 1763

A reorganization of the new North American and West Indian territories was set out in the Royal Proclamation of 1763, a key document in the constitutional evolution of Canada. In the Royal Proclamation, 1763, the new boundaries for the additions to British America were set out as follows:

Royal Proclamation, 1763 (Extracts)

October 7, 1763

First. The Government of Quebec, bounded on the Labrador Coast by the River St. John, and from thence by a Line drawn from the Head of that River through the Lake St. John to the South End of the Lake [Nipissing]; from whence the said Line crossing the River St. Lawrence and the Lake Champlain in Forty five Degrees of North Latitude, passes along the High Lands which divide the

Rivers that empty themselves into the said River St. Lawrence, from those which fall into the Sea; and also along the North Coast of the Baye des Chaleurs, and the Coast of the Gulf of St. Lawrence to Cape Rosieres, and from thence crossing the Mouth of the River St. Lawrence by the West End of the Island of Anticosti, terminates at the aforesaid River of St. John.

. . . .

Fourthly. ... And, to the End that the open and free Fishery of Our Subjects may be extended to and carried on upon the Coast of Labrador and the adjacent Islands, We have thought fit, with the Advice of Our said Privy Council, to put all that Coast, from the River St. John's to Hudson's Straights, together with the Islands of Anticosti and Madelaine[1], and all other smaller Islands lying upon the said Coast, under the Care and Inspection of Our Governor of Newfoundland.

We have also, with the Advice of Our Privy Council, thought fit to annex the Islands of St. John's[2], and Cape Breton or Isle Royale, with the lesser Islands adjacent thereto, to Our Government of Nova Scotia.

Consequences of the Royal Proclamation

As a result of the Royal Proclamation, 1763, the colony of Newfoundland was constituted to include the island of Newfoundland, the north coast of the Gulf of St. Lawrence, the Labrador Coast, and Anticosti Island and the Magdalen Islands. Nova Scotia was constituted to include both present day Nova Scotia as well as present day New Brunswick and Prince Edward Island. Quebec was contained within borders established between the St. John River westward to a point on the south side of Lake Nippissing and then south to the watershed divide between the St. Lawrence River basin and the Atlantic Ocean basin. The watershed divide was then followed east to and along the north coast of Chaleur Bay to Cap-des-Rosiers on the Gaspé peninsula and then across the mouth of the St. Lawrence River past the westernmost point of Anticosti Island back to the St. John River.

However, there was some subsequent uncertainty about the use of the St. John River as the boundary between Quebec and Newfoundland. In its historic 1927 judgment concerning the Labrador boundary, the Judicial Committee of the Privy Council, then the highest judicial body in both Canada and Newfoundland, decided that the proclamation actually meant the Romaine River when it described the St. John River as the eastern boundary of Quebec, stating:

> The contention that the territory annexed to Newfoundland was intended to run back to the watershed is supported by the fact that in the Proclamation of 1763 the province of Quebec is described as bounded on the north by a line drawn from the head of the river St. John to the westward—a description which leads to the inference that the land on the east or left bank of the river St. John from its head to the sea had been already allotted to the government of Newfoundland. It has been ascertained by recent surveys that the river St. John here mentioned does not in fact rise near the watershed, but at some point between the height of land and the sea; but it is plain from contemporary maps that the sources of the river Romaine, which rises at the watershed and runs parallel with the St. John, had been taken for the sources of the latter river, and that the eastern boundary of the new Province of Quebec at this point was intended to follow the course of the river Romaine from the watershed to the sea.[3]

These borders confined Quebec to the historic heartland of New France by cutting it off from both the east coast and from the Pays d'en Haut, the vast upper lake country that was the lifeblood of the fur trade. Instead, the Pays d'en Haut and the country farther south, west of the heights of the Appalachian mountain chain, were reserved for the aboriginal population and the Royal Proclamation prohibited British Americans, including those in the colonies newly acquired from France, from entering into land purchase arrangements with members of the aboriginal first nations. To the Crown alone was reserved the right to enter into land transactions in relation to aboriginal lands. The Royal Proclamation of 1763 has been lauded for its efforts to prevent abuses by colonists seeking to enter into land purchase arrangements with aboriginal first nations. However, such restrictions weighed heavily on the British Americans residing in the Atlantic littoral colonies who were eager to penetrate and occupy the western wilderness.

Thus, the thirteen years in which British America survived as a single political entity covering all of eastern North America remained uneasy years. In addition to the resentments spawned by the Proclamation Line, which restricted the westward expansion of the littoral colonies, British American sentiments in the Atlantic colonies were inflamed by the efforts of the Imperial Government to extract additional revenues from North America through customs and stamp duties. Hitherto, the main financial burden of the wars in North America had fallen on Great Britain itself, although the colonial legislatures had voted sums for the British war effort in the Seven Years War, and the colonies had supported their own colonial militias serving with the British forces. Now, however, with the French ousted from North America there was no longer a strategic need for maintaining substantial imperial forces in North America, and British American colonists did not want to pay for the garrison forces stationed in North America. Thus the determination of the Imperial Government to extract revenues from the colonies through customs and stamp duties riled the sentiments of the political elites in British America. Increasingly, British Americans began to see themselves as different from the British people in the mother country, although colonial politicians were careful to frame their demands for relief against imperial taxation by reference to the ancient liberties of Englishmen, and not as a radical departure from the existing constitutional norms.

The Quebec Act, 1774

The brooding crisis came to a head when the Imperial Parliament enacted a series of laws that agitators in the colonies termed the

Intolerable Acts. Perhaps chief among these new statutes was the Quebec Act of 1774, which greatly extended the borders of the province of Quebec, by reincorporating the Pays d'en Haut into the province and extending Quebec's boundaries further south, to the forks of the Ohio and Mississippi rivers:

Quebec Act, 1774 (Extracts)

That all the territories, islands, and countries in North America, belonging to the crown of Great Britain, bounded on the south by a line from the Bay of Chaleurs, along the high lands which divide the rivers that empty themselves into the river St. Lawrence from those which fall into the sea, to a point in 45° of northern latitude, on the eastern bank of the River Connecticut, keeping the same latitude directly West, through the Lake Champlain, until in the same latitude, it meets the River St. Lawrence; from thence up the eastern bank of the said river to the Lake Ontario; thence through the Lake Ontario, and the River commonly called Niagara; and thence along by the Eastern and South Eastern Bank of Lake Erie, following the said bank, until the same shall be intersected by the northern boundary, granted by the charter of the province of Pennsylvania, in case the same shall be so intersected; and from thence along the said northern and western boundaries of the said province, until the said Western boundary strike the Ohio: but in case the said bank of the said Lake shall not be found to be so intersected, then following the said bank until it shall arrive at that point of the said bank which shall be nearest to the northwestern angle of the said province of Pennsylvania, and thence, by a right line, to the said northwestern angle of the said province; and thence along the western boundary of the said province, until it strike the river Ohio; and along the bank of the said river, westward, to the banks of the Mississippi, and northward to the southern boundary of the territory granted to the merchants adventurers of England, trading to Hudson's Bay; and also all such territories, islands, and countries, which have, since 10 February, 1763, been made part of the government of Newfoundland, be and they are hereby during his Majesty's pleasure, annexed to, and made part and parcel of the province of Quebec, as created and established by the said Royal proclamation of 7 October, 1763.

Provided always, that nothing herein contained, relative to the boundary of the province of Quebec, shall in any wise affect the boundaries of any other colony.

Consequences of the Quebec Act

The hostility of the British American colonists in the littoral colonies to this extension of the Quebec boundary was exacerbated by the fact that the Seven Years War was still of recent memory, as was the memory of the many years in which the British colonies feared military attacks from French Canada. Now, the extension of Quebec into the far south not only seemed to block the land-hungry southern colonies from encroaching westward beyond the Appalachian Mountain chain but also resurrected the unhappy memory of the many conflicts between the French and the English in North America, and the recurring threat to the littoral colonies of an attack from the north. That the memories of the recent war were still fresh could be seen by the reaction of many of the colonial agitators in the littoral colonies toward the efforts to relieve the impediments to a full participation in civil life by the Roman Catholic inhabitants of Canada through reforms to the public oath statutes, and the restoration of the traditional French civil law, the Coutume de Paris, in place of the English common law that had been imposed in civil matters following the cession of New France.[4] Many of the agitators in the English-speaking colonies railed against the removal of what they called the English civil liberties in Quebec in favour of a return to what they deemed to be the forces of reaction.

By this point in time (1774) Britain and many of its American colonies were headed for a political collision although throughout the growing crisis there were statesmen on both sides of the Atlantic who sought compromise as a means of keeping the empire together. Unhappily, those efforts failed and when the spark was lit by a clash of arms in 1775 at Lexington and Concord, in the province of Massachusetts, the British and the British-American colonists in the Atlantic littoral colonies were set on a course for rebellion and war.

The American Revolutionary War of 1775-83 eventually broadened into a war not only between rebellious Americans and the British but also into a war involving the major European powers. Of the twenty British American colonies forming British America in 1775,[5] there were active rebellions in 14 of them. However, the short-lived rebellion in Nova Scotia, which was not supported by the majority of the population, was quickly suppressed and in each of Quebec, Newfoundland, St. John's Island, East Florida and West Florida loyalty to the Crown was maintained. Rupert's Land was too remote to be influenced by the politics in the south and, in any event, it possessed only an itinerant population. A long and extensive war was fought by the rebels in the thirteen rebellious Atlantic littoral colonies under the capable generalship of George Washington, who had earlier played such a prominent role in the spark that launched the Seven Years War in North America. Quebec was invaded in 1775, and Montreal taken, but at the fortress of Quebec the city's defences held although it was invested by two rebel armies and the rebellious British Americans were forced to withdraw. The following year, on July 4, 1776, the British Americans formally declared their independence from Great Britain.

The Treaty of Paris, 1783

With large armies tied down in a fruitless struggle in the thirteen colonies where a majority of the population no longer supported their colonial governments, and beset abroad by France and Spain, Great Britain found itself outdone by its enemies. After its catastrophic defeat at the battle of Yorktown by American forces under General Washington, and French naval forces under Admiral de Grasse, the Imperial Government bowed to the inevitable and entered into peace negotiations with the Americans and the European powers. Those negotiations eventually bore fruit and resulted in the Treaty of Paris of 1783 by which Great Britain recognized the independence of the United States of America and agreed to generous concessions concerning the new country's boundaries with British North America. The British made concessions to America out of a desire to restore the profitable trade relationship that had existed between the thirteen colonies and their mother country before the outbreak of the war.

The Treaty of Paris, 1783 (Extracts)

September 3, 1783

In the name of the most holy and undivided Trinity.

It having pleased the Divine Providence to dispose the hearts of the most serene and most potent Prince George the Third, by the grace of God, king of Great Britain, France, and Ireland, defender of the faith, duke of Brunswick and Lunebourg, arch-treasurer and prince elector of the Holy Roman Empire etc., and of the United States of America, to forget all past misunderstandings and differences that have unhappily interrupted the good correspondence and friendship which they mutually wish to restore, and to establish such a beneficial and satisfactory intercourse , between the two countries upon the ground of reciprocal advantages and mutual convenience as may promote and secure to both perpetual peace and harmony; and having for this desirable end already laid the foundation of peace and reconciliation by the Provisional Articles signed at Paris on the 30th of November 1782, by the commissioners empowered on each part, which articles were agreed to be inserted in and constitute the Treaty of Peace proposed to be concluded between the Crown of Great Britain and the said United States, but which treaty was not to be concluded until terms of peace should be agreed upon between Great Britain and France and his Britannic Majesty should be ready to conclude such treaty accordingly; and the treaty between Great Britain and France having since been concluded, his Britannic Majesty and the United States of America, in order to carry into full effect the Provisional Articles above mentioned, according to the tenor thereof, have constituted and appointed, that is to say his Britannic Majesty on his part, David Hartley, Esqr., member of the Parliament of Great Britain, and the said United States on their part, John Adams, Esqr., late a commissioner of the United States of America at the court of Versailles, late delegate in Congress from the state of Massachusetts, and chief justice of the said state, and minister plenipotentiary of the said United States to their high mightinesses the States General of the United Netherlands; Benjamin Franklin, Esqr., late delegate in Congress from the state of Pennsylvania, president of the convention of the said state, and minister plenipotentiary from the United States of America at the court of Versailles; John Jay, Esqr., late president of Congress and chief justice of the state of New York, and minister plenipotentiary from the said United States at the court of Madrid; to be plenipotentiaries for the concluding and signing the present definitive treaty; who after having reciprocally communicated their respective full powers have agreed upon and confirmed the following articles.

Article 1:

His Britannic Majesty acknowledges the said United States, viz., New Hampshire, Massachusetts Bay, Rhode Island and Providence Plantations, Connecticut, New York, New Jersey, Pennsylvania, Maryland, Virginia, North Carolina, South Carolina and Georgia, to be free sovereign and independent states, that he treats with them as such, and for himself, his heirs, and successors, relinquishes all claims to the government, propriety, and territorial rights of the same and every part thereof.

Article 2:

And that all disputes which might arise in future on the subject of *the boundaries of the said United States may be prevented, it is hereby agreed and declared, that the following are and shall be their boundaries, viz.; from the northwest angle of Nova Scotia, viz., that angle which is formed by a line drawn due north from the source of St. Croix River to the highlands; along the said highlands which divide those rivers that empty themselves into the river St. Lawrence, from those which fall into the Atlantic Ocean, to the northwesternmost head of Connecticut River; thence down along the middle of that river to the forty-fifth degree of north latitude; from thence by a line due west on said latitude until it strikes the river Iroquois or Cataraquy; thence along the middle of said river into Lake Ontario; through the middle of said lake until it strikes the communication by water between that lake and Lake Erie; thence along the middle of said communication into Lake Erie, through the middle of said lake until it arrives at the water communication between that lake and Lake Huron; thence along the middle of said water communication into Lake Huron, thence through the middle of said lake to the water communication between that lake and Lake Superior; thence through Lake Superior northward of the Isles Royal and Phelipeaux to the Long Lake; thence through the middle of said Long Lake and the water communication between it and the Lake of the Woods, to the said Lake of the Woods; thence through the said lake to the most northwesternmost point thereof, and from thence on a due west course to the river Mississippi; thence by a line to be drawn along the middle of the said river Mississippi until it shall intersect the northernmost part of the thirty-first degree of north latitude, South, by a line to be drawn due east from the determination of the line last mentioned in the latitude of thirty-one degrees of the equator, to the middle of the river Apalachicola or Catahouche; thence along the middle thereof to its junction with the Flint River, thence straight to the head of Saint Mary's River; and thence down along the middle of Saint Mary's River to the Atlantic Ocean; east, by a line to be drawn along the middle of the river Saint Croix, from its mouth in the Bay of Fundy to its source, and from its source directly north to the aforesaid highlands which divide the rivers that fall into the Atlantic Ocean from those which fall into the river*

Saint Lawrence; comprehending all islands within twenty leagues of any part of the shores of the United States, and lying between lines to be drawn due east from the points where the aforesaid boundaries between Nova Scotia on the one part and East Florida on the other shall, respectively, touch the Bay of Fundy and the Atlantic Ocean, excepting such islands as now are or heretofore have been within the limits of the said province of Nova Scotia.

Article 3:

It is agreed that the people of the United States shall continue to enjoy unmolested the right to take fish of every kind on the Grand Bank and on all the other banks of Newfoundland, also in the Gulf of Saint Lawrence and at all other places in the sea, where the inhabitants of both countries used at any time heretofore to fish. And also that the inhabitants of the United States shall have liberty to take fish of every kind on such part of the coast of Newfoundland as British fishermen shall use, (but not to dry or cure the same on that island) and also on the coasts, bays and creeks of all other of his Britannic Majesty's dominions in America; and that the American fishermen shall have liberty to dry and cure fish in any of the unsettled bays, harbors, and creeks of Nova Scotia, Magdalen Islands, and Labrador, so long as the same shall remain unsettled, but so soon as the same or either of them shall be settled, it shall not be lawful for the said fishermen to dry or cure fish at such settlement without a previous agreement for that purpose with the inhabitants, proprietors, or possessors of the ground.

. . . .

Article 7:

There shall be a firm and perpetual peace between his Britannic Majesty and the said states, and between the subjects of the one and the citizens of the other, wherefore all hostilities both by sea and land shall from henceforth cease. All prisoners on both sides shall be set at liberty, and his Britannic Majesty shall with all convenient speed, and without causing any destruction, or carrying away any Negroes or other property of the American inhabitants, withdraw all his armies, garrisons, and fleets from the said United States, and from every post, place, and harbor within the same; leaving in all fortifications, the American artillery that may be therein; and shall also order and cause all archives, records, deeds, and papers belonging to any of the said states, or their citizens, which in the course of the war may have fallen into the hands of his officers, to be forthwith restored and delivered to the proper states and persons to whom they belong.

Article 8:

The navigation of the river Mississippi, from its source to the ocean, shall forever remain free and open to the subjects of Great Britain and the citizens of the United States.

Article 9:

In case it should so happen that any place or territory belonging to Great Britain or to the United States should have been conquered by the arms of either from the other before the arrival of the said Provisional Articles in America, it is agreed that the same shall be restored without difficulty and without requiring any compensation.

Consequences of the Treaty of Paris

The consequences of the Treaty of Paris, 1783 were profound. British America was severed into two halves, with the northern half remaining under British sovereignty while the southern half became the independent United States of America.[6] Initially, the American negotiators, led by Benjamin Franklin, had sought the cession of Canada and Nova Scotia to the new United States but having successfully defended the northern colonies Britain had no desire to part with them. Nor did the majority of the inhabitants of the northern colonies exhibit any preference toward joining the United States.

The American negotiators then suggested that the border be established along the 45th parallel of latitude. However, the Americans had a weak claim to any lands lying north of the Great Lakes. None of the colonial charters granted by the Crown to any one of the thirteen colonies now to become independent included any of the lands lying north of the Great Lakes, which in any event had formed part of New France through most of the early colonial period. Finally, bowing to the inevitable, the American negotiators suggested that the Great Lakes formed a natural frontier between that United States and Canada and that it ought to become the international boundary between the two countries.[7] This proposal was acceptable to the British and thus Canada, or British North America as it was now called, achieved a defined international boundary that, in general, remains the permanent border between the two countries within the Great Lakes basin.

The two parties agreed that the border between the Province of Quebec and the United States would be placed through the midpoint of the St. Lawrence river west of the intersection of that river with the 45th parallel of latitude, and the mid-point of each of Lakes Ontario, Erie, Huron and Superior, and in the waterways that connect those lakes. The use of the midpoint of those bodies of water as the border between the two countries was equitable, in that it provided a roughly equal proportion of the freshwater resources to each country, and it was based on the principles of international law espoused by such notable authorities as Grotius and Vattel.[8] However, issues with respect to some of the islands in the lakes and rivers required further consideration at a later point in time.

In the east, the American negotiators were interested in obtaining Nova Scotia for their new nation but again the British demurred. Ultimately, the American negotiators accepted that Nova Scotia too, would remain under British sovereignty.[9] However, there were difficulties in defining the border between Nova Scotia (which then included New Brunswick) and Massachusetts (which then included Maine). The British and American negotiators had access to a map prepared in 1755 by John Mitchell, a map-maker who had been in the employ of the Crown, but Mitchell's map suffered from several inaccuracies.[10] One of the most prominent inaccuracies concerned the identification of the St. Croix River. There was, in fact, no river bearing that name and that uncertainty led to several rivers later being proposed as the true St. Croix River. This unsettled issue would be carried forward to a future date for resolution.

In the west, the British and American negotiators were at a particular disadvantage due to the paucity of reliable geographical knowledge of the rivers and land-forms of the west during this period of time. The border was defined westward to and through the Lake of the Woods "to the most north westernmost point thereof, and from thence on a due west course to the river Mississippi". The problem with this description was that the Mississippi River does not come far enough north to intersect with any point due west of the Lake of the Woods. At the time of the treaty the source of the Mississippi River was unknown, and it was only presumed to reach far enough north to enter into the territory remaining under the sovereignty of Great Britain. That this was not so would not be known for a number of years, and would eventually require a rectification in the description of the boundary.[11]

Nevertheless, despite its faults, the Treaty of Paris, 1783, succeeded in a practical way to accomplish the severing of British America into two new political entities, the United States of America, and British North America. The international border established by the Treaty of Paris, 1783, is, in the main, the southern border that exists at present between Canada and the United States of America.

The Jay Treaty, 1794

Following the Treaty of Paris, 1783, both Great Britain and the

United States found cause to breach its intent, and its terms. The American Revolutionary War was not only a war for independence but it was also a civil war, fought between Americans, and hard feelings remained on both the loyalist and patriot sides following the end of the war. In the United States, recommendations made to the states pursuant to the terms of the treaty for the restoration of property, or compensation for the losses incurred by American loyalists, went unanswered. Further, attempts by British creditors to recover outstanding monies owed to them from pre-war debts were also impeded, or frustrated, in the individual states.

In British North America the colonial authorities received the news of the province of Quebec's new southern border with some consternation. The southern border put several important border forts outside of British sovereignty and potentially jeopardized the ability of the colonial Indian Department to maintain its traditional relations and important alliances with the aboriginal first nations south of the Great Lakes. Therefore, from both a military perspective concerning colonial defences, and the political perspective of retaining the British hold on the aboriginal first nations in the continental interior, the British authorities in Canada simply decided to keep the existing forts in their possession after the cessation of hostilities following the American Revolutionary War. Thus, the border posts were retained at Fort au Fer and Dutchman's Point, on Lake Champlain, Fort Oswegatchie on the St. Lawrence River (at what is today Ogdensburg, New York), Fort Ontario at Oswego, New York, Fort Niagara on the Niagara River, Fort Miami on the Maumee River, in what is now Ohio, Fort Lernoult at Detroit, and Fort Mackinac, on Mackinac Island, which controlled the strategic Straits of Mackinac between Lake Huron and Lake Michigan. Naturally, the United States continued to object to the continuing presence of the British at these important border points.

To resolve the unsettled questions concerning the implementation of the Treaty of Paris, 1783, as well as to repair relations between the United States and Great Britain, President Washington dispatched the Chief Justice of the United States, John Jay, to negotiate a new treaty with Great Britain in the mid-1790's. Jay was successful, and a series of issues leftover from the American Revolutionary War, including issues pertaining to the boundary between Canada and the United States, were successfully resolved.

The Jay Treaty, 1794 (Extracts)

November 19, 1794

Treaty of Amity Commerce and Navigation, between His Britannic Majesty; and The United States of America, by Their President, with the advice and consent of Their Senate.

. . . .

2. His Majesty will withdraw all His Troops and Garrisons from all Posts and Places within the Boundary Lines assigned by the Treaty of Peace[12] to the United States. This Evacuation shall take place on or before the first Day of June One thousand seven hundred and ninety six, and all the proper Measures shall in the interval be taken by concert between the Government of the United States, and His Majesty's Governor General in America, for settling the previous arrangements which may be necessary respecting the delivery of the said Posts: The United States in the mean Time at Their discretion extending their settlements to any part within the said boundary line, except within the precincts or Jurisdiction of any of the said Posts. All Settlers and Traders, within the Precincts or Jurisdiction of the said Posts, shall continue to enjoy, unmolested, all their property of every kind, and shall be protected therein. They shall be at full liberty to remain there, or to remove with all or any part of their Effects; and it shall also be free to them to sell their Lands, Houses, or Effects, or to retain the property thereof, at their discretion; such of them as shall continue to reside within the said Boundary Lines shall not be compelled to become Citizens of the United States, or to take any Oath of allegiance to the Government thereof, but they shall be at full liberty so to do, if they think proper, and they shall make and declare their Election within one year after the Evacuation aforesaid. And all persons who shall continue there after the expiration of the said year, without having declared their intention of remaining Subjects of His Britannick Majesty, shall be considered as having elected to become Citizens of the United States.

. . . .

4. Whereas it is uncertain whether the River Mississippi extends so far to the Northward as to be intersected by a Line to be drawn due West from the Lake of the woods in the manner mentioned in the Treaty of Peace between His Majesty and the United States, it is agreed, that measures shall be taken in Concert between His Majesty's Government in America, and the Government of the United States, for making a joint Survey of the said River, from one Degree of Latitude below the falls of St Anthony to the principal Source or Sources of the said River, and also of the parts adjacent thereto, And that if on the result of such Survey it should appear that the said River would not be intersected by such a Line as is above mentioned; The two Parties will thereupon proceed by amicable negotiation to regulate the Boundary Line in that quarter as well as all other Points to be adjusted between the said Parties, according to Justice and mutual Convenience, and in Conformity, to the Intent of the said Treaty.

5. Whereas doubts have arisen what River was truly intended under the name of the River St. Croix mentioned in the said Treaty of Peace and forming a part of the boundary therein described, that question shall be referred to the final Decision of Commissioners to be appointed in the following Manner-Viz-

One Commissioner shall be named by His Majesty, and one by the President of the United States, by and with the advice and Consent of the Senate thereof, and the said two Commissioners shall agree on the choice of a third, or, if they cannot so agree, They shall each propose one Person, and of the two names so proposed one shall be drawn by Lot, in the presence of the two original Commissioners.

And the three Commissioners so appointed shall be Sworn impartially to examine and decide the said question according to such Evidence as shall respectively be laid before Them on the part of the British Government and of the United States. The said Commissioners shall meet at Halifax and shall have power to adjourn to such other place or places as they shall think fit. They shall have power to appoint a Secretary, and to employ such Surveyors or other Persons as they shall judge necessary. The said Commissioners shall by a Declaration under their Hands and Seals, decide what River is the River St Croix intended by the Treaty.

The said Declaration shall contain a description of the said River, and shall particularize the Latitude and Longitude of its mouth and of its Source. Duplicates of this Declaration and of the State meets of their Accounts, and of the Journal of their proceedings, shall be delivered by them to the Agent of His Majesty, and to the Agent of the United States, who may be respectively appointed and authorized to manage the business on behalf of the respective Governments. And both parties agree to consider such decision as final and conclusive, so as that the same shall never thereafter be called into question, or made the subject of dispute or difference between them.

Consequences of the Jay Treaty

The Jay Treaty, 1794, resolved the issue of the over-holding tenancy of Great Britain in the forts located south of the Great Lakes. Under the terms of the Jay Treaty Great Britain was required to vacate the border forts by June 1, 1796, an obligation which the British satisfied. For the purposes of the defence of Upper Canada[13] new forts were built by the British to replace those lost to the United States, such as the fort on St. Joseph's Island, which replaced the fort lost on Mackinac Island.

Relations between the British Crown and the aboriginal first nations located in the United States continued and the British maintained officers of the Indian Department at Fort Malden in Amherstburg, Upper Canada, for the purpose of maintaining the aboriginal-Crown relationship. Nevertheless, the transfer of the forts to the United States put the American government in a much better strategic position to obtain favourable terms in any future treaties between the US government and the aboriginal first nations located on US soil.

The Jay Treaty also attempted to resolve two outstanding issues with respect to the placement of the international border between British North America and the United States. Those two issues concerned firstly, the identification of the St. Croix River boundary between New Brunswick[14] and Massachusetts (Maine)[15] and secondly the question of whether the upper Mississippi River intersected the line established by the Treaty of Paris, 1783, as the boundary between the United States and British North America. In the first case the Jay Treaty provided for the establishment of a commission made up representatives of both sovereign powers to investigate the geographical issues and to determine the location of the boundary that was intended by the framers of the Treaty of Paris, 1783. In the second case it was provided that a joint survey would be conducted by the parties to determine whether the Mississippi river intersected the western extension of the international boundary.

The commission to determine the meaning of the reference to the St. Croix River in the Treaty of Paris, 1783 was subsequently convened and it represented an early use of international arbitration to resolve disputes between sovereign countries. The particular issue that the commissioners had to determine was the identification of the river that was referred to as the St. Croix River in the Treaty of Paris, 1783. Initially, there were three possibilities. Great Britain suggested that it meant [what was then called] the Cobscook River, which would have shifted the boundary between British North America and the United States well into Massachusetts (Maine). The Americans took the view that it meant the Magaguadavic River, which was well to the east and would have incorporated considerable lands that were ostensibly British into the United States, including a large part of Passamaquoddy Bay, as well as the loyalist settlement at St. Andrews, New Brunswick. Subsequently, the British claimed that [what was then called] the Schoodic River was the river specified in the Peace Treaty. Cases were presented to the commissioners, who also personally viewed the geography of the area. However, a resolution of the case proved to be more intractable then was first thought.

In his annual message to Congress for the year 1796 President Washington reported that:

> The commissioners appointed on the part of the United States and of Great Britain to determine which is the river St. Croix mentioned in the treaty of peace of 1783, agreed in the choice of Egbert Benson, esq., of New York, for the 3rd commissioner. The whole met at St. Andrew's, in Passamaquoddy Bay, in the beginning of October, and directed surveys to be made of the rivers in dispute; but deeming it impracticable to have these surveys completed before the next year, they adjourned to meet at Boston in August, 1797, for the final decision of the question.[16]

However, as President John Adams reported to Congress the following year: "They met, but the surveys requiring more time than had been supposed, and not being then completed, the commissioners again adjourned, to meet at Providence, in the State of Rhode Island, in June next, when we may expect a final examination and decision".[17] Subsequently, the Commissioners determined that they would have difficulty ascertaining the source of the St. Croix River by latitude and longitude, as intended by the framers of the Treaty of Paris, 1783. Accordingly, Great Britain and the United States jointly agreed to absolve the commissioners of that responsibility and to that end the two parties to the Jay Treaty, 1794 entered into an amending treaty to establish by way of an explanatory article that the commissioners were released from the obligation to ascertain the source of the St. Croix river by geographical coordinates.

Explanatory Article to Article 5 of the Jay Treaty, 1798
(Extract)

March 15, 1798

... whereas Difficulties have arisen with respect to the Execution of so much of the Fifth Article of the said Treaty as requires that the Commissioners appointed under the same should in their Description particularize the Latitude and Longitude of the source of the River which may be found to be the one truly intended in the Treaty of Peace between His Britannic Majesty and the United States under the name of the River St. Croix, by reason whereof it is expedient that the said Commissioners should be released from the obligation of conforming to the Provisions of the said Article in this respect. The . . . Plenipotentiaries ... have agreed and concluded and do hereby declare in the name of His Britannic Majesty and of the United States of America That the Commissioners appointed under the fifth Article of the above-mentioned Treaty shall not be obliged to particularize in their Description, the Latitude and Longitude of the source of the River which may be found to be the one truly intended in the aforesaid Treaty of Peace, under the name of the River St. Croix, but they shall be at liberty to describe the said River in such other manner as they may judge expedient ... [18]

Following this amendment to the duties of the commissioners appointed pursuant to the Jay Treaty, 1794, the commissioners were able to complete their work. To the members of the tribunal the case presented on behalf of Great Britain appeared to be conclusive as to the identification of the St. Croix River because archaeological examinations of the area disclosed evidence of the original French fort. That, and the evidence provided by the local aboriginal population, proved the identity of the St. Croix River.[19] It was, in fact, the river then known as the Schoodic River. However, the source of the river proved to be more difficult to determine because there were several lakes from which the river drew its water. The British contended that the most western spring feeding the lakes was the source while the Americans held that it was the Chiputneticook River that was the source of the river. The commissioners eventually compromised on the American position with the gloss that the western head of the Chiputneticook River was held to be the source of the St. Croix river. This compromise gave neither country all that they wished and so became an agreeable resolution of the border issue at this location.[20] The commissioners provided Great Britain and the United States with the following declaration:

Declaration of the Commissioners under Article 5 of the Jay Treaty

signed at Providence October 25, 1798

We the said Commissioners having been sworn impartially to examine and decide the said Question according to such evidence as should respectively be laid before Us on the part of the British Government, and of The United States. And having heard the evidence which hath been laid before Us by the Agent of His Majesty, and The Agent of The United States, respectively appointed and authorized to manage the business on behalf of the respective Governments – Have decided and hereby do decide the River herein after particularly described and mentioned to be the River truly intended under the name of The River Saint Croix in the said Treaty of Peace and forming a part of the Boundary therein described That is to say The Mouth of the said River is in Passamaquoddy Bay at a point of Land called Joe's Point, about one mile northward from the northern part of Saint Andrew's Island, and in the Latitude of forty five degrees, five minutes and five seconds north, and in the Longitude of sixty seven degrees twelve minutes and thirty seconds west from the Royal Observatory at Greenwich in Great-Britain, and three degrees, fifty four minutes and fifteen seconds east from Harvard College in the University of Cambridge, in the State of Massachusetts. And the course of the said River up from it's said Mouth is northerly to a point of Land called The Devil's-Head, then turning the said point is westerly to where it divides into two Streams the one coming from the westward, and the other coming from the northward, having the Indian name of Chiputnaticook or

Chibnitcook, as the same may be variously spelt, then up the said Stream so coming from the northward to its source, which is at a Stake near a yellow-Birch Tree trooped with Iron, and marked ST and IH 1797. by Samuel Titcomb and John Harris the Surveyors employed to survey the above mentioned Stream coming from the northward. And the said River is designated on the Map hereunto annexed and hereby referred to as farther descriptive of it by the Letters A. B. a. D. E. F. G. H. I. K. and L.–the Letter A being at it's said Mouth, and the Letter L being at it's said Source. And the course and distance of the said source from the Island at the Confluence of the abovementioned two Streams is as laid down on the said Map north five degrees and about fifteen minutes west by the magnet, about forty eight miles and one quarter.

Consequences of the Jay Treaty (St Croix River Arbitration)

The successful resolution of the St. Croix River boundary dispute through a process of conciliation and arbitration showed that border disputes between British North America and the United States could be resolved peacefully based on evidence jointly ascertained by the two states. The early use of this dispute resolution process by the United States and Great Britain established a precedent for the future peaceful resolution of boundary disputes between those two sovereign states.

As for the Mississippi River, a joint survey of its source was not carried out by the United States and Great Britain despite the clause in the Jay Treaty stipulating that such a survey would take place. It slowly became apparent that the river did not intersect with the boundary prescribed by the Treaty of Paris, 1783, although it would take some time before the source of the river was finally discovered. Initially, Lieutenant Zebulon Pike of the US Army, who explored the territory now forming the state of Minnesota, reported in 1806 that the source of the Mississippi river was Leech Lake. Later, in 1820, another expedition identified Cass Lake as the source. But it wasn't until 1832 that Henry Schoolcraft determined that the source of the Mississippi river was located in Lake Itasca, Minnesota. That is the generally accepted source of the river today. Notably, the lakes that were named at various times as the sources of the river are all located considerably south of the boundary line projected by the Treaty of Paris, 1783, and thus the location of the southern border in the west would ultimately require further diplomatic negotiations between Great Britain and the United States.

The Nootka Sound Conventions 1790-94

While Great Britain and the United States of America were negotiating and implementing the Jay Treaty, a different issue concerning the southern border arose in the far west along the Pacific coast. Spain had slowly expanded north along the Pacific rim of North America, spurred on by the imprimatur of the Papal Bull *Inter Cateras* and by the Treaty of Tordesillas, which had divided the world for exploration purposes between Spain and Portugal in the early days of exploration in the New World. The Spanish under Pérez had reached Nootka Sound on what is now Vancouver Island in 1774, and the following year under Bodega y Quadra and Bruno de Heceta the Spanish reached as far north as Russian America (Alaska). Meanwhile, the British were exploring the western coast of North America under James Cook, who reached the west coast in 1778. Both the Hudson's Bay Company and the Northwest Company had important fur-trading interests in the Pacific region of North America.

A failed naval officer and British trader named Meares established a trading post at Nootka in 1788, seeking pelts that could be sold in the China fur trade. However, a Spanish expedition discovered his post and evicted him in 1789, seizing both the Nootka post and a ship belonging to the Meares expedition. The Spanish claimed territorial sovereignty over the entire region. When the British learned of these events an exercise in saber-rattling occurred and Spain was forced to give way to the demands of the British that Spain give up possession of the occupied post at Nootka, and make reparations for British property losses (which amounted to an admission that the Spanish actions at Nootka were contrary to international law). The negotiations between the two powers were formalized in a series of agreements known as the Nootka Conventions.

There was an agreement that Britain and Spain could each establish posts on the western coast where the lands were not occupied by the other power, and there would be free access to the settlements established by either power for the subjects of the other power. The conventions also provided for some regulation of the fisheries. The Nootka Conventions did not ultimately settle the boundaries of the territories between the two powers along what later became the British Columbia coast but it did stop the saber-rattling and prevented the outbreak of a war between Great Britain and Spain.

The Nootka Sound Convention, 1790

October 28, 1790

Their Britannic and Catholic Majesties being desirous of terminating, by a speedy and valid agreement, the differences which have lately arisen between the two Crowns, have considered that the best way of attaining this salutary object would be that of an amicable arrangement which, setting aside all retrospective discussions of the rights and pretensions of the two parties, should regulate their respective positions for the future on the bases which would be conformable to their true interests as well as to the mutual desires with which Their said Majesties are animated, of establishing with each other, in everything and in all places, the most perfect friendship, harmony, and good correspondence. With this in view they have named and constituted for their plenipotentiaries, to wit, on the part of His Britannic Majesty, Alleyne Fitzherbert, of the privy council of His said Majesty in Great Britain and Ireland, and his ambassador extraordinary and minister plenipotentiary to His Catholic Majesty; and on the part of His Catholic Majesty, Don Joseph Moñino Count of

Floridablanca, Knight Grand Cross of the Royal Spanish Order of Charles III., counsellor of state to His said Majesty, and his principal secretary of state and of the cabinet, who, after having communicated to each other their full powers, have agreed on the following articles:

I. *It is agreed that the buildings and tracts of land situated on the Northwest Coast of the continent of North America, or on the islands adjacent to that continent, of which the subjects of His Britannic Majesty were dispossessed about the month of April, 1789, by a Spanish officer, shall be restored to the said British subjects.*

II. *Further, a just reparation shall be made, according to the nature of the case, for every act of violence or hostility which may have been committed since the said month of April, 1789, by the subjects of either of the contending parties against the subjects of the other; and in case their lands, buildings, vessels, merchandise, or any other objects of property on the said continent or on the seas or islands adjacent, they shall be replaced in possession of them or a just compensation shall be made to them for the losses which they have sustained.*

III. *And in order to strengthen the bonds of friendship and to preserve in the future a perfect harmony and good understanding between the two contracting parties, it is agreed that their respective subjects shall not be disturbed or molested either in navigating or carrying on their fisheries in the Pacific Ocean or in the South Seas, or in landing on the coasts of those seas in places not already occupied, for the purpose of carrying on their commerce with the natives of the country or of making establishments there; the whole subject, nevertheless, to the restrictions and provisions which shall be specified in the three following articles.*

IV. *His Britannic Majesty engages to employ the most effective measures to prevent the navigation and fishery of his subjects in* the Pacific Ocean or in the South Seas from being made a pretext for illicit trade with the Spanish settlements; and with this in view it is moreover expressly stipulated that British subjects shall not navigate nor carry on their fishery in the said seas within the distance of 10 maritime leagues from any part of the coast already occupied by Spain.

V. It is agreed that as well in the places which are to be restored to British subjects by virtue of the first article as in all other parts of the Northwest Coast of North America or of the islands adjacent, situated to the north of the parts of the said coast already occupied by Spain, wherever the subjects of either of the two powers shall have made settlements since the month of April, 1789, or shall hereafter make any, the subjects of the other shall have free access and shall carry on their commerce without disturbance or molestation.

VI. It is further agreed with respect to the eastern and western coasts of South America and the islands adjacent, that the respective subjects shall not form in the future any establishment on the parts of the coast situated to the south of the parts of the same coast and of the islands adjacent already occupied by Spain; it being understood that the said respective subjects shall retain the liberty of landing on the coasts and islands so situated for objects connected with their fishery and of erecting thereon huts and other temporary structures serving only those objects.

VII. In all cases of complaint or infraction of the articles of the present convention the officers of either party without previously permitting themselves to commit any act of violence or assault shall be bound to make an exact report of the affair and of its circumstances to their respective Courts, who will terminate the differences in an amicable manner.

VIII. The present convention shall be ratified and confirmed within the space of six weeks, to be counted from the day of its signature, or sooner if possible.

SECRET ARTICLE

Since by article 6 of the present convention it has been stipulated, respecting the eastern and western coasts of South America, that the respective subjects shall not in the future form any establishment on the parts of these coasts situated to the south of the parts of the said coasts actually occupied by Spain, it is agreed and declared by the present article that this stipulation shall remain in force only so long as no establishment shall have been formed by the subjects of any other power on the coasts in question. This secret article shall have the same force as if it were inserted in the convention.

Consequences of the Nootka Sound Convention, 1790

A second convention between Great Britain and Spain was subsequently entered into by them to fix the quantum of the reparations that had to be paid by Spain to John Meares, whose ship and port facility had been seized by the Spanish at Nootka Sound. However, that convention, the Nootka Claims Convention, signed on February 12, 1793, did not by its terms affect the territorial positions of either state on the west coast of North America.

In Britain, Prime Minister William Pitt inserted instructions into the orders of Captain George Vancouver, who was then preparing a voyage of exploration to the west coast of North America, to require him to accept the transfer of Meares' seized post from the Spanish representative at Nootka. Vancouver arrived at Nootka on August 28, 1792, where he was lavishly entertained by Juan Francisco de Bodega y Quadra, the Spanish commandant. Bodega y Quadra sought to delay the transfer to the British and even to portray it as a temporary withdrawal that did not affect the existence of Spanish sovereignty at Nootka Sound.[21] In fact, his instructions from the Spanish government were to negotiate to establish the Strait of Juan de Fuca as the future boundary between Spanish America and British North America.

However, Vancouver lacked specific instructions on the creation of an international boundary between the two empires on the Pacific coast and therefore he sought to refer the Question of the boundary back to London, for consideration by the British government. In the meantime, Vancouver continued with his important surveys of the west coast during 1793, and during that summer he surveyed the Dean Channel near the mouth of the Bella Coola river.[22] Some 48 days before, Alexander Mackenzie, arriving at the same spot had written: "Alex MacKenzie from Canada by land 22d July 1793", thus completing the historic first crossing of North America by land.

Back in Europe, Britain and Spain addressed the territorial sovereignty question relating to the west coast in the third and final Nootka Convention. By the terms of The Convention for the Mutual Abandonment of Nootka, Spain and Britain agreed that a formal transfer of the seized Meares property would take place at Nootka and British sovereignty would be restored, following which Nootka Sound would essentially become a free port and neither state would assert sovereignty over it. No permanent structures would be permitted but temporary structures to facilitate commerce with the aboriginal population would be allowed. Both states would prevent any other country from asserting sovereignty at Nootka.[23]

In March of 1795 Lieutenant Thomas Pearce of the Royal Marines went to Nootka Sound and took possession of the site from the Spanish commandant, General Manuel de Alva. The British flag was raised over the site of Meares' former post and then lowered and placed into the safekeeping of the Chief of the local aboriginal first nation, Maquinna, with instructions to raise it if a foreign ship entered the sound. Fort San Miguel, the Spanish fort, was taken apart and the Spanish garrison departed, as did the British under Lieutenant Pearce. With that, the Nootka crisis that had threatened war between Great Britain and Spain came to an end.

The Convention for the Mutual Abandonment of Nootka, 1794

January 11, 1794

Their Catholic and Britannic Majesties desiring to remove and obviate all doubt and difficulty relative to the execution of article I of the convention concluded between Their said Majesties on the 28th of October, 1790, have resolved and agreed to order that new instructions be sent to the officials who have been respectively commissioned to carry out the said article, the tenor of which instructions shall be as follows:

That within the shortest time that may be possible after the arrival of the said officials at Nootka they shall meet in the place, or near, where the buildings stood which were formerly occupied by the subjects of His Britannic Majesty, at which time and in which place they shall exchange mutually the following declaration and counter declaration:

DECLARATION

"I, N____ N____ in the name and by the order of His Catholic Majesty, by means of these presents restore to N____ N____ the buildings and districts of land situated on the Northwest Coast of the continent of North America, or the islands adjacent to that continent, of which the subjects of His Britannic Majesty were dispossessed by a Spanish officer toward the month of April, 1789. In witness whereof I have signed the present declaration, sealing it with the seal of my arms. Done at Nootka on the ____ day of ____ 179__."

COUNTER DECLARATION

"I, N____ N____, in the name and by the order of His Britannic Majesty, by means of these presents declare that the buildings and tracts of land on the Northwest Coast of the continent of North America, or on the islands adjacent to that continent, of which the

subjects of His Britannic Majesty were dispossessed by a Spanish officer toward the month of April, 1789, have been restored to me by N____ N____, which restoration I declare to be full and satisfactory. In witness whereof I have signed the present counter declaration, sealing it with the seal of my arms. Done at Nootka on the ____ day of ____, 179__."

That then the British official shall unfurl the British flag over the land so restored in sign of possession. And that after these formalities the officials of the two Crowns shall withdraw, respectively, their people from the said port of Nootka.

Further, Their said Majesties have agreed that the subjects of both nations shall have the liberty of frequenting the said port whenever they wish and of constructing there temporary buildings to accommodate them during their residence on such occasions. But neither of the said parties shall form any permanent establishment in the said port or claim any right of sovereignty or territorial dominion there to the exclusion of the other. And Their said Majesties will mutually aid each other to maintain for their subjects free access to the port of Nootka against any other nation which may attempt to establish there any sovereignty or dominion.

Consequences of the Nootka Sound Convention, 1794 (The Convention for the Mutual Abandonment of Nootka)

While the Nootka Conventions did not establish a firm boundary between British North America and Spanish America it did oust Spain from the geographical territory that ultimately became British Columbia. As a practical matter, the Spanish Empire fell back below the Straits of Juan de Fuca and, as a declining empire, it was no longer capable of projecting its power northwards. Soon it ceased to engage in the China trade and was subsequently embroiled in the Napoleonic Wars, which weakened the Spanish Empire further. After the conclusion of the Napoleonic Wars the Spanish Empire in the Americas collapsed, as the provinces of

Latin America rebelled, and successfully sought their independence.

Great Britain was able reinforce its claim to establish settlements on the Pacific coast of North America and reinforced the British position in the Columbia District of the Hudson Bay Company. The dispute with Spain helped to firm up a British intention to maintain its territorial position on the west coast of North America despite conflicting claims by Spain, Russia, and later the United States of America. By the time of confederation in 1867, and the subsequent promises made by Canada to build a transcontinental railway to the colony of British Columbia, only the Columbian coast surveyed by George Vancouver, including Nootka sound, remained under British control.

The Treaty of San Ildefonso, 1800

After the Nootka Conventions pushed the Spanish Empire back below the Straits of Juan de Fuca the only remaining territory possessed by Spain within the borders of what is presently Canada was a slice of territory along the northern boundary of the Louisiana territory. That formerly French territory had been transferred to Spain by the Treaty of Fontainebleau, signed on November 3, 1762. As Spanish Louisiana (or Luisiana, as the Spanish spelled the name of their colony) it was somewhat haphazardly administered by Spanish officials in New Orleans and St. Louis. The French had made expansive claims to territory defined by the watershed basin of the Mississippi-Missouri river system which the Spanish had inherited. Thus the boundaries of Spanish Luisiana extended as far as the 50th parallel of latitude, incorporating the water basins drained by the Milk River and the Poplar River in what is now southern Saskatchewan, and southern Alberta.

Europe was increasingly in conflict due to the French revolution, a condition that was exacerbated after a young general, Napoleon Bonaparte, seized power in Paris on November 9, 1799. Under pressure from Napoleon, Spain agreed to return the portion of the Louisiana territory that it had received from France by the Treaty of Fontainebleau in 1762.[24] In return, France was to provide territory in Italy as a kingdom for a prince of the Spanish royal house. Napoleon wanted a return of the Louisiana territory because he dreamed of using it as a base to recover the lost provinces France had formerly possessed in North America, particularly New France. The transfer was provided for in the Treaty of San Ildefonso concluded on October 1, 1800, sometimes described as the Third Treaty of San Ildefonso, to distinguish it from other treaties between France and Spain bearing the same name. In entering into this treaty France made an oral pledge to Spain, not embodied within the terms of the treaty itself, in which France promised not to alienate the colony of Louisiana to a third nation. Should France wish to give up Louisiana again it promised that it would revert Louisiana to Spain. However, as subsequent events showed, that was a promise that Napoleon felt no compunction to keep.

The Third Treaty of San Ildefonso was subsequently confirmed by Spain and France in the Treaty of Aranjuez, signed on March 21, 1801.

Treaty of San Ildefonso (Extracts)

October 1, 1800

His Catholic Majesty having always manifested an earnest desire to procure for His Royal Highness the Duke of Parma an aggrandizement which would place his domains on a footing more consonant with his dignity; and the French Republic on its part having long since made known to His Majesty the King of Spain its desire to be again placed in possession of the colony of Louisiana; and the two Governments having exchanged their views on these two subjects of common interest, and circumstances permitting them to assume obligations in this regard which, so far as depends on them, will assure mutual satisfaction, they have authorized for this purpose the following: the French Republic, the Citizen Alexandre Berthier General in Chief, and His Catholic Majesty, Don Mariano Luis de Urquijo, knight of the Order of Charles III, and of that of St. John of Jerusalem, a Counselor of State, his Ambassador Extraordinary and Plenipotentiary appointed near the Batavian Republic, and his First Secretary of State ad interim, who, having exchanged their powers, have agreed upon the following articles, subject to ratification.

I. The French Republic undertakes to procure for His Royal Highness the Infant Duke of Parma an aggrandizement of territory which shall increase the population of his domains to one million inhabitants, with the title of King and with all the rights which attach to the royal dignity; and the French Republic undertakes to obtain in this regard the assent of His Majesty the Emperor and King and that of the other interested states that His Highness the Infant Duke of Parma may be put into possession of the said territories without opposition upon the conclusion of the peace to be made between the French Republic and His Imperial Majesty.

II. The aggrandizement to be given to His Royal Highness the Duke of Parma may consist of Tuscany, in case the present negotiations of the French Government with His Imperial Majesty shall permit that Government to dispose thereof; or it may consist of the three Roman legations or of any other continental provinces of Italy which form a rounded state.

III. His Catholic Majesty promises and undertakes on his part to retrocede to the French Republic, six months after the full and entire execution of the above conditions and provisions regarding His Royal Highness the Duke of Parma, the colony or province of Louisiana, with the same extent that it now has in the hands of Spain and that it had when France possessed it, and such as it ought to be according to the treaties subsequently concluded between Spain and other states.

Consequences of the Treaty of San Ildefonso

The Third Treaty of San Ildefonso reintroduced France to an imperial mission in North America. It ended Spanish control over any territory that subsequently became modern Canada, and briefly, very briefly indeed, once again restored France to *de jure* sovereignty over a portion of territory that became modern Canada.

However, in order to effect his dreams of restoring the French North American empire Napoleon Bonaparte needed to ensure that France would have available to it the revenues from sugar operations in the Caribbean to support French military operations in North America. To that end Napoleon had to recover the French colony of Saint-Domingue, on the island of Hispaniola, which was the scene of a recently successful slave rebellion. A French army was sent to the island but it became bogged down in fighting and tropical diseases took a tremendous toll on the army's strength. Foreseeing that he would be not be successful in restoring French sugar fortunes in the Caribbean Napoleon concluded that Louisiana would be of little value to him and he decided to cut his losses by entering into a transaction to sell Louisiana to the United States of America.

France's changing fortunes and the mercurial strategies of Napoleon delayed the physical transfer of Louisiana to France from Spain, and for a period of time Spain continued to administer the colony on behalf of France. The formal transfer of Louisiana from Spain to France occurred in two stages. In the first, at a ceremony conducted in New Orleans on November 30, 1803, the southern district of Spanish Louisiana (Baja Luisiana) was transferred from Spanish to French control. The northern district of Spanish Louisiana (Alta Luisiana) was transferred to France on March 9, 1804, in a flag-raising ceremony held at St. Louis but there the French flag flew over the settlement for only 24 hours before the transfer of Louisiana from France to the United States took place. The Treaty of San Ildefonso provided for the last transfer of territory in North America solely between European powers. Henceforth, any transfers occurring in North America would involve European and North American states.

The Louisiana Purchase Treaty, 1803

The news that Spain had agreed to transfer Spanish Louisiana back to France caused consternation in Washington, D.C. President Thomas Jefferson was perturbed by the prospect of France obtaining control of New Orleans because France could control marine traffic on the Mississippi River from New Orleans. Furthermore, the President clearly perceived that France was a much more powerful potential adversary than the declining Spanish Empire. Accordingly, he dispatched diplomatic representatives to Paris to determine if Napoleon would be open to selling New Orleans to the United States.

The mission of the American diplomats coincided with a growing realization by Napoleon that he would be unable to successfully reestablish the French Empire in North America because of the difficulties encountered by French arms in their attempt to retake France's former sugar colony on the island of Hispaniola. Accordingly, Napoleon decided to cut his losses in the New World by instructing his treasury minister, Barbé-Marbois, to negotiate for the sale of the entire territory to the United States. Negotiations ensued between Barbé-Marbois and the American representatives, Robert Livingston and James Monroe. The French offered to sell the entire territory to the United States for the sum of 15 million dollars, which was a very favourable price. The American negotiators quickly agreed to the French proposal and a treaty was signed on April 30, 1803.

The Louisiana Purchase Treaty (Extracts)

April 30, 1803

I. Whereas by the Article the third of the Treaty concluded at St Ildefonso the 9th Vendamiaire on 1st October 1800 between the

First Consul of the French Republic and his Catholic Majesty it was agreed as follows.

"His Catholic Majesty promises and engages on his part to cede to the French Republic six months after the full and entire execution of the conditions and Stipulations herein relative to his Royal Highness the Duke of Parma, the Colony or Province of Louisiana with the Same extent that it now has in the hand of Spain, & that it had when France possessed it; and Such as it Should be after the Treaties subsequently entered into between Spain and other States"

And whereas in pursuance of the Treaty and particularly of the third article the French Republic has an incontestable title to the domain and to the possession of the said Territory–The First Consul of the French Republic desiring to give to the United States a strong proof of his friendship doth hereby cede to the United States in the name of the French Republic for ever and in full Sovereignty the said territory with all its rights and appurtenances as fully and in the Same manner as they have been acquired by the French Republic in virtue of the above mentioned Treaty concluded with his Catholic Majesty.

II. In the cession made by the preceding article are included the adjacent Islands belonging to Louisiana all public lots and Squares, vacant lands and all public buildings, fortifications, barracks and other edifices which are not private property.–The Archives, papers & documents relative to the domain and Sovereignty of Louisiana and its dependencies will be left in the possession of the Commissaries of the United States, and copies will be afterwards given in due form to the Magistrates and Municipal officers of such of the said papers and documents as may be necessary to them.

III. The inhabitants of the ceded territory shall be incorporated in the Union of the United States and admitted as soon as possible according to the principles of the federal Constitution to the enjoyment of all these rights, advantages and immunities of citizens of the United States, and in the mean time they shall be maintained and protected in the free enjoyment of their liberty, property and the Religion which they profess.

IV. There Shall be Sent by the Government of France a Commissary to Louisiana to the end that he do every act necessary as well to receive from the Officers of his Catholic Majesty the Said country and its dependencies in the name of the French Republic if it has not been already done as to transmit it in the name of the French Republic to the Commissary or agent of the United States.

V. Immediately after the ratification of the present Treaty by the President of the United States and in case that of the first Consul's shall have been previously obtained, the commissary of the French Republic shall remit all military posts of New Orleans and other parts of the ceded territory to the Commissary or Commissaries named by the President to take possession–the troops whether of France or Spain who may be there shall cease to occupy any military post from the time of taking possession and shall be embarked as soon as possible in the course of three months after the ratification of this treaty.

VI. The United States promise to execute Such treaties and articles as may have been agreed between Spain and the tribes and nations of Indians until by mutual consent of the United States and the said tribes or nations other Suitable articles Shall have been agreed upon.

Consequences of the Louisiana Purchase Treaty

The main consequence of the Louisiana Purchase Treaty of 1803 from a British North American perspective was that an international boundary in the west now existed between the United States of America and Rupert's Land. Furthermore, territory between the 49th parallel and the 50th parallel of latitude in what is now south-western Saskatchewan and southern Alberta became

American territory by the terms of the treaty. That is the only place where territory that now forms part of Canada was at one time part of the territory of the United States of America.

The Treaty of Ghent, 1814

Despite the Jay Treaty of 1794, which attempted to resolve outstanding border issues, and to promote harmony between Great Britain and the United States, there remained a strong undercurrent of fear and antipathy toward Great Britain on the part of a large segment of the political elite in the United States. That attitude was particularly prevalent among the Virginians who occupied the presidency almost continuously between 1789 and 1825.[25] Many Americans with strong memories of the American Revolution still sought the ouster of Great Britain from all of North America and perceived Great Britain as an existential threat to the survival of the United States although some others, particularly in New England, favoured cordial relations with Great Britain. Land hunger also played an important role in relations between the United States and British North America. Many Americans still desired to annex Upper Canada[26] because of its favourable climate and agricultural prospects. In fact, many Americans emigrated to Upper Canada because farmland there was readily available. So many former Americans lived in Upper Canada by the second decade of the nineteenth century that some Americans thought they could rely upon the Upper Canadian population to rise up against British rule if American troops entered the country.

In the western states there remained a great fear of the aboriginal population and a great temptation to take the unsurrendered aboriginal lands for settlement by the burgeoning American population. A great aboriginal leader emerged in the form of Tecumseh who worked to forge an aboriginal confederacy in the western lands given over to the United States by the Treaty of Paris, 1783. The western population in the United States feared such a development because of the effects it could have on the westward movement of the United States. Strained relations between the US government and the aboriginal first nations in the west was increased by the fact that the aboriginal nations continued to maintain strong ties with the British Crown. Americans resented the continued support of the British Crown for the aboriginal first nations in the western parts of the United States and this fact contributed to a deterioration in relations between the two countries.

On the high seas there was also conflict between Great Britain and the United States over the Royal Navy's practice of impressing seamen into military service on the high seas. Several incidents involving the stopping of American flagged vessels and the forcible transfer of seamen into British warships inflamed American public opinion who saw in such practices a failure by Great Britain to respect the flag of the United States. During this period Great Britain was involved in the long and costly Napoleonic Wars, the last in a long series of wars for dominance in Europe and the world by Great Britain and France. Britain depended upon the Royal Navy to insulate the island kingdom from an invasion by France and to keep open its sea lanes to foreign countries but a continuing shortage of seamen drove Britain to forcefully seize anyone who could not prove that they were not British from among the seamen serving in the ships of neutral countries. Britain also curtailed trade between the United States and France through its control of the seas, which created an additional of contentious issue between the United States and Great Britain.

Thus, a litany of American grievances would underlie a decision by President Madison and the US Congress to declare war on Great Britain (and by extension, on British North America) in June 1812. The War of 1812 is sometimes referred to in the United States as the Second War of Independence but it was far from that. Stripped of its maritime grievances the war was primarily one of territorial aggrandizement against Upper Canada and a war against the aboriginal first nations in the west. Although the United States held the military and economic advantage in North

America, and Great Britain could ill-afford to send a substantial body of troops to North America while the wars with Napoleon raged in Europe, the British nevertheless succeeded in seizing the initial advantage. Naval control of Lake Erie by the Provincial Marine allowed the British commander of the Army of Upper Canada, Major General Isaac Brock, to launch a lightning attack on the border at Detroit that resulted in the seizure of the Michigan Territory by the Crown. American attacks further eastward at Queenston Heights on the Niagara peninsula were repulsed by Brock and his officers, at the cost of Brock's life. Thereafter, the war settled into a period of frontier maneuvers without significant military conquests by either side until the Battle of Lake Erie in 1813, in which an entire naval squadron of the Royal Navy was defeated and captured, thus opening the upper Great Lakes to American naval control and forcing the Army of Upper Canada to withdraw eastwards, pursued by the US Army. At the Battle of Moraviantown on the Thames River, Major General Henry Proctor and the Army of Upper Canada were defeated and routed. The great aboriginal leader Tecumseh fell in this battle and with his death the dreams of an aboriginal confederacy that could resist the encroachment of white settlers onto Indian lands in the west died with him.

Although the US Army's lines of supply prevented it from moving sufficiently eastward to threaten the Niagara peninsula, or York (today's Toronto) it did succeed in devastating western Upper Canada, which the British had abandoned. However, the campaigns by the US army in eastern Upper Canada, and in Lower Canada south of Montreal in 1814, ended in failure and an American withdrawal. The armies of the United States and those defending British North America essentially fought each other to a stalemate along the border. But the defeat of Napoleon in 1814 released imperial troops for North American service and Great Britain now began to reinforce British North America as well as to embark on substantial amphibious operations on the east coast of the United States and on the American southern coast. By this time the populations of both countries were exhausted by war and although President Madison wanted to make one more attempt to conquer Upper Canada by force of arms the US Congress was averse to granting further war appropriations, and the United States and Great Britain entered into peace negotiations at the city of Ghent, in the low countries.

Those negotiations bore fruit and a peace treaty was signed in December 1814. Delays in communication allowed the US army to achieve a significant late war victory over the British army at the Battle of New Orleans and that victory, together with several successes on the high seas by the US Navy, allowed the Americans to end the war on a high note. But the real victor in the war was British North America which preserved its separate existence despite the heavy military odds against it. Indeed, the British commander-in-chief in the European war against Napoleon, the Duke of Wellington, expressed surprise that his colleagues in the British army had been able to forestall the conquest of Canada by the United States in the War of 1812.

The War of 1812 represents the last formal military conflict between the United States of America and British North America and a diplomatic peace has been preserved for more than 200 years since the end of that conflict. However, the peace treaty of Ghent did not mark the end of all conflicts in North America and insurgencies would occur on two further occasions in the nineteenth century. Nevertheless the Treaty of Ghent was an important historical development in the relations between the North American states and both sides, desirous of putting to rest any border controversies between them, agreed upon new treaty provisions to finalize their eastern borders.

Treaty of Ghent, 1814 (Extracts)

December 24, 1814

His Britannic Majesty and the United States of America desirous of terminating the war which has unhappily subsisted between the two Countries, and of restoring upon principles of perfect reciprocity, Peace, Friendship, and good Understanding between them, have for that purpose appointed their respective Plenipotentiaries, that is to say, His Britannic Majesty on His part has appointed the Right Honourable James Lord Gambier, late Admiral of the White now Admiral of the Red Squadron of His Majesty's Fleet; Henry Goulburn Esquire, a Member of the Imperial Parliament and Under Secretary of State; and William Adams Esquire, Doctor of Civil Laws: And the President of the United States, by and with the advice and consent of the Senate thereof, has appointed John Quincy Adams, James A. Bayard, Henry Clay, Jonathan Russell, and Albert Gallatin, Citizens of the United States; who, after a reciprocal communication of their respective Full Powers, have agreed upon the following Articles.

I. There shall be a firm and universal Peace between His Britannic Majesty and the United States, and between their respective Countries, Territories, Cities, Towns, and People of every degree without exception of places or persons. All hostilities both by sea and land shall cease as soon as this Treaty shall have been ratified by both parties as hereinafter mentioned. All territory, places, and possessions whatsoever taken by either party from the other during the war, or which may be taken after the signing of this Treaty, excepting only the Islands hereinafter mentioned, shall be restored without delay and without causing any destruction or carrying away any of the Artillery or other public property originally captured in the said forts or places, and which shall remain therein upon the Exchange of the Ratifications of this Treaty, or any Slaves or other private property; And all Archives, Records, Deeds, and Papers, either of a public nature or belonging to private persons, which in the course of the war may have fallen into the hands of the Officers of either party, shall be, as far as may be practicable, forthwith restored and delivered to the proper authorities and persons to whom they respectively belong. Such of the Islands in the Bay of Passamaquoddy as are claimed by both parties shall remain in the possession of the party in whose occupation they may be at the time of the Exchange of the

Ratifications of this Treaty until the decision respecting the title to the said Islands shall have been made in conformity with the fourth Article of this Treaty. No disposition made by this Treaty as to such possession of the Islands and territories claimed by both parties shall in any manner whatever be construed to affect the right of either.

. . . .

IV. Whereas it was stipulated by the second Article in the Treaty of Peace of one thousand seven hundred and eighty three between His Britannic Majesty and the United States of America that the boundary of the United States should comprehend "all Islands within twenty leagues of any part of the shores of the United States and lying between lines to be drawn due East from the points where the aforesaid boundaries between Nova Scotia on the one part and East Florida on the other shall respectively touch the Bay of Fundy and the Atlantic Ocean, excepting such Islands as now are or heretofore have been within the limits of Nova Scotia, and whereas the several Islands in the Bay of Passamaquoddy, which is part of the Bay of Fundy, and the Island of Grand Manan in the said Bay of Fundy, are claimed by the United States as being comprehended within their aforesaid boundaries, which said Islands are claimed as belonging to His Britannic Majesty as having been at the time of and previous to the aforesaid Treaty of one thousand seven hundred and eighty three within the limits of the Province of Nova Scotia: In order therefore finally to decide upon these claims it is agreed that they shall be referred to two Commissioners to be appointed in the following manner: viz: One Commissioner shall be appointed by His Britannic Majesty and one by the President of the United States, by and with the advice and consent of the Senate thereof, and the said two Commissioners so appointed shall be sworn impartially to examine and decide upon the said claims according to such evidence as shall be laid before them on the part of His Britannic Majesty and of the United States respectively. The said Commissioners shall meet at St Andrews in the Province of New Brunswick, and shall have power to adjourn to such other place or places as they shall think fit. The said Commissioners shall by a declaration or report under their hands and seals decide to which of the two Contracting parties the several Islands aforesaid do respectely belong in conformity with the true intent of the said Treaty of Peace of one thousand seven hundred and eighty three. And if the said Commissioners shall agree in their decision both parties shall consider such decision as final and conclusive. It is further agreed that in the event of the two Commissioners differing upon all or any of the matters so referred to them, or in the event of both or either of the said Commissioners refusing or declining or willfully omitting to act as such, they shall make jointly or separately a report or reports as well to the Government of His Britannic Majesty as to that of the United States, stating in detail the points on which they differ, and the grounds upon which their respective opinions have been formed, or the grounds upon which they or either of them have so refused declined or omitted to act. And His Britannic Majesty and the Government of the United States hereby agree to refer the report or reports of the said Commissioners to some friendly Sovereign or State to be then named for that purpose, and who shall be requested to decide on the differences which may be stated in the said report or reports, or upon the report of one Commissioner together with the grounds upon which the other Commissioner shall have refused, declined or omitted to act as the case may be. And if the Commissioner so refusing, declining, or omitting to act, shall also willfully omit to state the grounds upon which he has so done in such manner that the said statement may be referred to such friendly Sovereign or State together with the report of such other Commissioner, then such Sovereign or State shall decide ex parse upon the said report alone. And His Britannic Majesty and the Government of the United States engage to consider the decision of such friendly Sovereign or State to be final and conclusive on all the matters so referred.

V. Whereas neither that point of the Highlands lying due North from the source of the River St Croix, and designated in the former Treaty of Peace between the two Powers as the North West Angle *of Nova Scotia, nor the North Westernmost head of Connecticut River has yet been ascertained; and whereas that part of the boundary line between the Dominions of the two Powers which extends from the source of the River St Croix directly North to the above mentioned North West Angle of Nova Scotia, thence along the said Highlands which divide those Rivers that empty themselves into the River St Lawrence from those which fall into the Atlantic Ocean to the North Westernmost head of Connecticut River, thence down along the middle of that River to the forty fifth degree of North Latitude, thence by a line due West on said latitude until it strikes the River Iroquois or Cataraquy, has not yet been surveyed: it is agreed that for these several purposes two Commissioners shall be appointed, sworn, and authorized to act exactly in the manner directed with respect to those mentioned in the next preceding Article unless otherwise specified in the present Article. The said Commissioners shall meet at St Andrews in the Province of New Brunswick, and shall have power to adjourn to such other place or places as they shall think fit. The said Commissioners shall have power to ascertain and determine the points above mentioned in conformity with the provisions of the said Treaty of Peace of one thousand seven hundred and eighty three, and shall cause the boundary aforesaid from the source of the River St Croix to the River Iroquois or Cataraquy to be surveyed and marked according to the said provisions. The said Commissioners shall make a map of the said boundary, and annex to it a declaration under their hands and seals certifying it to be the true Map of the said boundary, and particularizing the latitude and longitude of the North West Angle of Nova Scotia, of the North Westernmost head of Connecticut River, and of such other points of the said boundary as they may deem proper. And both parties agree to consider such map and declaration as finally and conclusively fixing the said boundary. And in the event of the said two Commissioners differing, or both, or either of them refusing, declining, or willfully omitting to act, such reports, declarations, or statements shall be made by them or either of them, and such reference to a friendly Sovereign or State shall be made in all respects as in the latter part of the fourth Article is contained, and in as full a manner as if the same was herein repeated.*

VI. Whereas by the former Treaty of Peace that portion of the boundary of the United States from the point where the forty fifth degree of North Latitude strikes the River Iroquois or Cataraquy to the Lake Superior was declared to be "along the middle of said River into Lake Ontario, through the middle of said Lake until it strikes the communication by water between that Lake and Lake Erie, thence along the middle of said communication into Lake Erie, through the middle of said Lake until it arrives at the water communication into the Lake Huron; thence through the middle of said Lake to the water communication between that Lake and Lake Superior" and whereas doubts have arisen what was the middle of the said River, Lakes, and water communications, and whether certain Islands lying in the same were within the Dominions of His Britannic Majesty or of the United States: In order therefore finally to decide these doubts, they shall be referred to two Commissioners to be appointed, sworn, and authorized to act exactly in the manner directed with respect to those mentioned in the next preceding Article unless otherwise specified in this present Article. The said Commissioners shall meet in the first instance at Albany in the State of New York, and shall have power to adjourn to such other place or places as they shall think fit. The said Commissioners shall by a Report or Declaration under their hands and seals, designate the boundary through the said River, Lakes, and water communications, and decide to which of the two Contracting parties the several Islands lying within the said Rivers, Lakes, and water communications, do respectively belong in conformity with the true intent of the said Treaty of one thousand seven hundred and eighty three. And both parties agree to consider such designation and decision as final and conclusive. And in the event of the said two Commissioners differing or both or either of them refusing, declining, or willfully omitting to act, such reports, declarations, or statements shall be made by them or either of them, and such reference to a friendly Sovereign or State shall be made in all respects as in the latter part of the fourth

Article is contained, and in as full a manner as if the same was herein repeated.

VII. It is further agreed that the said two last mentioned Commissioners after they shall have executed the duties assigned to them in the preceding Article, shall be, and they are hereby, authorized upon their oaths impartially to fix and determine according to the true intent of the said Treaty of Peace of one thousand seven hundred and eighty three, that part of the boundary between the dominions of the two Powers, which extends from the water communication between Lake Huron and Lake Superior to the most North Western point of the Lake of the Woods;-to decide to which of the two Parties the several Islands lying in the Lakes, water communications, and Rivers forming the said boundary do respectively belong in conformity with the true intent of the said Treaty of Peace of one thousand seven hundred and eighty three, and to cause such parts of the said boundary as require it to be surveyed and marked. The said Commissioners shall by a Report or declaration under their hands and seals, designate the boundary aforesaid, state their decision on the points thus referred to them, and particularize the Latitude and Longitude of the most North Western point of the Lake of the Woods, and of such other parts of the said boundary as they may deem proper. And both parties agree to consider such designation and decision as final and conclusive. And in the event of the said two Commissioners differing, or both or either of them refusing, declining, or willfully omitting to act, such reports, declarations or statements shall be made by them or either of them, and such reference to a friendly Sovereign or State shall be made in all respects as in the latter part of the fourth Article is contained, and in as full a manner as if the same was herein revealed.

VIII. The several Boards of two Commissioners mentioned in the four preceding Articles shall respectively have power to appoint a Secretary, and to employ such Surveyors or other persons as they shall judge necessary. Duplicates of all their respective reports, declarations, statements, and decisions, and of their accounts, and of the Journal of their proceedings shall be delivered by them to the Agents of His Britannic Majesty and to the Agents of the United States, who may be respectively appointed and authorized to manage the business on behalf of their respective Governments. The said Commissioners shall be respectively paid in such manner as shall be agreed between the two contracting parties, such agreement being to be settled at the time of the Exchange of the Ratifications of this Treaty. And all other expenses attending the said Commissions shall be defrayed equally by the two parties. And in the case of death, sickness, resignation, or necessary absence, the place of every such Commissioner respectively shall be supplied in the same manner as such Commissioner was first appointed; and the new Commissioner shall take the same oath or affirmation and do the same duties. It is further agreed between the two contracting parties that in case any of the Islands mentioned in any of the preceding Articles, which were in the possession of one of the parties prior to the commencement of the present war between the two Countries, should by the decision of any of the Boards of Commissioners aforesaid, or of the Sovereign or State so referred to, as in the four next preceding Articles contained, fall within the dominions of the other party, all grants of land made previous to the commencement of the war by the party having had such possession, shall be as valid as if such Island or Islands had by such decision or decisions been adjudged to be within the dominions of the party having had such possession.

Consequences of the Treaty of Ghent

The Treaty of Ghent is a classical example of the principle of *status quo ante bellum* in the crafting of peace treaties because it essentially restored both parties to the territorial positions that each possessed prior the outbreak of hostilities. However, Great Britain and the United States both recognized that additional work was required to define the boundary between the United States of America and British North America. To that end, the treaty provided for a number of commissions to attempt a resolution of border questions. In fact, the Treaty of Ghent is sometimes referred to as the treaty of boundaries because so much of the treaty text was taken up with the subject of building dispute resolution clauses into the treaty to resolve the outstanding border issues. The treaty provided for four two-member commissions, with one member appointed by Great Britain and the other member to be appointed by the United States. The purpose of the commissions was to determine the location of the international boundary between British North America and the United States of America through four of its segments:

1) the disputed islands in Passamaquoddy Bay,

2) from the source of the St. Croix River to the headlands separating the drainage into the St. Lawrence River from the drainage into the Atlantic Ocean and from there to the head of the Connecticut River then west along the 45th parallel of latitude to its point of intersection with the St. Lawrence River,

3) from the point of intersection between the 45th parallel of latitude and the St. Lawrence River westward through the Great Lakes to Sault Ste. Marie, and

4) from Sault Ste. Marie westward through Lake Superior to the Lake of the Woods.

It was apparent from the outset that unanimity among the commissioners would be required in order for an effective decision to be made. If the commissioners could not agree on a particular resolution of boundary issues the treaty provided that the issue could be referred to the sovereign of a mutually acceptable third country.

At issue in the first segment was the ownership of certain islands in Passamaquoddy Bay. That issue had been left over from the earlier arbitration of the St. Croix River boundary made under the Jay Treaty, 1794. Thomas Barclay, who had served as the British commissioner in the Jay Treaty arbitration was once again appointed as the British commissioner under the Treaty of Ghent and his American counterpart was John Holmes. The two commissioners held a series of meetings to determine the issue. British North America was well served by the skillful negotiations of Barclay who essentially took advantage of the American commissioner's desire to depart from his appointed task to take up a seat in the US House of Representatives by foisting upon him the choice of either a compromise along British lines, or taking the risk of an international arbitration with a foreign sovereign. The American commissioner chose the former, which left British North America with both Campobello Island and Grand Manan Island, although some of the other lesser islands, which were actually inhabited by Americans, were acknowledged to be US territory. This compromise was accepted by both countries.[27]

Decision of the Commissioners under Article 4 of the Treaty of Ghent

November 24, 1817

By Thomas Barclay and John Holmes Esquires.

Commissioners, appointed by virtue of the fourth Article of the Treaty of Peace and Amity between His Britannic Majesty and The United States of America concluded at Ghent on the twenty fourth day of December One Thousand eight hundred and fourteen to decide to which of the two Contracting parties to the said Treaty the several Islands in the Bay of Passamaquoddy which is part of the Bay of Fundy and the Island of Grand Manan in the said Bay of Fundy do respectively belong in conformity with the true intent of the second Article of the Treaty of Peace of One Thousand seven hundred and eighty three between His said Britannic Majesty and the aforesaid United States of America.

We the said Thomas Barclay and John Holmes Commissioners as aforesaid having been duly sworn impartially to examine and decide upon the said claims according to such evidence as should be laid before us on the part of His Britannic Majesty and The

United States respectively Have decided and do decide that Moose Island, Dudley Island, and Frederick Island, in the Bay of Passamaquoddy which is part of the Bay of Fundy do and each of them does belong to The United States of America and we have also decided and do decide that all the other Islands and each and every of them in the said Bay of Passamaquoddy which is part of the Bay of Fundy and the Island of Grand Manan in the said Bay of Fundy do belong to His said Britannic Majesty in conformity with the true intent of the said second Article of said Treaty of One Thousand seven hundred and eighty three.

However, the commissioners appointed to determine the location of the border lying between the St. Lawrence river and the source of the St. Croix River (again including Thomas Barclay on the British side) were unable to come to an agreement. That commission had the complex task of:

1) locating the northwest angle of Nova Scotia,

2) defining the watershed division between the waters that drained into the St. Lawrence River from the waters that drained into the Atlantic Ocean,

3) locating of the head of the Connecticut River, and

4) tracing the 45th parallel of latitude from the head of the Connecticut River to its point of intersection with the St. Lawrence River.

The British disputed the American claim that the northwest angle of the old province of Nova Scotia was located north of the St. John River and the Americans disputed the 45th parallel after precise calculations by both the British and American surveyors disclosed that the colonial Collins-Valentine survey line (surveyed in 1771-73) which had been presumed to be the actual boundary between the old Province of Quebec and the southern littoral provinces of the former colonial British America, was erroneous. As a result of more accurate surveys it was discovered that the important American fortress at Rouse's Point on Lake Champlain was acutally in British North American territory.

The British commissioner, Thomas Barclay, correctly perceived that the problems along this section of the border were political, as well as technical, and that the various American states lying along this section of the border would erupt in acrimony if any part of their territory was compromised in favour of protecting US territory located in another state. Consequently, this particular commission was unable to complete its task and, therefore, under the terms of the Treaty of Ghent, the unresolved boundary issue was eventually referred to King William I of the Netherlands for his disposition. However, when the King's award was issued in 1831, it was found that the award exceeded the limits of the defined subject-matter that had been submitted to the king for arbitration. As a consequence, the arbitral award was not accepted, and the border issue between Maine and Lower Canada remained an open issue.

A further area of concern related to the fixing of the border through the Great Lakes maritime boundary. The principle of using an equidistant line had been established by the Treaty of Paris, 1783 but that treaty did not deal with the river islands, or the navigable and non-navigable channels in the rivers. Great Britain adhered rigorously to the equidistant principle, with exceptions for islands in the stream but the United States favoured what subsequently came to be known as the Thalweg Principle. Under the Thalweg Principle where a water boundary involves multiple channels it is the deepest channel (and presumably the channel that is most navigable) that forms the division point between two sovereign entities. Thus, the border between such states will be located in the middle of the deepest navigable channel between them.

Important work was done by the commission to resolve the issues relating to this part of the southern border. The commissioners jointly accepted that the boundary through this part of the border would solely be a water boundary, and thus no island would be divided between British North America and the United States of America. The uncertainties presented by multiple river channels would be resolved by choosing the navigable channel (or the most navigable channel) within a river but where more than one channel was navigable the boundary would be located within the channel possessing the greatest volume of water that was nearest the centre line of the river, always provided that sufficient navigability would exist for both countries.[28] But, ultimately, the commissioners could not find agreement on an overall resolution of the boundary issues for this particular segment. Nevertheless, an important principle that both sides accepted was that the international boundary should not divide islands and therefore where the equidistant principle bisected an island the country in which the greater portion lay would obtain sovereignty over the whole island.[29]

The practical impact of the dispute over the application of the equidistant principle really concerned several small islands in the Detroit River between Lake Erie and Lake St. Clair, and in the St. Mary's River between Lake Huron and Lake Superior. A compromise was worked out for the Detroit River islands under which Bois Blanc Island would remain British and the Sugar, Stoney and Fox islands would go to the United States (and in which case the boundary would pass between Bois Blanc Island and the American islands).[30] Thus, this portion of the boundary was resolved but the commissioners were unable to fix the location of the boundary through the Neebish Channel between Lake Huron and Lake Superior, which also involved the ownership of St. George Island. The inability of the commissioners to successfully resolve that issue prevented them from making a formal decision under Article VI of the Treaty of Ghent and the issue of the definition of the boundary through the St. Mary's River would await a disposition at a later time, as neither party wished to refer this dispute to a third party sovereign for resolution.

The commission was also unable to agree on the precise location of the boundary from Lake Superior to the Lake of the Woods and this too remained an outstanding issue despite an attempt made in the Treaty of Ghent to resolve it. A suggestion by the United States in 1839 that the matters be put to international arbitration went unanswered by the British government.[31]

The Anglo-American Convention of 1818

The conclusion of the War of 1812 began a long detente between Great Britain and the United States of America on the North American continent. Both countries desired to establish cordial relations and realized that outstanding border issues were continuing to prevent the development of satisfactory relations between them. Negotiations to resolve some of the outstanding issues between the two countries took place in London in the aftermath of the war and resulted in a treaty in 1818 that reorganized the international boundary between British North America and the United States of America westward from the Lake of the Woods to the Rocky Mountains. Beyond the Rocky Mountains the two countries agreed that the Columbia District (called the Oregon Country in the United States) should be treated as a territorial condominium.

Convention of 1818 between the United States and Great Britain (Extracts)

October 20, 1818

II. It is agreed that a Line drawn from the most North Western Point of the Lake of the Woods, along the forty Ninth Parallel of North Latitude, or, if the said Point shall not be in the Forty Ninth Parallel of North Latitude, then that a Line drawn from the said Point due North or South as the Case may be, until the said Line shall intersect the said Parallel of North Latitude, and from the Point of such Intersection due West along and with the said Parallel shall be the Line of Demarcation between the Territories of the United States, and those of His Britannic Majesty, and that the said Line shall form the Northern Boundary of the said

Territories of the United States, and the Southern Boundary of the Territories of His Britannic Majesty, from the Lake of the Woods to the Stony Mountains.

III.   It is agreed, that any Country that may be claimed by either Party on the North West Coast of America, Westward of the Stony Mountains, shall, together with it's Harbours, Bays, and Creeks, and the Navigation of all Rivers within the same, be free and open, for the term of ten Years from the date of the Signature of the present Convention, to the Vessels, Citizens, and Subjects of the Two Powers: it being well understood, that this Agreement is not to be construed to the Prejudice of any Claim, which either of the Two High Contracting Parties may have to any part of the said Country, nor shall it be taken to affect the Claims of any other Power or State to any part of the said Country; the only Object of The High Contracting Parties, in that respect, being to prevent disputes and differences amongst Themselves.

Consequences of the Anglo-American Convention of 1818

This treaty removed the sovereignty of the United States from that portion of the Missouri Territory lying above the 49th parallel, which the United States had acquired from France in the Louisiana Purchase Treaty of 1803. The territory ceded by the United States included the watershed basins of the Milk River, Poplar River and Big Muddy Creek systems, all of which drain southwards into the Gulf of Mexico. That portion of the Missouri Territory now forms part of southern Saskatchewan and southern Alberta.

In return the portion of Rupert's Land, and more particularly the portion of the Red River Colony that lay below the 49th parallel, was ceded by Great Britain to the United States.[32] In terms of total land area the United States acquired more territory from Great Britain than Britain acquired from the United States. However, the decision to adopt a straight-line border along the 49th parallel of latitude provided for a rational southern boundary in the west, and avoided the difficulties that would have arisen in attempting to define the border by watershed boundaries – an especially difficult process on the flat prairie landscape of western North America.

The United States and Great Britain also arrived at a temporary arrangement concerning the Columbia District/Oregon Country west of the Rocky Mountains that set aside rival claims to sovereignty over the Pacific coast of North America. Both Great Britain and the United States agreed that each country would continue to exercise their sovereign powers over their own subjects or citizens within the Oregon Country for ten years, or until a final resolution of the international boundary in the far west could be agreed upon. This agreement represented an early example of the creation of a political condominium, a type of governance structure that accommodates the undifferentiated sovereignty of more than one country over a particular territory.

This convention also created one minor aberration in the long southern boundary between British North America and the United States. Probably due to some uncertainty regarding the location of the Lake of the Woods Article II provided that a line was to be drawn from the northwestern point of the lake to the 49th parallel and then westward to the mountains. However, the northwest point of the Lake of the Woods is 271 miles north of the 49th parallel of latitude. Therefore the effect of the line drawn by the convention was to sever an area of land that jutted into the lake and to create an exclave of US territory lying above the 49th parallel. This American exclave, known today as the Northwest Angle of Minnesota, is the only portion of US sovereign territory that lies above the 49th parallel outside of Alaska.

The Adams – Onis Treaty, 1819

The Adams – Onis Treaty was a treaty between the United States of America and the Kingdom of Spain under which Spain abandoned and transferred to the United States the Spanish claims to western North America above the 42nd degree of latitude.

Adams – Onis Treaty (Extracts)

February 22, 1819

The United States of America and His Catholic Majesty, desiring to consolidate, on a permanent basis, the friendship and good correspondence which happily prevails between the two parties, have determined to settle and terminate all their differences and pretensions, by a treaty, which shall designate, with precision, the limits of their respective bordering territories in North America.

. . . .

III. The boundary-line between the two countries, west of the Mississippi, shall begin on the Gulf of Mexico, at the mouth of the river Sabine, in the sea, continuing north, along the western bank of that river, to the 32d degree of latitude; thence, by a line due north, to the degree of latitude where it strikes the Rio Roxo of Nachitoches, or Red River; then following the course of the Rio Roxo westward, to the degree of longitude 100 west from London and 23 from Washington; then, crossing the said Red River, and running thence, by a line due north, to the river Arkansas; thence, following the course of the southern bank of the Arkansas, to its source, in latitude 42 north; and thence, by that parallel of latitude, to the South Sea. The whole being as laid down in Melish's map of the United States, published at Philadelphia, improved to the first of January, 1818. But if the source of the Arkansas River shall be found to fall north or south of latitude 42, then the line shall run from the said source due south or north, as the case may be, till it meets the said parallel of latitude 42, and thence, along the said parallel, to the South Sea: All the islands in the Sabine, and the said Red and Arkansas Rivers, throughout the course thus described. to belong to the United States; but the use of the waters, and the navigation of the Sabine to the sea, and of the said rivers Roxo and Arkansas, throughout the extent of the said boundary, on their respective banks, shall be common to the respective inhabitants of both nations.

The two high contracting parties agree to cede and renounce all their rights, claims, and pretensions to the territories described by the said line, that is to say: The United States hereby cede to His Catholic Majesty, and renounce forever, all their rights, claims, and pretensions, to the territories lying west and south of the above-described line; and, in like manner, His Catholic Majesty cedes to the said United States all his rights, claims, and pretensions to any territories east and north of the said line, and for himself, his heirs, and successors, renounces all claim to the said territories forever.

Consequences of the Adams – Onis Treaty

The main consequence of the Adams – Onis Treaty was the final retreat of Spain from western North America above San Francisco (the United States gave up claims to Texas in return[33]). The United States had obtained a northern limitation of Spanish claims in the Pacific Northwest to latitude 42 degrees north (the present northern boundary of the state of California). At the same time, Spain transferred its outstanding claims to the Oregon Country to the United States, which reinforced the American claims to the Oregon Country.

Although the practical effect of the Nootka Conventions had been to force the Spanish back below the 49th parallel of latitude Spain had never relinquished its claims to the whole of the Oregon Country up to the boundary with Russian America. Although Spain no longer had the strength to assert such claims the United States did increasingly have such power, and the disposition of the Oregon Country would become a serious irritant in relations between Great Britain and the United States as the nineteenth century progressed.

The Anglo-American Convention of 1827

When the ten-year limit to the arrangements made in the Anglo-American Convention of 1818 for the Columbia District/Oregon

Country approached neither country wished to attempt to settle the final sovereignty of the territory. Substantial developments were occurring in the western half of North America following the trail blazing explorations of Sir Alexander Mackenzie and the Lewis and Clark Expedition, each the first of their countrymen to reach the Pacific coast of North America by an overland journey. The Hudson's Bay Company continued to expand its economic penetration of the Columbia District/Oregon Country during this period, while American immigration into the southern Oregon Country, particularly near the mouth of the Columbia River, continued to increase the number of Americans in the Oregon Country.

Subsequent to the Adams-Onis Treaty of 1819, which permanently removed Spain from the northwestern Pacific coast of North America, Mexico had revolted against the Spanish Empire and achieved its independence on August 24, 1821, at which point it succeeded to the remaining Spanish claims to the North American mainland. A substantial American immigration into Texas, then part of Mexico, was also occurring during these years. With continuing ferment and change occurring in western North America, it appeared wise to the statesmen of the period to maintain the status quo.

As a temporary expedient the condominium arrangement that Great Britain and the United States had put in place for the Columbia District/Oregon Country had proven to be effective, and both parties evinced a desire to continue the arrangement. Accordingly, a new treaty was entered into to provide for the continuation of the condominium for the Columbia District/ Oregon Country.

The Anglo-American Convention, 1827 (Extracts)

August 6, 1827

The United States of America, and his Majesty the King of the

United Kingdom of Great Britain and Ireland, being equally desirous to prevent, as far as possible, all hazard of misunderstanding between the two nations, with respect to the territory on the northwest coast of America west of the Stoney or Rocky Mountains, after the expiration of the third article of the Convention concluded between them on 20 October 1818; and also with a view to give further time for maturing measures which shall have for their object a more definite settlement of the claims of each party to the said territory, have respectively named their plenipotentiaries to treat and agree concerning a temporary renewal of the said article, that is to say:

. . . .

I. All the provisions of the third article of the Convention concluded between the United States of America, and his Majesty the King of the United Kingdom of Great Britain and Ireland, on 20 October 1818, shall be, and they are hereby, further indefinitely extended and continued in force, in the same manner as if all the provisions of the said article were specifically recited.

II. It shall be competent, however, to either of the contracting parties, in case either should think fit, at any time after 20 October 1828, on giving due notice of 12 months to the other contracting party, to annul and abrogate this Convention: and it shall, in such case, be accordingly entirely annulled and abrogated, after the expiration of the said term of notice.

III. Nothing contained in this Convention, or in the third article of the Convention of 20 October 1818, hereby continued in force, shall be construed to impair, or in any manner affect, the claims which either of the contracting parties may have to any part of the country westward of the Stoney or Rocky Mountains.

Consequences of the Anglo-American Convention of 1827

This treaty continued the condominium arrangement put in place for the Columbia District, or Oregon Country as it was called in the United States. Neither Great Britain or the United States were prepared to tackle the reorganization of their interests in the Columbia District/Oregon Country and therefore the continuation of the existing arrangements served the interests of both nations. The treaty provided for an indefinite continuation of the condominium with a provision allowing either party to exit the arrangement upon giving twelve months notice to the other party.

St. Croix – St. Lawrence Arbitration Treaty 1827

The Treaty of Ghent, 1814, provided that commissioners from both Great Britain and the United States would meet and seek to determine the precise location of the international border in three regions; the ownership of islands in Passamaquoddy Bay, the location of the boundary lying between the St. Lawrence River and the source of the St. Croix River, and the fixing of the border through the Great Lakes maritime boundary as far west as the Lake of the Woods. The commissioners were successful with respect to the first issue but not with respect to the second or the third issues. Under the terms of the Treaty of Ghent unresolved issues could be sent to a third-party sovereign or foreign state for international arbitration of the issue. While Great Britain and the United States did not perceive it convenient to submit the Great Lakes – Lake of the Woods boundary issue to international arbitration there was a need to resolve the eastern boundary and accordingly the parties decided to submit the issue of the boundary between the source of the St. Croix River and the St. Lawrence River to international arbitration. For that purpose the King of the Netherlands, William I, was selected as an arbitrator and a treaty was entered into between the United States and Great Britain to provide for arbitration of the St. Croix – St. Lawrence boundary issue.

St. Croix – St. Lawrence Boundary Arbitration Treaty, 1827 (Extracts)

September 29, 1827

I. It is agreed that the points of difference which have arisen in the settlement of the boundary between the American and British dominions, as described in the fifth article of the Treaty of Ghent, shall be referred, as therein provided, to some friendly sovereign or state, who shall be invited to investigate, and make a decision upon, such points of difference.

The two contracting powers engage to proceed in concert, to the choice of such friendly sovereign or state, as soon as the ratifications of this convention shall have been exchanged, and to use their best endeavours to obtain a decision, if practicable, within two years after the arbiter shall signify his consent to act as such.

. . . .

VII. The decision of the arbiter, when given, shall be taken as final and conclusive; and it shall be carried without reserve into immediate effect, by commissioners appointed for that purpose by the contracting parties.

Arbitral Award of King William I of the Netherlands
(Extracts)

January 10, 1831

We ARE OF OPINION:

That it will be suitable [il conviendra] to adopt, as the boundary of the two States, a line drawn due north from the source of the river St. Croix to the point where it intersects the middle of the thalweg of the river St. John; thence, the middle of the thalweg of that river, ascending it, to the point where the river St. Francis empties itself into the river St John; thence, the middle of the thalweg of the river St. Francis, ascending it, to the source of its south westernmost branch, which source we indicate on the Map A, by the letter X, authenticated by the signature of our Minister of Foreign Affairs; thence, a line drawn due west, to the point where it unites with the line claimed by the United States of America, and delineated on the Map A; thence, said line to the point at which, according to said map, it coincides with that claimed by Great Britain; and thence, the line traced on the map by the two Powers, to the north westernmost source of Connecticut River.

As regards the second point, to wit: the question, which is the North westernmost head of Connecticut river:

. . . .

We are of opinion:

That the stream situated farthest to the northwest among those which fall into the northernmost of the three Lakes, the last of which bears the name of Connecticut Lake, must be considered as the north westernmost head of Connecticut river.

And as to the third point, to wit: the question, which is the boundary to be traced from the river Connecticut, along the parallel of the 45th degree of north latitude to the river St. Lawrence, named in the Treaties Iroquois or Cataraguy:

. . . .

We are of opinion:

That it will be suitable [il conviendra] to proceed to fresh operations to measure the observed latitude, in order to mark out the boundary from the river Connecticut along the parallel of the 45th degree of north latitude to the river St- Lawrence, named in the Treaties Iroquois or Cataraguy, in such a manner, however, that, in all cases, at the place called Rouse's Point, the territory of the United States of America shall extend to the fort erected at that place, and shall include said fort and its Kilometrical radius [rayon Kilométrique.]

Consequences of the Arbitral Award of the King of the Netherlands

The parties had chosen King William I of the Netherlands as the arbiter of the dispute. However, when the King released his award on January 10, 1831, the United States was immediately disappointed with the result. The Dutch King admitted his inability to determine the boundary issue predicated on any fixed principles arising from the previous treaties between Great Britain and the United States concerning this subject and he provided a compromise solution to the dispute.

The United States of America objected to the arbitral award because King William I had not answered the arbitral question put before him. Rather, finding that the evidence did not disclose sufficient grounds for the King to make a determination according to legal principles, he chose instead to effect a compromise between the views of Great Britain and the views of the United States concerning the location of the border from the source of the St. Croix River to the St. Lawrence River.[34]

One subsequent commentator has stated that:

> [In] the Northeastern Boundary Arbitration, the royal arbitrator frankly admitted his inability to render a judicial decision and recommended a compromise line, a course which amounted to such a clear departure from the terms of the submission that the United States refused to abide by the award and Great Britain acquiesced in this decision.[35]

Thus, despite article VII of the arbitration treaty, which stipulated that the decision of the arbitrator would be final, the United States took the view that the arbitrator had exceeded his jurisdiction in the matter by producing a result that was not based upon the specific issue put before him for determination. Rather, the arbitrator had attempted to create a compromise solution based on more subjective equitable principles rather than a strict adherence to legal principles. There was a perception at the time that the

King of the Netherlands was influenced by the need of the Netherlands to retain the cordial support of Great Britain during a difficult period in Dutch history. The southern provinces of the Netherlands had declared their independence as the kingdom of Belgium and the King may have been motivated by a desire to retain the friendship of Britain with respect to any border issues between Belgium and Holland that might emerge now that Belgium had separated.[36] Many observers presumed that the compromise line avoided the necessity of the King siding with the United States on grounds of principle, which would have been to the territorial detriment of British North America.

Such an arbitral result the United States was, of course, averse to accepting and Great Britain acquiesced to the American position after the Crown legal officers confirmed that the submission to arbitration made by the two countries precluded the King, as arbitrator, from developing compromise positions in lieu of a principled legal judgment.[37] Thus, the issue of the St. Croix – St. Lawrence boundary continued to remain an open issue between the two countries.

The Webster-Ashburton Treaty, 1842

During the 1830's an element of discord crept into Anglo-American relations which was brought about by the 1837 rebellions in both Lower and Upper Canada. Although the rebellions were swiftly suppressed by the colonial governments in Canada the situation prevailing in British North America was taken advantage of by those Americans who still sought territorial aggrandizement north of the border. So-called Hunters Lodges were organized in the United States with their membership open to disaffected Canadians although they mainly consisted of young American men who were persuaded that the conquest of Canada would be an adventure. A border insurgency resulted which led to active combat operations between insurgents entering British North America from the United States and the colonial garrison. Several battles were fought, culminating in the Battle of the

Windmill in eastern Upper Canada, which crushed the border incursions from the United States. However, a preemptive strike by colonial forces across the border from the Niagara Peninsula resulted in the destruction of an American-flagged vessel, the *Caroline*, severely straining diplomatic relations between Great Britain and the United States.

For a time it appeared that war between the two powers was possible but restraint on both sides allowed war to be averted. Ultimately, a decision by the Imperial Government to adopt the recommendations made in a report delivered by Lord Durham, a Governor General of Canada, in which he suggested that Lower Canada and Upper Canada be combined into a single province, and granted a responsible government, ameliorated the political dissent in the colony, and eliminated any justification for an insurgency. Firm action south of the border by the US Federal Government, ultimately including the suppression of the Hunters Lodges, greatly assisted in the reestablishment of a peaceful border between British North America and the United States.

The dispute over the *Caroline* was subsequently resolved through diplomatic negotiations and compensation was paid by Great Britain for the American losses. The *Caroline* incident subsequently became an important precedent in international law with respect to the legality of preemptive strikes.[38]

Further east , the unresolved boundary between the province of New Brunswick and the state of Maine led to incidents in the backwoods north of the Aroostook River. The so-called Aroostook War in 1839 resulted from conflicting lumbering operations in that disputed region. Militia forces were called out on both sides of the border, and all along the New Brunswick-Maine section of the international boundary armed forces were placed on a war-footing. However, President Van Buren dispatched General Winfield Scott to the border to cool the passions that had arisen and a prior cordial relationship that Scott had formed with the Lieutenant Governor of New Brunswick,

Sir John Harvey, allowed officials on both sides of the border to reduce tensions and the crisis dissipated.[39]

Both Great Britain and the United States realized that to avoid potential clashes in the future it was imperative to resolve outstanding boundary issues between British North America and the United States. Accordingly, in 1842, the two countries embarked upon a major diplomatic negotiation with a view to finally resolving the boundary between the United States of America and British North America. Those negotiations became known as the Webster-Ashburton negotiations after the two representatives of the parties, US Secretary of State Daniel Webster and the British representative Lord Ashburton. Daniel Webster was one of the leading legal and political figures in the United States during the first half of the nineteenth century. His British counterpart was Alexander Baring, Lord Ashburton, who was instrumental in the growth of Baring Brothers, an important British banking firm. Ashburton had lived in the United States as a young man where he had been tasked with looking after the British bank's interests in that country, and Ashburton had developed a positive perspective on the young republic. He had also married into a wealthy, and politically connected Philadelphia family, and he retained his American connections after returning to live in the United Kingdom.

Daniel Webster was concerned to resolve the boundary issues involving Maine and to that end he began to shape the direction of elite public opinion in that state. He had come into possession of a map that was produced contemporaneously with the Treaty of Paris, 1783, and that had supposedly been in the possession of Benjamin Franklin at the time. It showed a boundary line that supported the maximal British claims to the disputed territory in Maine. Webster now used that map in secret to soften up the opposition being expressed by the key political figures in Maine to what Webster hoped would be a mutually acceptable compromise settlement of the boundary.[40] For his part, Lord Ashburton was instructed to hold the boundary at the St. John

River at the eastern end of the disputed territory, and to attempt to push the Americans farther way at the western end of the disputed Maine border, where it could approach too closely to Quebec City, the strategic fortress city whose possession could control the country. The British objective was to maintain a road connection between Lower Canada and New Brunswick for military defence purposes and therefore it was necessary to keep the United States as far away from the St. Lawrence River as possible.[41]

The boundary in this region had been disputed since the Treaty of Paris, 1783, and a substantial amount of goodwill would be necessary on both sides if a resolution was to be obtained. Webster made an important decision by inviting the states of Maine and Massachusetts (which had originally possessed Maine as its dependency) to establish state boundary commissions to assist in facilitating a settlement. Allowing some participation by the states in the boundary resolution process was a brilliant negotiating maneuver because it opened up the prospect that the states could be co-opted into a final settlement that would minimize the potential for their concerns to be subsequently raised in the Senate, which was the legislative body in Washington that would ultimately bear constitutional responsibility for approving any treaty between the two countries.

Some hard bargaining ensued but nevertheless in a cordial atmosphere. The compromise boundary agreed upon largely followed the award made by King William I of the Netherlands but departed from his award by moving the border away from the line of hills that approached Quebec City and the St. Lawrence River. The new border was fixed northwest of the St. John River but southeast of the line that had been created in the King of the Netherlands' award. Of the disputed territory the United States received 7015 square miles and British North America received 5012 square miles. The British also conceded the Collins-Valentine line for the border between Vermont, New Hampshire, New York and Lower Canada, which resulted in the United States retaining Fort Montgomery, its misplaced fortress at Rouses's

Point, New York, that had originally been inadvertently constructed on Canadian lands lying north of the 45th parallel of latitude. The Rouse's Point concession by Great Britain resolved a significant defence issue for the United States. Maine and Massachusetts were also given the right to bring logs down the St. John River into and through New Brunswick.[42] Although the state commissioners, particularly those from Maine, initially demurred from this resolution they ultimately acceded to it and the treaty was signed.

Webster and Ashburton also resolved the boundary through the Great Lakes to the Lake of the Woods, large parts of which had been approved *de facto* by the commissions established under the Treaty of Ghent. The Thalweg Principle was employed to establish the location of the boundary and the navigable channels adjacent to the Long Sault Islands and Barnhart Island in the St. Lawrence River, and the channels adjacent to Bois Blanc Island in the Detroit River. As well, it was decided that the western channel in Lake St. Clair (which was navigable) where it entered the St. Clair River would be open to the citizens and subjects of both countries.[43] In the St. Mary's River the border was placed in the Eastern Neebish Channel, which was navigable.[44] St. George's island in the St. Mary's River was assigned to the United States. Further west it was agreed that the boundary would follow the Pigeon River from south of Hunter's Island to the Lake of the Woods, with the citizens and subjects of both countries allowed to use the historic Grand Portage, and the other customary portages between Lake Superior and the Lake of the Woods. The work of Webster and Ashburton on this particular segment of the boundary was greatly eased because maps for this part of the border already existed – they had been prepared by the great Scottish-Canadian geographer David Thompson as part of his work for the border commissions established under the Treaty of Ghent in the 1820's.[45]

Finally, Lord Ashburton and Secretary Webster came to an accommodation on how to treat the *Caroline* incident, in which an American vessel had been destroyed in American waters by the British during the Patriot Insurgency and thus both states were able to move past that unfortunate incident in their mutual relations.[46]

The Webster-Ashburton Treaty, 1842 (Extracts)

August 9, 1842

A Treaty to settle and define the Boundaries between the Territories of the United States and the possessions of Her Britannic Majesty, in North America: For the final Suppression of the African Slave Trade: and For the giving up of Criminals fugitive from justice, in certain cases.

Whereas certain portions of the line of boundary between the United States of America and the British Dominions in North America, described in the second article of the Treaty of Peace of 1783, have not yet been ascertained and determined, notwithstanding the repeated attempts which have been heretofore made for that purpose, and whereas it is now thought to be for the interest of both Parties, that, avoiding further discussion of their respective rights, arising in this respect under the said Treaty, they should agree on a conventional line in said portions of the said boundary, such as may be convenient to both Parties, with such equivalents and compensations, as are deemed just and reasonable: ... The United States of America and Her Britannic Majesty, having resolved to treat on these several subjects, have for that purpose appointed their respective Plenipotentiaries to negotiate and conclude a Treaty, that is to say: the President of the United States has, on his part, furnished with full powers, Daniel Webster, Secretary of State of the United States; and Her Majesty the Queen of the United Kingdom of Great Britain and Ireland, has, on her part, appointed the Right honorable Alexander Lord Ashburton, a peer of the said United Kingdom, a member of Her Majesty's most honorable Privy Council, and Her Majesty's Minister Plenipotentiary on a Special Mission to the United States;

who, after a reciprocal communication of their respective full powers, have agreed to and signed the following articles:

I. It is hereby agreed and declared that the line of boundary shall be as follows: Beginning at the monument at the source of the river St. Croix, as designated and agreed to by the Commissioners under the fifth article of the Treaty of 1794, between the Governments of the United States and Great Britain; thence, north, following the exploring line run and marked by the Surveyors of the two Governments in the years 1817 and 1818, under the fifth article of the Treaty of Ghent to its intersection with the river St. John, and to the middle of the channel thereof: thence, up the middle of the main channel of the said river St. John, to the mouth of the river St. Francis; thence up the middle of the channel of the said river St. Francis, and of the lakes through which it flows, to the outlet of the Lake Pohenagamook; thence, southwesterly, in a straight line to a point on the northwest branch of the river St. John, which point shall be ten miles distant from the main branch of the St. John, in a straight line, and in the nearest direction; but if the said point shall be found to be less than seven miles from the nearest point of the summit or crest of the highlands that divide those rivers which empty themselves into the river Saint Lawrence from those which fall into the river Saint John, then the said point shall be made to recede down the said northwest branch of the river St. John, to a point seven miles in a straight line from the said summit or crest; thence, in a straight line, in a course about south eight degrees west, to the point where the parallel of latitude of 46°25' north, intersects the southwest branch of the St. John's; thence, southerly, by the said branch, to the source thereof in the highlands at the Metjarmette Portage; thence, down along the said highlands which divide the waters which empty themselves into the river Saint Lawrence from those which fall into the Atlantic Ocean, to the head of Hall's Stream; thence, down the middle of said Stream, till the line thus run intersects the old line of boundary surveyed and marked by Valentine and Collins previously to the year 1774, as the 45th degree of north latitude, and which has been known and understood to be the line of actual division between the States of New York and Vermont on one side, and the British Province of Canada on the other; and, from said point of intersection, west along the said dividing line as heretofore known and understood, to the Iroquois or St. Lawrence river.

II. It is moreover agreed, that from the place where the joint Commissioners terminated their labors under the sixth article of the Treaty of Ghent, to wit: at a point in the Neebish Channel, near Muddy Lake, the line shall run into and along the ship channel between Saint Joseph and St. Tammany Islands, to the division of the channel at or near the head of St. Joseph's Island; thence, turning eastwardly and northwardly, around the lower end of St. George's or Sugar Island, and following the middle of the channel which divides St. George's from St. Joseph's Island; thence, up the east Neebish channel, nearest to St. George's Island, through the middle of Lake George;-thence, west of Jonas' Island, into St. Mary's river, to a point in the middle of that river, about one mile above St. George's or Sugar Island, so as to appropriate and assign the said Island to the United States; thence, adopting the line traced on the maps by the Commissioners, thro' the river St. Mary and Lake Superior, to a point north of Ile Royale in said Lake, one hundred yards to the north and east of Ile Chapeau, which last mentioned Island lies near the northeastern point of Ile Royale, where the line marked by the Commissioners terminates; and from the last mentioned point, southwesterly, through the middle of the Sound between Ile Royale and the northwestern mainland, to the mouth of Pigeon river, and up the said river to, and through, the north and south Fowl Lakes, to the Lakes of the height of land between Lake Superior and the Lake of the Woods; thence, along the water-communication to Lake Saisaginaga, and through that Lake; thence, to and through Cypress Lake, Lac du Bois Blanc, Lac la Croix, Little Vermilion Lake, and Lake Namecan, and through the several smaller lakes, straights, or streams, connecting the lakes here mentioned, to that point in Lac la Pluie, or Rainy Lake, at the Chaudiere Falls, from which the Commissioners traced the line to the most northwestern point of the Lake of the Woods,-thence, along the said line to the said most northwestern point, being in latitude 49° 23'55" north, and in longitude 95°14'38" west from the Observatory at Greenwich; thence, according to existing treaties, due south to its intersection with the 49th parallel of north latitude, and along that parallel to the Rocky Mountains. It being understood that all the water-communications, and all the usual portages along the line from Lake Superior to the Lake of the Woods; and also Grand Portage, from the shore of Lake Superior to the Pigeon river, as now actually used, shall be free and open to the use of the citizens and subjects of both countries.

III. In order to promote the interests and encourage the industry of all the inhabitants of the countries watered by the river St. John and its tributaries, whether living within the State of Maine or the Province of New Brunswick, it is agreed that, where, by the provisions of the present treaty, the river St. John is declared to be the line of boundary, the navigation of the said river shall be free and open to both Parties, and shall in no way be obstructed by either: That all the produce of the forest, in logs, lumber, timber, boards, staves, or shingles, or of agriculture not being manufactured, grown on any of those parts of the State of Maine watered by the river St. John, or by its tributaries, of which fact reasonable evidence shall, if required, be produced, shall have free access into and through the said river and its said tributaries, having their source within the State of Maine, to and from the seaport at the mouth of the said river St. John's, and to and round the Falls of the said river, either by boats, rafts, or other conveyance: That when within the Province of New Brunswick, the said produce shall be dealt with as if it were the produce of the said province: That, in like manner, the inhabitants of the Territory of the Upper St John determined by this Treaty to belong to her Britannic Majesty, shall have free access to and through the river for their produce, in those parts where the said river runs wholly through the State of Maine: provided always, that this agreement shall give no right to either party to interfere with any regulations not inconsistent with the terms of this treaty which the Governments, respectively, of Maine or of New Brunswick, may make respecting the navigation of the said river, where both banks thereof shall belong to the same Party.

IV. All grants of land heretofore made by either Party, within the limits of the territory which by this Treaty falls within the dominions of the other Party, shall be held valid, ratified, and confirmed to the persons in possession under such grants, to the same extent as if such territory had by this Treaty fallen within the dominions of the Party by whom such grants were made: And all equitable possessory claims, arising from a possession and improvement of any lot or parcel of land by the person actually in possession, or by those under whom such person claims, for more than six years before the date of this Treaty, shall, in like manner, be deemed valid, and be confirmed and quieted by a release to the person entitled thereto, of the title to such lot or parcel of land, so described as best to include the improvements made thereon; and in all other respects the two contracting Parties agree to deal upon the most liberal principles of equity with the settlers actually dwelling upon the Territory falling to them, respectively, which has heretofore been in dispute between them.

V. Whereas, in the course of the controversy respecting the disputed Territory on the northeastern boundary, some moneys have been received by the authorities of Her Britannic Majesty's Province of New Brunswick, with the intention of preventing depredations on the forests of the said Territory, which moneys were to be carried to a fund called the " Disputed Territory Fund ", the proceeds whereof, it was agreed, should be hereafter paid over to the Parties interested, in the proportions to be determined by a final settlement of boundaries: It is hereby agreed, that a correct account of all receipts and payments on the said fund, shall be delivered to the Government of the United States, within six months after the ratification of this Treaty; and the proportion of the amount due thereon to the States of Maine and Massachusetts, and any bonds or securities appertaining thereto, shall be paid and delivered over to the Government of the United States; and the Government of the United States agrees to receive for the use of, and pay over to the States of Maine and Massachusetts, their respective portions of said Fund: And further to pay and satisfy said States, respectively, for all claims for expenses incurred by them in protecting the said heretofore disputed Territory, and making a survey thereof, in 1838; the Government of the United States agreeing with the States of Maine and Massachusetts to pay them the further sum of three hundred thousand dollars, in equal moieties, on account of their assent to the line of boundary described in this Treaty, and in consideration of the conditions and equivalents received therefor, from the Government of Her Britannic Majesty.

VI. It is furthermore understood and agreed, that for the purpose of running and tracing those parts of the line between the source of the St. Croix and the St. Lawrence river, which will require to be run and ascertained, and for marking the residue of said line by proper monuments on the land, two Commissioners shall be appointed, one by the President of the United States, by and with the advice and consent of the Senate thereof, and one by Her Britannic Majesty: and the said commissioners shall meet at Bangor, in the State of Maine, on the first day of May next, or as soon thereafter as may be, and shall proceed to mark the line above described, from the source of the St. Croix to the river St. John; and shall trace on proper maps the dividing line along said river, and along the river St. Francis, to the outlet of the Lake Pohenagamook; and from the outlet of the said Lake, they shall ascertain, fix, and mark by proper and durable monuments on the land, the line described in the first article of this Treaty; and the said Commissioners shall make to each of their respective Governments a joint report or declaration, under their hands and seals, designating such line of boundary, and shall accompany such report or declaration with maps certified by them to be true maps of the new boundary.

VII. It is further agreed, that the channels in the river St. Lawrence, on both sides of the Long Sault Islands and of Barnhart Island; the channels in the river Detroit, on both sides of the

Island Bois Blanc, and between that Island and both the American and Canadian shores; and all the several channels and passages between the various Islands lying near the junction of the river St. Clair with the lake of that name, shall be equally free and open to the ships, vessels, and boats of both Parties.

Consequences of the Webster-Ashburton Treaty

As a slate-cleaning exercise the Webster-Ashburton Treaty of 1842 represents a significant and successful milestone in the history of relations between Great Britain (and Canada) and the United States of America. At a single stroke it resolved the outstanding border definition issues that had perplexed the diplomatic relations between the two countries for almost six decades since the Treaty of Paris, 1783. The boundary between British North America and the United States of America from Passamaquoddy Bay on the Atlantic coast westward to the Rocky Mountains had now been ascertained. It was a significant achievement albeit one that built upon the work of previous negotiators and officials on both sides of the border. In Maine, the United States obtained less than the entirety of its claim (and even less than what was awarded to them by the King of the Netherlands in the arbitral award that America had spurned) but British North America had conceded the Collins-Valentine line, which meant that the United States could retain the fortress at Rouse's Point that it had built at great expense. Further west, the United States was given St. George's island in the St. Mary's River, and Britain compromised on the boundary from Lake Superior to the Lake of the Woods.

In both the United States and Great Britain there were critics of the Webster-Ashburton Treaty and several pointed to various maps, including secret maps that had been dug out of archives but not publicly released during the negotiations. But none of those maps conclusively proved anything, and ultimately the Webster-Ashburton Treaty came to be seen in all three countries, Great Britain, Canada, and the United States of America, as a wise and judicious outcome, a "monumental accomplishment" in the words of one historian who has extensively studied the negotiations.[47]

Manifest Destiny and the Oregon Treaty, 1846

The concept of Manifest Destiny, a belief by Americans that their republic was destined to govern all of North America, was itself an outgrowth of American exceptionalism, which was a sense that America held a special place in the world as a result of its revolutionary origins, belief in individual liberty, and the trajectory of its history as an independent country. In the middle of the nineteenth century many Americans assumed that it was natural and inevitable that the United States would expand over the entire North American continent, and some even saw such a development as one that was divinely inspired. The phraseology of Manifest Destiny has been attributed to an American columnist, John O'Sullivan, in his writings in the late 1830's and early 1840's, although the concept was present in an unfocused form well before that date.[48] The United States was seen by many of its citizens as the torch bearer of liberty in contrast to the authoritarian monarchies of the Old World. Manifest Destiny thus became a shared myth of many Americans, although it was never articulated as official policy.[49] However, it was also a way to camouflage the burning desire of many Americans for the acquisition of new land.[50] It has been viewed by one academic observer as "bold and aggressive" though on balance taking fewer lives than the expansionist dreams that drove other, comparable, great powers.[51]

Canada was an early object of the efforts by Americans to implement Manifest Destiny, although the phrase had not yet been coined when the invasions of the War of 1812-14 occurred. The Virginian presidencies that dominated the politics of the early republic looked with fear and loathing upon the British control of northern North America and saw in the continued British presence a clear and present danger to the survival of their republic. Earlier memories of the French threat from the north were also still within the living memory of Americans, and so the desire for an expansion into the north was clearly present in American politics. The potential for expansion into British North America was one of the drivers of the Patriot Insurgency by American Hunter Lodges that provided both sanctuary for the failed Canadian leaders of the 1837 rebellions in Lower and Upper Canada, as well as a focal point for the recruitment of young Americans into the insurgency. Canada was a prize that American filibusters sought to seize from Great Britain.[52] Manifest Destiny was seen as a way to counter British influence and to protect the United States, while also acquiring new lands.

However, Great Britain consistently protected its British North American colonies from American encroachment throughout the nineteenth century, reinforcing the local garrison with troops from Europe whenever American expansionism presented a threat to the British possessions. Additionally, Britain combated Manifest Destiny by diplomacy.[53] The negotiations that led to the Webster-Ashburton Treaty were an important element of this process. Great Britain also lent diplomatic support to the Republic of Texas after it won its independence from Mexico, and encouraged both that country as well as the Kingdom of Hawaii, where Americans were establishing substantial economic interests, to remain independent of the United States.

The one part of North America where Manifest Destiny was an important element in defining Canada's southern border concerned the Oregon Territory, or the Columbia District as it was known in British North America. That territory was ruled jointly by the United States and Great Britain as a condominium, with the citizens and subjects of both parties entitled to settle within it by right. In the earlier years there was little in the way of local government in the territory other than the Hudson Bay Company, which maintained its main base at Fort Vancouver, at the mouth of the Columbia River. British North American fur traders were active along the Columbia River but there was little British presence south of the Columbia and north of the 42nd parallel, the boundary with the Mexican province of Alta California.

Although Great Britain and the United States had developed the condominium approach to forestall, or delay, the resolution of the dispute over sovereignty with respect to the Oregon Country, increasing American immigration and developing economic interests in the Pacific region threatened to upset the balance of power in the territory. By 1845 perhaps 5000 Americans resided in the Oregon Country, particularly in the Willamette Valley, and the American whaling industry was anxious to secure port facilities on Puget Sound.[54] American settlers began to form a local government as the American population mushroomed.[55] Meanwhile British efforts to foster development in the Columbia District through the Hudson Bay Company had not borne fruit.[56]

Initially, the British had proposed that the border follow the 49th parallel of latitude until it reached the Columbia River and then follow that river to the ocean, a little above the 46th parallel. The United States rejected this suggestion because it sought a port on the Pacific coast and with San Francisco owned by Mexico the next best alternative appeared to be Puget Sound.[57] The United States thus sought to place the border on the 49th parallel, including a division of Vancouver Island, which Great Britain would not accept. Both President John Tyler and his successor, President James K. Polk, publicly claimed the entire Columbia District/Oregon Country for the United States, raising diplomatic tensions between Great Britain and the United States.[58] Democratic Party extremists in the United States began chanting the slogan of fifty-four forty or fight, by which they meant that if Great Britain did not surrender the whole of the Columbia District/ Oregon Country the US should take it by force. However, the Imperial Government in London refused to surrender its claims and in the rising tensions it appeared that a third war between Great Britain and the United States was possible.

Ultimately, however, cooler tempers prevailed and a solution to the crisis was found in a proposal made by the American Ambassador to the United Kingdom, Edward Everett, who suggested that the border be fixed at the 49th parallel to the Pacific coast but then follow the Strait of Juan de Fuca, thus giving all of Vancouver Island to Great Britain.[59] That solution protected the interests of the Hudson Bay Company, which had by then transferred its main administrative post in the Columbia District/Oregon Country from Fort Vancouver, at the mouth of the Columbia River, to a new post on the southern part of Vancouver Island.[60]

While President Polk initially held firm on American claims to the entire country, he was primarily interested in expanding the United States into the sparsely populated northern territories of Mexico. To that end, he fomented a war with Mexico between 1846-48, which saw Mexico lose approximately 40% of its territory. The United States took all of the Mexican territory north of the Rio Grande River, including the province of Alta California, and also annexed the Republic of Texas. Realizing that the United States could not fight two major wars at the same time, Polk decided to compromise with Great Britain on the Oregon question and it was the compromise that Edward Everett had initially proposed that both countries agreed-to.

Oregon Treaty, 1846

June 15, 1846

The United States of America and her Majesty the Queen of the United Kingdom of Great Britain and Ireland, deeming it to be desirable for the future welfare of both countries that the state of doubt and uncertainty which has hitherto prevailed respecting the sovereignty and government of the territory on the northwest coast of America, lying westward of the Rocky or Stony Mountains, should be finally terminated by an amicable compromise of the rights mutually asserted by the two parties over the said territory, have respectively named plenipotentiaries to treat and agree concerning the terms of such settlement-that is to say: the

President of the United States of America has, on his part, furnished with full powers James Buchanan, Secretary of State of the United States, and her Majesty the Queen of the United Kingdom of Great Britain and Ireland has, on her part, appointed the Right Honorable Richard Pakenham, a member of her Majesty's Most Honorable Privy Council, and her Majesty's Envoy Extraordinary and Minister Plenipotentiary to the United States; who, after having communicated to each other their respective full powers, found in good and due form, have agreed upon and concluded the following articles:—-

I. From the point on the forty-ninth parallel of north latitude, where the boundary laid down in existing treaties and conventions between the United States and Great Britain terminates, the line of boundary between the territories of the United States and those of her Britannic Majesty shall be continued westward along the said forty-ninth parallel of north latitude to the middle of the channel which separates the continent from Vancouver's Island, and thence southerly through the middle of the said channel, and of Fuca's Straits, to the Pacific Ocean: Provided, however, That the navigation of the whole of the said channel and straits, south of the forty-ninth parallel of north latitude, remain free and open to both parties.

II. From the point at which the forty-ninth parallel of north latitude shall be found to intersect the great northern branch of the Columbia River, the navigation of the said branch shall be free and open to the Hudson's Bay Company, and to all British subjects trading with the same, to the point where the said branch meets the main stream of the Columbia, and thence down the said main stream to the ocean, with Free access into and through the said river or rivers, it being understood that all the usual portages along the line thus described shall, in like manner, be free and open. In navigating the said river or rivers, British subjects, with their goods and produce, shall be treated on the same footing as citizens of the United States; it being, however, always understood that nothing in this article shall be construed as preventing, or intended to prevent, the government of the United States from making any regulations respecting the navigation of the said river or rivers not inconsistent with the present treaty.

III. In the future appropriation of the territory south of the forty-ninth parallel of north latitude, as provided in the first article of this treaty, the possessory rights of the Hudson's Bay Company, and of all British subjects who may be already in the occupation of land or other property lawfully acquired within the said territory, shall be respected.

IV. The farms, lands, and other property of every description, belonging to the Puget's Sound Agricultural Company, on the north side of the Columbia River, shall be confirmed to the said company. In case, however, the situation of those farms and lands should be considered by the United States to be of public and political importance, and the United States government should signify a desire to obtain possession of the whole, or of any part thereof, the property so required shall be transferred to the said government, at a proper valuation, to be agreed upon between the parties.

V. The present treaty shall be ratified by the President of the United States, by and with the advice and consent of the Senate thereof, and by Her Britannic Majesty; and the ratifications shall be exchanged at London, at the expiration of six months from the date hereof, or sooner, if possible.

Consequences of the Oregon Treaty

The Oregon Treaty resolved the last major outstanding border issue involving the southern boundary between British North America and the United States of America. Both sides obtained territory of value to satisfy their interests. The United States obtained the richer agricultural lands south of the 49th parallel, as well as Puget Sound, despite the longer historical presence of British interests in that portion of the territory between the

Columbia River and the 49th parallel. The northern part of the Columbia District was of greater value to the Hudson Bay Company's fur trading interests and, in the long run, the port of Vancouver would prove to be the best commercial harbour north of San Francisco. The agreement not to divide Vancouver Island was consistent with the approach taken by the commissioners who fixed the southern boundary through the Great Lakes, who had decided as a matter of principle that where an island in the Great Lakes would be divided by the location of the equidistant border the country that would have received the greater share of the island would in fact receive the whole island, with the other country compensated elsewhere.[61] Despite some early intransigence on both sides neither country wished to enter another war with the other country again and the logic of following the 49th parallel to Pacific tidewater was an obvious solution. Despite the stridency of Manifest Destiny claims in the United States to the entire territory the settlement was accepted in both countries with little dissent.

Manifest Destiny would continue to play an important role in the territorial expansion of the United States but at the expense of Mexico and the aboriginal first nations of the Great Plains, rather than of British North America.[62] Still, many Americans continued to hope that British North America would be absorbed into the United States, although they expected that to happen on consent by the choice of the people living in the British colonies. Nevertheless, as late as 1893, American observers still cited Manifest Destiny as a basis for the hoped-for annexation of Canada.[63] As it happened, Canadians began to fashion their own destiny following the grant of responsible government to the British North American provinces in the 1840's. Soon a northern confederation would be created and the new country of Canada would rapidly expand by incorporating the remaining territories of British North America into a new federation, and then take the road from internal autonomy to external independence. The Columbia District that Great Britain preserved in the Oregon Treaty would play an important role in the Canadian confederation after 1871, as the province of British Columbia.

Commissioners were appointed by both Great Britain and the United States to locate the boundary provided for in the treaty and, after conducting and producing border surveys, their maps were approved by a declaration issued by US Secretary of State Hamilton Fish and the British Minister to the United States, Edward Thornton, at Washington, D.C. on February 24, 1870.[64]

Cession of Horseshoe Reef, 1850

During the late 1840's an issue concerning the navigability of the Niagara River at Lake Erie led to a minor cession of British North American territory to the United States. The United States desired to construct a lighthouse to assist navigation on the Niagara River at the port of Buffalo, New York. A survey disclosed that the best location for the lighthouse was a partially submerged reef known as Horseshoe Reef in Lake Erie, which was within the territory of Upper Canada. Representations were made to Great Britain by the United States about this matter, and, after consulting with the local Canadian authorities, the Imperial Government agreed to cede Horseshoe Reef to the United States to accommodate the construction of the lighthouse.

Cession of Horseshoe Reef

December 9, 1850

Protocol of a Conference held at the Foreign Office, December 9, 1850, ceding Horseshoe Reef to the United States

Abbott Lawrence, Esq., envoy extraordinary and minister plenipotentiary of the United States of America at the court of Her Britannic Majesty and Viscount Palmerston, Her Britannic Majesty's principal Secretary of State for Foreign Affairs, having met together at the Foreign Office:

Mr. Lawrence stated that he was instructed by his government to call the attention of the British Government to the dangers to which the important commerce of the Great Lakes of the interior of America, and more particularly that concentrating at the town of Buffalo near the entrance of the Niagara River from Lake Erie, and that passing Welland Canal, is exposed from the want of a lighthouse near the outlet of Lake Erie. Mr. Lawrence stated that the current of the Niagara River is at that spot very strong, and increases in rapidity as the River approaches the falls; and as that part of the River is necessarily used for the purpose of a harbor, the Congress of the United States, in order to guard against the danger arising from the rapidity of the current, and from other local causes, made an appropriation for the construction of a lighthouse at the outlet of the lake. But on a local survey being made, it was found that most eligible site for the erection of the lighthouse was our reef known by the name of the "Horse-Shoe reef", which is within the dominions of Her Britannic Majesty; and Mr. Lawrence was therefore instructed by the Government of the United States to ask whether the Government of Her Britannic Majesty will cede to the United States the Horse-Shoe reef, or such part thereof as may be necessary for the purpose of erecting a lighthouse; and if not, whether the British Government will itself erect and maintain a lighthouse on the said reef.

Viscount Palmerston stated to Mr. Lawrence in reply, that Her Majesty's government concurs in opinion with the Government of the United States, that the proposed lighthouse would be a great advantage to all vessels navigating the Lakes; and that Her Majesty's government is prepared to advise Her Majesty to cede to the United States such portion of the Horse-Shoe Reef as may be found requisite for the intended lighthouse, and to maintain a light therein; and provided no fortification be erected on the said reef.

Mr. Lawrence and Viscount Palmerston, on the part of their respective Governments, accordingly agreed that the British Crown should make this cession, and that the United States should accept it, on the above mentioned conditions.

Abbott Lawrence

Palmerston

Consequences of the Cession of Horseshoe Reef

The cession of Horseshoe Reef involved less than an acre of Upper Canadian territory for the purposes of a lighthouse that would be of benefit to both countries with respect to navigation on the Great Lakes. The willingness of British North America to assist in this endeavour was an example of the improving relations between the two North American countries, and between the United States and Great Britain. Increasingly, both countries would cooperate with each other to improve the navigability of the Great Lakes as a shipping conduit that served both nations.[65] Subsequently, in the twentieth century, Canada and the United States would join together to construct and maintain the St. Lawrence Seaway to afford ocean-going vessels the ability to access the Great Lakes marine transportation system, and to thereby increase international trade.

Treaty of Washington, 1871

The decade of the 1860's was crucial in North American history. The sectional pressures that had long bedeviled the politics of the United States finally reached a point where it burst asunder the bonds of union between the states of the United States, and a terrible civil war resulted. The US Civil War began as a war over states rights but as it progressed it became a war to abolish slavery, the fundamental social relationship upon which the aristocratic societies of the southern states were built. Along with the northern states, which did not permit slavery, British North America, where slavery had been completely abolished by 1833, was largely sympathetic to the union cause. However, economic and geopolitical interests caused the Imperial Government in London to initially favour the political aspirations of the southern states, at least until President Abraham Lincoln characterized the war as a war to end slavery when he issued the Emancipation Proclamation in 1863.

As a result of Great Britain's early tilt toward the Confederacy, the Confederate Navy was allowed to build war vessels in Great Britain, in defiance of Great Britain's professed neutrality during the US Civil War. Confederate sea raiders caused significant economic damage to the United States and hardened feelings among Americans toward Great Britain. During the US Civil War the threat of an American attack on British North America had caused the Imperial Government to reinforce the garrison in the British provinces, though Great Britain realized that the waxing power of the United States meant that any future Anglo-American war could be catastrophic. Even Queen Victoria had confided in her diary to the " . . . impossibility of our being able to hold Canada . . . "[66] After the war was prosecuted to a successful conclusion by the Union a blind eye was cast by the US Government over demobilized Irish-American soldiers who organized themselves as the Fenian societies and who then launched insurgent attacks upon British North America in what proved to be a vain attempt to force Great Britain to retreat from Ireland. Several pitched battles were fought on the frontier between the Canadian militia and British troops against the Fenian invaders.

In British North America, the burgeoning strength on display in the union armies as they conquered the south acted as a catalyst to create a union of the British North American territories. In a now famous series of conferences at Charlottetown, Quebec City, and London, England, representatives of British North America hammered out the basic structure of a federal state that would incorporate the disparate British territories into one country. Although Prince Edward Island and Newfoundland initially decided not to join, a new country under the name of Canada was born on July 1, 1867, welding together the provinces of Ontario (Upper Canada), Quebec (Lower Canada), New Brunswick, and Nova Scotia. Spurred on by the fear of American annexation, the new country would rapidly expand from its eastern Canadian origins east, west and north by the incorporation of Prince Edward Island, British Columbia, and Rupert's Land and the North-

Western territory into Confederation. In less than a decade Canada came to occupy almost all of the mainland territory of North America north of the 49th parallel.

With the creation of Canada, Great Britain sought to reduce its military presence in North America. To do that required a slate-cleaning diplomatic exercise, in order to eliminate the bitter fallout in Anglo-American relations left over from the US Civil War. The administration of President Ulysses S. Grant proved to be amenable to a resolution of the outstanding matters dividing the two countries and commissioners were appointed by both countries to meet at Washington in 1871. For the first time Canada was officially represented in a British diplomatic mission to the United States, with the presence of Prime Minister Sir John A. Macdonald as part of the British delegation.

The resulting Treaty of Washington, 1871, is famous for its use of international arbitration to resolve the so-called Alabama claims, which involved satisfaction for the economic losses incurred by Americans due to the depredations of the Confederate raider *CSS Alabama*, and other vessels of war constructed in Britain for the Confederacy. A number of other important issues were dealt with in the treaty, including the right of American vessels to access the St. Lawrence River to and from the Great Lakes waterways. The treaty is a milestone in the development of peaceful relations between the United States, Great Britain and Canada.

The Treaty of Washington, 1871, is also important from the perspective of the southern border of Canada with the United States because it established a framework for the location of the border through the Strait of Juan de Fuca between British Columbia and Washington state. A dispute had emerged just prior to the US Civil War over the ownership of the San Juan Islands located in the Strait of Juan de Fuca. Both sides claimed the islands based on differing interpretations of the Oregon Treaty, 1846. The dispute resulted in the ridiculous Pig War of 1859, when the killing by an American settler of a foraging pig owned by a British inhabitant of San Juan Island led to a rush of US troops under the command of Captain George Pickett (later to win fame as a Confederate general at the battle of Gettysburg) to the island, as well as the landing of Royal Marines on the islands from the Royal Navy's Pacific Squadron. President Buchanan dispatched US General Winfield Scott to the Pacific Northwest where that officer, who had calmed the border at the height of the Patriot Insurgency in 1838, once again employed his diplomatic skills to achieve a *modus vivendi* under which both American and British forces jointly occupied San Juan Island pending a diplomatic resolution. Such a resolution was deferred during the US Civil War but afterwards the time was ripe to resolve this outstanding issue.

In the negotiations at Washington it was decided that the location of the boundary was unclear and that it should be submitted to international arbitration for resolution. Ultimately, Kaiser Wilhelm I, the Emperor of Germany, was selected as the arbitrator. He was faced with a choice between the American-preferred Haro Channel, the British-preferred Rosario Channel or a compromise between the two. After receiving and considering the submissions of both sides the German Emperor found in favour of the American position in his award and the boundary was located through the Haro Channel, thus giving all of the San Juan Islands to the United States.

The Treaty of Washington, 1871 (Extracts)

May 8, 1871

Treaty between Her Majesty and the United States of America, for the Amicable Settlement of all Causes of Difference between the two Countries

. . . .

XXXIV. Whereas it was stipulated by Article I of the Treaty concluded at Washington on the 15th of June, 1846, between Her

Britannic Majesty and the United States, that the line of boundary between the territories of Her Britannic Majesty and those of the United States, from the point on the 49th parallel of north latitude up to which it had already been ascertained, should be continued westward along the said parallel of north latitude " to the middle of the channel which separates the continent from Vancouver's Island, and thence southerly, through the middle of the said channel and of Fuca Straits, to the Pacific Ocean; " and whereas the Commissioners appointed by the two High Contracting Parties to determine that portion of the boundary which runs southerly through the middle of the channel aforesaid were unable to agree upon the same; and whereas the Government of Her Britannic Majesty claims that such boundary line should, under the terms of the Treaty above recited, be run through the Rosario Straits, and the Government of the United States claims that it should be run through the Canal de Haro, it is agreed that the respective claims of the Government of Her Britannic Majesty and of the Government of the United States shall be submitted to the arbitration and award of His Majesty the Emperor of Germany, who, having regard to the above-mentioned Article of the said Treaty shall decide thereupon, finally and without appeal, which of those claims is most in accordance with the true interpretation of the Treaty of June 15, 1846.

XXXV. The award of His Majesty the Emperor of Germany shall be considered as absolutely final and conclusive; and full effect shall be given to such award without any objection, evasion, or delay whatsoever. Such decision shall be given in writing and dated; it shall be in whatsoever form His Majesty may choose to adopt; it shall be delivered to the representatives or other public agents of Great Britain and of the United States respectively, who may be actually at Berlin, and shall be considered as operative from the day o f the date of the delivery thereof.

XXXVI. The written or printed case of each of the two parties, accompanied by the evidence offered in support of the same , shall be laid before His Majesty the Emperor of Germany within six months from the date of the exchange of the ratifications of this Treaty, and a copy of such case and evidence shall be communicated by each party to the other, through their respective representatives at Berlin. The High Contracting Parties may include, in the evidence to be considered by the Arbitrator, such documents, official correspondence, and other official or public statements bearing on the subject of the reference as they may consider necessary to the support of their respective cases. After the written or printed case shall have been communicated by each Party to the other, each Party shall have the power of drawing up and laying before the arbitrator a second and definitive statement, if it think fit to do so, in reply to the case of the other Party so communicated, which definitive statement shall be so laid before the arbitrator, and also be mutually communicated in the same manner as aforesaid, by each Party to the other, within six months from the date of laying the first statement of the case before the arbitrator.

XXXVII. If, in the case submitted to the arbitrator, either Party shall specify or allude to any report or document in its own exclusive possession without annexing a copy, such Party shall be bound, if the other Party thinks proper to apply for it, to furnish that Party with a copy thereof, and either Party may call upon the other through the arbitrator, to produce the originals or certified copies of any papers adduced as evidence giving in each instance such reasonable notice as the arbitrator may require. And if the arbitrator should desire further elucidation or evidence with regard to any point contained in the statements laid before him, he shall be at liberty to require it from either Party, and he shall be at liberty to hear one counsel or agent for each Party, in relation to any matter and at such time, and in such manner, as he may think fit.

XXXVIII. The representatives or other public agents of Great Britain and of the United States at Berlin respectively, shall be considered as the agents of their respective Governments to conduct their cases before the arbitrator, who shall be requested to address all his communications, and give all his notices, to such Representatives or other public agents, who shall represent their respective Governments generally in all matters connected with the arbitration.

XXXIX. It shall be competent to the arbitrator to proceed in the said arbitration, and all matters relating thereto, as and when he shall see fit, either in person, or by a person or persons named by him for that purpose, either in the presence or absence of either or both agents, and either orally or by written discussion, or otherwise.

XL. The arbitrator may, if he think fit, appoint a secretary or clerk, for the purposes of the proposed arbitration, at such rate of remuneration as he shall think proper. This, and all other expenses of and connected with the said arbitration, shall be provided for as hereinafter stipulated.

XLI. The arbitrator shall be requested to deliver, together with his award, an account of all the costs and expenses which he may have been put to in relation to this matter, which shall forthwith be repaid by the two Governments in equal moieties.

XLII. The arbitrator shall be requested to give his award in writing as early as convenient after the whole case on each side shall have been laid before him, and to deliver one copy thereof to each of the said agents.

XLIII. The present Treaty shall be duly ratified by Her Britannic Majesty, and by the President of the United States of America, by and with the advice and consent of the Senate thereof, and the ratifications shall be exchanged either at London or at Washington within six months from the date hereof, or earlier if possible.

The Arbitral Award provided for in the treaty was rendered by the Emperor Wilhelm I of Germany one year later, in 1872.

San Juan Islands Arbitral Award[67]

October 21, 1872

Award of the Emperor of Germany on the interpretation of the Treaty between Her Majesty and the United States of America of 15th June, 1846. Water Boundary between Vancouver's Island and the Mainland (San Juan),

Berlin, October 21, 1872.

We, William, by the Grace of God, German Emperor, King of Prussia, etc.

After examination of the Treaty between the Governments of Her Britannic Majesty and that of the United States of America, dated at Washington, May 8, 1871, by virtue of which the above-named Governments have submitted to our Arbitration the question at issue between them, viz., whether the line of boundary which, according to the Treaty dated at Washington, June 15, 1846, after it had been continued westward along the 49th parallel of north latitude to the middle of the channel which separates the continent from Vancouver's Island, shall be further drawn southerly through the middle of the said channel and of Fuca's Straits to the Pacific Ocean, should run, as claimed by the Government of Her Britannic Majesty, through the Rosario Straits, or through the canal of Haro, as claimed by the Government of the United States, in order that we should decide finally and without appeal which of these claims is most in accordance with the true interpretation of the Treaty of June 15, 1846:– Have, after taking into consideration the statement of the experts and jurists appointed by us to report upon the contents of the respective cases and counter-cases, with their inclosures, given the following decision:–

The claim of the Government of the United States, viz., that the line of boundary between the dominions of Her Britannic Majesty and the United States should be run through the canal of Haro–is most in accordance with the true interpretation of the Treaty concluded between the

Government of Her Britannic Majesty and that of the United States of America, dated at Washington, June 15, 1846.

Given under our hand and seal at Berlin, October 21, 1872.

WILLIAM

Consequences of the Treaty of Washington

The Treaty of Washington, 1871, is very important in the history of the diplomatic relations between Great Britain, Canada, and the United States of America. It swept away the lingering bitterness in the United States at the actions of the British Government in giving limited succor to the rebellious Confederate States of America during the US Civil War. It established new principles of international law concerning neutrality, and it marked the first occasion that a representative of the new country of Canada, in the person of Prime Minister Macdonald, engaged in formal diplomatic negotiations with the United States of America.

It is also important from a territorial perspective for its resolution of the San Juan Islands border. In this instance, the German Emperor found in favour of the United States, rejecting both the British position, as well as a potential compromise resolution that had been mooted during earlier diplomatic discussions which would have left San Juan Island itself in British Columbia. The main impact of the arbitral award was to place the United States closer to Vancouver Island and thus to confer a military advantage on the United States. At this time the Esquimalt naval base was in operation as the northern base of the British Pacific Squadron and the Royal Navy would have preferred that the boundary traverse the Rosario Channel in order to keep the US military farther away from the main Pacific naval base in the eastern Pacific Ocean. However, the resolution of the boundary issue, as well as the resolution of the other important issues dealt with in the Treaty of Washington, 1871, ushered in an era of improved relations between Great Britain, Canada, and the United States, ultimately reducing the prospect of any future military conflict between them.

Summary

With the issuance of the San Juan Islands Award by Emperor Wilhelm I, the southern boundary of Canada was essentially determined. Minor adjustments subsequently occurred as a result of demarcation of the border but for all intents and purposes the southern border had been agreed upon.[68] It was a monumental achievement that involved multiple negotiations extending across time for almost ninety years beginning with the negotiations that recognized American independence in the Treaty of Paris, 1783, and ending with the Treaty of Washington, 1871, and the subsequent arbitral award involving the San Juan Islands in 1872. Today, the southern border remains one of the longest international borders in the world. At approximately 6416 kilometers it is exceeded at the present time in length only by the length of the international border between Russia and Kazakhstan, at approximately 6,846 kilometers in length.[69]

ENDNOTES

[1] Now the Magdalen islands in the province of Quebec.

[2] Now the province of Prince Edward Island.

[3]   https://www.heritage.nf.ca/articles/politics/pdf/labrador-boundary-dispute-documents.pdf, p. 1016 [accessed June 26, 2018]

[4] The *British North America (Quebec) Act* of 1774 did not affect the application of English public and criminal law in Quebec, which had also been imposed after the war. However, the English

civil law relating to contracts, property, and estates caused disruption after its imposition and the British authorities finally agreed that the inhabitants of Quebec should be allowed to apply the traditional French law that they understood and were accustomed to.

[5] St. John's Island (now Prince Edward Island) was separated from Nova Scotia in 1769 and was thus added to the list of British American colonies outlined in chapter 2.

[6] By a separate treaty with Spain the sovereignty over East Florida and West Florida was transferred from the United Kingdom back to Spain, which had been the sovereign power before 1763.

[7] Richard Kluger, *Seizing Destiny: How America Grew from Sea to Shining Sea*, Alfred A. Knopf, New York, 2007, pp 168-69.

[8] Don Courtney Piper, *The International Law of the Great Lakes, A Study of Canadian-United States Co-operation*, Duke University Press, Durham (N.C.), 1967, p. 9.

[9] Reginald C. Stuart, *United States Expansionism and British North America, 1775-1871*, Univ. North Carolina Press, Chapel Hill, 1988, pp. 25-6.

[10] D.G.G. Kerr (ed.) *A Historical Atlas of Canada, 2nd ed.*, Thomas Nelson & Sons, Don Mills (Ont.), 1966, p. 35.

[11] The Treaty of Paris, 1783 provided for reciprocal navigation by the citizens or subjects of both countries on the Mississippi river. However, this did not have any practical utility for Canadians, since the Mississippi's source lies too far to the south of Canada.

[12] The Treaty of Paris, 1783.

[13] The Province of Quebec was divided in half at the Ottawa River by the *Constitutional Act, 1791*. The eastern portion was named Lower Canada and included the capital at Quebec and the important commercial centre of Montreal. The western half became Upper Canada, largely populated by loyalist refugees from the American Revolutionary War.

[14] Following the American Revolutionary War the Imperial Parliament severed the inland portion of Nova Scotia and created it as the new Province of New Brunswick. Cape Breton Island was also severed from Nova Scotia and made into a separate colony but Nova Scotia reacquired Cape Breton Island in 1820.

[15] Maine was only separated from Massachusetts and admitted to the union as a separate state in its own right in 1820.

[16] George Washington, *Eighth Annual Message of George Washington*, Philadelphia, December 7, 1796, from the Avalon Project, Yale University

[17] John Adams, *First Annual Message of John Adams*, Philadelphia, November 22, 1797, from the Avalon Project, Yale University.

[18] From the Avalon Project, Yale University

[19] Francis M Caroll, *A Good and Wise Measure, The Search for the Canadian-American boundary, 1783-1842*, University of Toronto Press, Toronto, 2001, p. 16

[20] Ibid, p. 17.

[21] Walter A McDougall, *Let the Sea Make a Noise, A History of the North Pacific from Magellan to MacArthur*, Harper Collins (Basic Books) New York, 1993, p. 95.

[22] Barry Gough, *Fortune's A River: The Collision of Empires in*

Northwest America, Harbour Publications, Madeira Park (British Columbia), 2007, page 42.

[23] Gough, p. 126.

[24] The eastern portion of La Louisiane, as France described it, was transferred to Great Britain under the Treaty of Paris, 1763.

[25] Except for the presidency of John Adams in the late 1790's.

[26] Under the *Constitutional Act, 1791*, the province of Quebec was split into two separate colonies along the Ottawa river. The western colony was named Upper Canada and the eastern colony, which incorporated the historic lands of French settlement in Canada was named Lower Canada.

[27] Carroll, pp. 43-44.

[28] Carroll, p. 113-14.

[29] An exception to this principle occurred in relation to Wolfe Island near Kingston. The Admiralty objected to this island being assigned to the United States because of its proximity to the naval base at Kingston. An arrangement was made whereby British North America would receive Wolfe Island and the United States in return would receive Grand Island in the Niagara river and the Long Sault islands near Cornwall, Upper Canada (Michael F. Scheuer, *From the St. Lawrence to Lake Superior: The Anglo-American Joint Commission of 1816-1822 and the Charting of the Canadian – American Boundary*, Masters Thesis, Carleton University, 1982, at page 76).

[30] Carroll, p. 115-16.

[31] Carroll, p. 144.

[32] A small portion of land that drained into the Hudson Bay near

Triple Creek Divide Mountain further west in what is now the state of Montana was also ceded by the United States. The rivers in that portion of the drainage basin ceded by the United States are the Belly River, Saint Mary River, and the Waterton River.

[33] Amy S. Greenberg, *Manifest Destiny and American Territorial Expansion*, Bedford/St. Martin's, Boston, 2012, p.8.

[34] Carroll, pp. 179-80

[35] William Cullen Dennis, *Compromise–The Great Defect of Arbitration*, Columbia Law Review, Vol. 11, No. 6 (Jun., 1911), p. 493 at 496.

[36] Carroll, pp. 181-83.

[37] Carroll, p. 184.

[38] Peter W Noonan, *Peace on the Lakes, Canada and the Rush-Bagot Agreement*, Magistralis, Ottawa, 2016, pp. 155-56.

[39] Carroll, pp. 210-11

[40] Carroll, pp. 257-599. Subsequently, the British would locate other maps that supported the American claim (Carroll, p. 298) but in neither case was there definite proof that one of these maps represented the agreement of the negotiators in the Treaty of Paris, 1783.

[41] Carroll, pp. 251, 254-55.

[42] Carroll, pp 273-74.

[43] Piper, pp. 48-49.

[44] Piper, p. 14.

[45] Carroll, p. 280

[46] Noonan, pp. 155-56.

[47] Carroll, p. 286.

[48] Greenberg, p. 15.

[49] Greenberg, pp. 4-5.

[50] Greenberg, p. 16

[51] Hill, p. 12

[52] Greenberg, pp. 26-27

[53] Greenberg, p. 20

[54] Stuart, p. 104.

[55] Kluger, p. 406

[56] Stuart, p. 103.

[57] Kluger, p. 403.

[58] Kluger, p. 410, 415-16

[59] Kluger, p. 409.

[60] Stuart, p. 103.

[61] Piper, p. 11

[62] Greenberg, p. 2

[63] Hill, p. 12

[64] *United States Treaties and International Agreements: 1776-1949*, Library of Congress, Washington DC (https://www.loc.gov/law/help/us-treaties/bevans/b-gb-ust000012-0157.pdf) [accessed March 29, 2018].

[65] The American guard ship on the Great Lakes, *USS Michigan*, helpfully towed a caisson to Pelee Island for the Upper Canada government in 1857 to facilitate the construction of the Pelee Island lighthouse (Noonan, p. 173).

[66] H.M. Queen Victoria, *The Letters of Queen Victoria – vol 1*, George Buckle (ed.), John Murray (pub.), New York, 1926, p. 250. The Queen did go on to say in her diary that, despite the odds, Great Britain would have to try to save Canada if it came to war.

[67]   https://www.marshall.edu/special-collections/css_alabama/pdf/treaty_washington.pdf [accessed March 29/18]

[68] In the Treaty of February 4, 1925, that established the permanent International Boundary Commission, the United States ceded to Canada a two and one-half acre water territory in the Lake of the Woods that a demarcation of the boundary had disclosed was completely surrounded by Canadian territory.

[69] The total length of the international border between Canada and the United States makes it the longest international border in the world when the length of the border between Alaska and British Columbia/Yukon is added to the total for the southern boundary.

5.

THE WESTERN BOUNDARY

Introduction

While Great Britain and France were contesting for control of the eastern half of North America during the eighteenth century, another major European power was expanding into northwestern North America. Early explorations by Vitus Bering and Alexei Chirikov led to the eventual establishment of Russian settlements in Alaska, as Russian traders were drawn to the region by the potential for trade in sea otter pelts. Eventually, the Russian-American Company, modelled on the Hudson's Bay Company, was created to administer and exploit the new territory, although Russia mostly confined its economic activities to the coastal areas of the province and did not venture extensively into the interior. By 1800 Russian sovereignty in the northwestern part of North America was firmly established.

The Russian-American Convention of 1824

Although Russia did establish trading posts outside of Alaska, as far south as Fort Ross, in Alta California, and in Hawaii, its main activities were confined to Alaska. In 1821, by means of an Imperial Ukase Tsar Alexander I claimed Russian sovereignty over the Pacific coast of North America as far south as 51 degrees north latitude.[1] That claim would have placed the extent of Russian North American sovereignty close to the northern tip of Vancouver Island. Both Great Britain and the United States, who then jointly exercised sovereignty over the Columbia District/Oregon Country through a condominium, were alarmed by the extent of the claims made by the Russian Empire but it was the United States that acted first. As the country west of the Rocky Mountains was a condominium between the United States and Great Britain, the United States had acquired territorial rights concerning the whole of what it termed the Oregon Country. The United States therefore entered into negotiations with the Russian Empire to limit the unilateral southward extension of the Russian Empire in North America. Those negotiations bore fruit and resulted in a treaty between the two countries limiting the extent of Russian territorial claims in North America

Russian-American Convention, 1824 (Extract)

April 17, 1824

ARTICLE THIRD. It is moreover agreed, that hereafter there shall not be formed by the citizens of the United States, or under the authority of the said States, any establishment upon the Northwest Coast of America, nor in any of the Islands adjacent, to the north of fifty-four degrees and forty minutes of north latitude; and that, in the same manner, there shall be none formed by Russian subjects, or under the authority of Russia, south of the same parallel.

Consequences of the Russian-American Convention of 1824

In the Adams-Onis Treaty of 1819 the United States of America had obtained a cession of all of Spain's rights to the west coast of North America above the 42nd parallel of north latitude. While ostensibly this included the territory up to the northern limits of Spain's exploration of the Pacific coast, Great Britain remained dominant in the area above the mouth of the Columbia River, having secured the removal of the Spanish from the coast in the earlier Nootka Conventions. Nevertheless, the United States had inherited at least a notional Spanish claim to the Pacific coast north of the Columbia. The Spanish had reached as far north as the 60th parallel of north latitude in the explorations of Juan Pérez in 1774, and US Secretary of State John Quincy Adams used that exploratory voyage to claim the 60th parallel as the border between Russian America and the Anglo-American Oregon condominium. His Russian counterpart, Count Nesselrode, was amenable to Adam's claim, provided that all of Prince of Wales Island remained under Russian jurisdiction, which meant an adjustment of the border to 54 degrees, 40 minutes north latitude.[2]

The Russian-American Convention established a precedent concerning the southernmost boundaries of the territory of Russian America. That precedent has governed the southern extent of Alaska since its inception. The negotiation of the Russian-American Convention of 1824 spurred the British Government to proceed to conclude its own similar treaty for the condominium with the Russian Empire, which it did in the following year.

Anglo-Russian Convention of 1825

Great Britain, unlike the United States, entered into negotiations to establish borders between Russian America and the Columbia/ Oregon condominium that would confine Russian America not only with respect to its southernmost extension but which would also establish the limits of its eastward extension. That was important to Great Britain in order to preserve the rights of the Hudson's Bay Company to exploit the interior of the Columbia District/Oregon Country and Hudson Bay Company's commercial control of the territory northwest of Rupert's Land.[3]

Anglo-Russian Convention, 1825 (Extracts)

February 28, 1825

III. The line of demarcation between the Possessions of the High Contracting Parties, upon the Coast of the Continent, and the Islands of America to the North-West, shall be drawn in the following manner:-

Commencing from the Southern-most Point of the Island called

Prince of Wales Island, which Point lies in the parallel of 54 degrees 40 minutes, North Latitude, and between the 131st and 133d Degree of West Longitude (Meridian of Greenwich), the said line shall ascend to the North along the Channel called Portland Channel, as far as the Point of the Continent where it strikes the 56th Degree of North Latitude; from this last mentioned Point the line of demarcation shall follow the summit of the mountains situated parallel to the Coast, as far as the point of intersection of the 141st Degree of West Longitude (of the same Meridian); and, finally, from the said point of intersection, the said Meridian Line of the 141st Degree, in its prolongation as far as the Frozen Ocean, shall form the limit between the Russian and British Possessions on the Continent of America to the North West.

IV. With reference to the line of demarcation laid down in the preceding Article it is understood;

1st That the island called Prince of Wales Island shall belong wholly to Russia.

2d That wherever the summit of the mountains which extend in a direction parallel to the Coast, from the 56th degree of north Latitude to the point of intersection of the 141st degree of West Longitude, shall prove to be at the distance of more than ten marine leagues from the Ocean, the limit between the British Possessions and the line of Coast which is to belong to Russia, as above-mentioned, shall be formed by a line parallel to the windings of the Coast, and which shall never exceed the distance of ten marine leagues therefrom.

V. It is moreover agreed, that no Establishment shall be formed by either of the Two Parties within the limits assigned by the two preceding Articles to the Possessions of the Other: consequently, British Subjects shall not form any Establishment, either upon the Coast, or upon the border of the Continent comprised within the limits of the Russian Possessions, as designated in the two

Preceding Articles; and, in like manner, no Establishment shall be formed by the Russian Subjects beyond the said limits.

VI. It is understood that the Subjects of his Britannic Majesty, from whatever Quarter they may arrive, whether from the Ocean, or from the interior of the Continent, shall for ever enjoy the right of navigating freely, and without any hindrance whatever, all the rivers and streams which, in their course towards the Pacific Ocean, may cross the line of demarcation upon the line of coast described in Article 3 of the present Convention.

Consequences of the Anglo-Russian Convention of 1825

The Anglo-Russian Convention established the boundary between Russian America and British North America. The southern boundary was set at the same point that the Russian Empire had agreed to in its treaty with the United States but the British also succeeded in establishing the eastern border of the Russian Empire in North America. The southern border was fixed at 54 degrees, forty minutes north latitude as in the US treaty. The eastern border followed the Portland Canal (a natural fjord) to 56 degrees north latitude and then along the heights of the mountains that were parallel to the coastline, and located within ten leagues of the ocean, until the boundary line reached the 141st meridian of longitude which it then followed north to the Arctic Ocean. In the result, Russian expansionism in North America was limited and the Russian territories remained confined to a less-hospitable part of North America.

The Hudson's Bay Company maintained a commercial relationship with the Russian-American Company and provided the latter company with many of its necessary supplies. As time progressed however, the Russian-American company became less viable economically and it increasingly relied on subsidies from the Imperial Government in St. Petersburg to sustain its commercial operations.

The Alaska Purchase Treaty, 1867

The declining economic importance of Russian America to the Russian Empire began to weigh upon the Imperial Government in St. Petersburg. The territory was far from metropolitan Russia and was not hospitable for settlement. Russia had been part of the international coalition with Great Britain that defeated Napoleon in the early nineteenth century but as the century wore on Russian territorial ambitions clashed with the interests of Great Britain along the periphery of the Russian Empire. When ongoing decline within the Ottoman Empire encouraged Russian aggression in the Near East Great Britain and France came to the succor of the Ottomans, resulting in the Crimean War (1853-56). Realizing that Russian America was exposed to attack in North America by Great Britain Russia declared the Russian-American territory to be neutral territory, a declaration that Great Britain accepted. Thus, despite the existence of a state of war, no hostilities ensued between the two empires in western North America.[4]

The vulnerability of Russian America that was underscored by the strategic realities of the Crimean War led to an increased consideration in St. Petersburg concerning the future of Russian America. The strength of cordial relations with Great Britain was obviously impacted by the Crimean War, while relations between the United States and Russia generally remained good. However, America's westward expansion, predicated on the concept of Manifest Destiny, also concerned the Russians. Although Great Britain had forestalled American attempts to secure the entire west coast of North America in the Oregon Treaty it was by no means clear in the mid-nineteenth century that the Oregon settlement would prove to be permanent. American migration into western North America was reaching flood levels while comparatively few British subjects were settling in the British territories in western North America. Russian officials foresaw a time when the United States might seize Russian America.[5] It seemed to Russian officials that the best outcome for Russia would be to sell Russian America to the United States.

Informal discussions began between American and Russian interlocutors in 1860, but no formal negotiations took place because of the looming sectional crisis in American internal relations. South Carolina's secession in 1860, and the subsequent outbreak of the US Civil War the following spring, put off any consideration by the United States of the acquisition of Russian America. However, the new US Secretary of State, William H. Seward, was a vigorous American expansionist who believed in America's Manifest Destiny and he became receptive to the idea of acquiring Russian America when the subject was once again broached following the conclusion of the US Civil War in 1865.

In March 1867, Seward received word that the Russians were interested in a sale of Russian America to the United States and Seward jumped at the chance. Possession of Alaska would put an immense part of the Pacific coast in American hands and it could facilitate future efforts to annex British Columbia to the United States. Negotiations with the Russian Ambassador were hurriedly conducted and a sale price of 7.2 million US dollars was agreed upon. The Alaska Purchase Treaty sailed through the US Senate and on October 18, 1867, the sovereignty of Alaska (as the Americans renamed it) passed from Russia to the United States of America.

Alaska Purchase Treaty, 1867 (Extracts)

March 30, 1867

I. His Majesty the Emperor of all the Russias, agrees to cede to the United States, by this convention, immediately upon the exchange of the ratifications thereof, all the territory and dominion now possessed by his said Majesty on the continent of America and in adjacent islands, the same being contained within the geographical limits herein set forth, to wit: The eastern limit is the line of demarcation between the Russian and the British possessions in North America, as established by the convention between Russia and Great Britain, of February 28—16, 1825, and described in Articles III and IV of said convention, in the following terms:

"III Commencing from the southernmost point of the island called Prince of Wales Island, which point lies in the parallel of 54 degrees 40 minutes north latitude, and between the 131st and 133d degree of west longitude (meridian of Greenwich), the said line shall ascend to the north along the channel called Portland Channel, as far as the point of the continent where it strikes the 56th degree of north latitude; from this last-mentioned point, the line of demarcation shall follow the summit of the mountains situated parallel to the coast, as far as the point of intersection of the 141st degree of west longitude (of the same meridian); and finally, from the said point of intersection, the said meridian line of the 141st degree, in its prolongation as far as the Frozen Ocean.

"IV With reference to the line of demarcation laid down in the preceding article, it is understood—

"1st That the island called Prince of Wales Island shall belong wholly to Russia" (now, by this cession to the United States).

"2d That whenever the summit of the mountains which extend in a direction parallel to the coast, from the 56th degree of north latitude to the point of intersection of the 141st degree of west longitude, shall prove to be at the distance of more than ten marine leagues from the ocean, the limit between the British possessions and the line of coast which is to belong to Russia as above mentioned (that is to say, the limit to the possessions ceded by this convention), shall be formed by a line parallel to the winding of the coast, and which shall never exceed the distance of ten marine leagues therefrom."

The western limit within which the territories and dominion conveyed are contained passes through a point in Behring's Straits on the parallel of sixty-five degrees thirty minutes north latitude, at its intersection by the meridian which passes midway between the islands of Krusenstern of Ignalook, and the island of Ratmanoff, or Noonarbook, and proceeds due north without limitation, into the same Frozen Ocean. The same western limit, beginning at the same initial point, proceeds thence in a course nearly southwest, through Behring's Straits and Behring's Sea, so as to pass midway between the northwest point of the island of St. Lawrence and the southeast point of Cape Choukotski, to the meridian of one hundred and seventy-two west longitude; thence, from the intersection of that meridian, in a southwesterly direction, so as to pass midway between the island of Attou and the Copper Island of the Kormandorski couplet or group, in the North Pacific Ocean, to the meridian of one hundred and ninety-three degrees west longitude, so as to include in the territory conveyed the whole of the Aleutian Islands east of that meridian.

II. In the cession of territory and dominion made by the preceding article, are included the right of property in all public lots and squares, vacant lands, and all public buildings, fortifications, barracks, and other edifices which are not private individual property. It is, however, understood and agreed, that the churches which have been built in the ceded territory by the Russian Government, shall remain the property of such members of the Greek Oriental Church resident in the territory as may choose to worship therein. Any Government archives, papers, and documents relative to the territory and dominion aforesaid, which may now be existing there, will be left in the possession of the agent of the United States; but an authenticated copy of such of them as may be required, will be, at all times, given by the United States to the Russian Government, or to such Russian officers or subjects as they may apply for.

III. The inhabitants of the ceded territory, according to their choice, reserving their natural allegiance, may return to Russia within three years; but if they should prefer to remain in the ceded territory, they, with the exception of uncivilized native tribes, shall be admitted to the enjoyment of all the rights, advantages, and immunities of citizens of the United States, and shall be maintained and protected in the free enjoyment of their liberty, property, and religion. The uncivilized tribes will be subject to such laws and regulations as the United States may from time to time adopt in regard to aboriginal tribes of that country.

IV. His Majesty, the Emperor of all the Russias, shall appoint, with convenient dispatch, an agent or agents for the purpose of formally delivering to a similar agent or agents, appointed on behalf of the United States, the territory, dominion, property, dependencies, and appurtenances which are ceded as above, and for doing any other act which may be necessary in regard thereto. But the cession, with the right of immediate possession, is nevertheless to be deemed complete and absolute on the exchange of ratifications, without waiting for such formal delivery.

V. Immediately after the exchange of the ratifications of this convention, any fortifications or military posts which may be in the ceded territory shall be delivered to the agent of the United States, and any Russian troops which may be in the territory shall be withdrawn as soon as may be reasonably and conveniently practicable.

VI. In consideration of the cession aforesaid, the United States agree to pay at the Treasury in Washington, within ten months after the exchange of the ratifications of this convention, to the diplomatic representative or other agent of His Majesty the Emperor of all the Russias, duly authorized to receive the same, seven million two hundred thousand dollars in gold. The cession of territory and dominion herein made is hereby declared to be free and unencumbered by any reservations, privileges, franchises, grants, or possessions, by any associated companies, whether corporate or incorporate, Russian or any other; or by any parties, except merely private individual property-holders; and the cession hereby made conveys all the rights, franchises, and privileges now belonging to Russia in the said territory or dominion, and appurtenances thereto.

. . . .

Consequences of the Alaska Purchase Treaty

Although the Alaska purchase was popularly characterized as Seward's Folly by those in the United States who opposed the purchase of Russian America it was a veritable political coup by the United States. It occurred in the same year as the Confederation of Canada and undoubtedly as Canada moved westward Canadian statesmen would have viewed it as highly desirable for Canada to obtain title to Russian America. The United States not only forestalled Canada from acquiring the territory for itself but the acquisition of Alaska also put the future of British Columbia in play. The Americans now controlled the western coast of North America from the northern limits of the Baja Peninsula to Point Barrow in Alaska with the exception of the British Columbia coastline. Seward hoped to obtain a cession of British Columbia from Great Britain (he even asked for it as part of the negotiations that resulted in the Treaty of Washington, 1871) and he thought that the acquisition of Alaska would further that cause. America's Manifest Destiny designs on British Columbia were not lost on Canadian politicians and Prime Minister Sir John A. Macdonald worked assiduously to bring the colony of British Columbia into Confederation, including the making of a promise to build a transcontinental railway. Although there was some sentiment in British Columbia for annexation by the United States the bulk of the population favoured confederation with Canada and, in 1871, in return for the promise to build a railway to the Pacific coast, British Columbia opted into the Canadian federation. Secretary Seward was philosophical about losing British Columbia to Canada. Although he favoured American expansion, and the acquisition of British Columbia by the United States, he thought that any merger between British Columbia and the United States should only occur by mutual consent. After leaving office he toured the west coast in 1869 and found nothing to dissuade him from the view that the United States should eventually acquire British Columbia in order to complete its control of the continent's western coast.[6]

From a Canadian perspective the importance of the Alaska Purchase Treaty was that it removed the last European power with colonial territory on the mainland of North America.[7] The only remaining (non-British) European colonial possessions in North America were islands, the French in St. Pierre and Miquelon, and the Danes in Greenland. Henceforth Canada would have a land border in both the south and the west with one country – the United States. In addition, the combined southern and western border between Canada and the United States now became the longest international border in the world.

The Boundaries Treaty, 1892, and the Boundaries Treaty, 1894

Although Canada had wished to define the western border more precisely after the acquisition of Alaska by the United States, the American Government had demurred due to the cost of conducting surveys. However, in 1892, there was a change of heart in the United States and the US Government proposed that a treaty be entered into to conduct a joint survey of the Alaskan-British Columbia border. A treaty to survey the Alaskan-British Columbia border (among other matters) was therefore agreed-to by the United Kingdom (acting on behalf of Canada) and the United States. The treaty provided for either a joint survey of the border or separate coincident surveys of the border. These surveys were eventually undertaken by eleven American survey parties, and four Canadian survey parties.[8]

Boundaries Treaty (Extracts)

July 22, 1892

I. The high contracting parties agree that a coincident or joint survey [as may be found in practice most convenient] shall be made of the territory adjacent to that part of the boundary line of the United States of America and the Dominion of Canada dividing the territory of Alaska from the province of British Columbia and the Northwest Territories of Canada, from the latitude of 54° 40 minutes north to the point where the said boundary encounters the 141st degree of longitude westward from the meridian of Greenwich, by commissions to be appointed severally by the high contracting parties, with a view to the ascertainment of the facts and data necessary to the permanent delimitation of said boundary line in accordance with the spirit and intent of the existing treaties in regard to it between Great Britain and Russia and between the United States and Russia.

Application will be made without delay to the respective legislative bodies for the appropriations necessary for the prosecution of the survey, and the commissions to be appointed by the two governments shall meet at Ottawa within two months after said appropriation shall have been made, and shall proceed as soon as practicable thereafter to the active discharge of their duties.

The respective commissions shall complete the survey and submit their final reports thereof within two years from the date of their first meeting.

The commissions shall, so far as they may be able to agree, make a joint report to each of the two governments, and they shall also report, either jointly or severally, to each government on any points upon which they may be unable to agree.

Each government shall pay the expenses of the commission appointed by it.

Each government engages to facilitate in every possible way any operations which, in pursuance of the plan to be agreed upon by the commissions, may be conducted within its territory by the commission of the other.

The high contracting parties agree that, as soon as practicable after the report or reports of the commissions shall have been received, they will proceed to consider and establish the boundary line in question.

However, the commissions found it impossible to complete their tasks within the allotted two-year period so another treaty in 1894 extended the time frame by a further thirteen months.

Boundaries Treaty 1894 (Extract)

February 3, 1894

I. The third paragraph of article 1 of the Convention of July 22, 1892, states that the respective commissions shall complete the survey and submit their final reports thereof within two years from the date of their first meeting. The Joint Commissioners held their first meeting November 28, 1892; hence the time allowed by that Convention expires November 28, 1894. Believing it impossible to complete the required work within the specified period, the two governments hereby mutually agreed to extend the time to December 31, 1895.

Consequences of the Boundaries Treaties of 1892 and 1894

The Canadian and American survey parties completed their work by 1896 and submitted a report to both the Canadian and American governments. The original intention of the two governments was that a joint committee would consider the survey reports and come to a satisfactory conclusion. However, the discovery of gold in the Klondike region, and the resulting gold rush, put off consideration of the survey reports by the commissioners.[9]

The problem in defining the Alaska-British Columbia boundary concerned the vague language of the Anglo-Russian Treaty, 1825. Under the terms of that treaty the boundary was to be determined by reference to "the summit of the mountains situated parallel to the coast" but the summit line had to be no "more than ten marine leagues from the ocean." If the summit of the mountains proved to be more than ten marine leagues from the coast, the boundary was to be formed by "a line parallel to the winding of the coast," but that line was also not to exceed ten marine leagues from the coast. It was not clear what the treaty meant by the coast, i.e., was it the mainland coastline, or the westerly island chain, and what was meant by "the mountains situated parallel to the coast," as the actual terrain did not provide a continuous mountain chain that was parallel to the coast.

The Exchange of Notes Concerning the Alaska-Canada Provisional Boundary, 1898

The Klondike Gold Rush excited public opinion about northwestern North America and many Canadians and Americans left their homes to seek their fortunes in the gold fields. Although there was an overland route from Edmonton to the Yukon it was a difficult route to take and many people struck by gold fever opted for an easier route by taking a steamer from Seattle, or Vancouver, to the town of Skagway, Alaska. From there, gold-seekers could trek overland over the Chilkoot Trail. The influx of miners elevated the issue of the location of the international boundary. It was necessary to establish a Canadian border post and initially one was put in place at Tagish Lake but that was considered to be too far inland by the Canadian authorities. Consequently, the border post was pushed further west to the summit of the mountains.[10] The members of the North-West Mounted Police, who manned the border post, suffered privations but continuously maintained a Canadian post at the summit of the mountains from February 1898.[11]

These actions taken by local officials established a provisional boundary until there was an agreement between the Canadian and American authorities on its precise location.

Exchange of Notes Concerning The Alaska and Canada Provisional Boundary

October 20, 1899

The Secretary of State to the British chargé d'affaires's,

Department of State,

Washington, October 20, 1899

Sir: your note of the 13th instant was duly received, in which you submit to me, under instructions from the Marquis of Salisbury, a modified form of agreement relative to a provincial boundary between the territory of Alaska and the Dominion of Canada in the region about the head of Lynn Canal.

I have given careful consideration to the modifications indicated in your note, and am prepared, on the part of the Government of the United States, to accept the same as a provisional agreement respecting the boundary in the localities stated. In examining the text of the proposed agreement enclosed with your note of the 13th instant, I have, however, noted some verbal changes which it seems desirable should be made and which in no wise affect the terms of the agreement. I therefore submit the following as the text of the agreement to be observed by the two governments:

"It is hereby agreed between the Governments of the United States and Great Britain that the boundary line between Canada and the Territory of Alaska in the region about the head of Lynn Canal shall be provisionally fixed as follows, without prejudice to the claims of either party in the permanent adjustment of the international boundary:

"In the region of the Dalton Trail, a line beginning at the peak west of Porcupine Creek, marked on the map No. 10 of the United States commission December 31, 1895, and on sheet No. 18 of the British commission December 31, 1895, with the number 6500; thence running to the Klehini [or Klaheela] River in the direction of the peak north of that river, marked 5020 on the aforesaid United States map, and 5025 on the aforesaid British map; thence following the high or right bank of the said Klehini River to the junction there off with the Chilkat River, a mile and a half, more

or less, north of Klukwan; provided that persons proceeding to or from Porcupine Creek shall be freely permitted to follow the trail between the said Creek and the said junction of the rivers into and across the territory on the Canadian side of the temporary line wherever the trail crosses to such side, and, subject to such reasonable regulations for the protection of the revenue as the Canadian Government may prescribe, to carry with them over such part or parts of the trail between the said points as may lie on the Canadian side of the temporary line such goods and articles as they desire without being required to pay any customs duties on such goods and articles; and from said junction to the summit of the peak east of the Chilkat River, marked on the aforesaid map No. 10 of the United States commission with the number 5410, and on map No. 17 of the aforesaid British commission with the number 5490.

"On the Dyea and Skagway trails, the summits of the Chilkoot and White Passes. "It is understood, as formerly set forth in communications of the Department of State of the United States, that the citizens or subjects of either power, found by this arrangement within the temporary jurisdiction of the other, shall suffer no diminution of the rights and privileges which they now enjoy.

"The Government of the United States will at once appoint an officer or officers, in conjunction with an officer or officers to be named by the Government of Her Britannic Majesty, to mark the temporary line agreed upon by the erection of posts, stakes, or other appropriate temporary marks."

It shall be understood that the foregoing agreement is binding upon the two Governments from the date of your written acceptance of its terms.

I have, etc.,

John Hay

[REPLY]

The British chargé d'affaires's to the Secretary of State,

British Embassy,

Washington, October 20, 1899

Sir: I have the honor to acknowledge the receipt of your note number 1589 on the 20th instant, submitting the following as the text of the agreement to be observed by the two governments as a provisional boundary between the Territory of Alaska and the Dominion of Canada in the region about the head of Lynn Canal:

[for content see the US note, above.]

It shall be understood that the foregoing agreement is binding upon the two Governments from the date of this my written acceptance of its terms.

I have, etc.,

Reginald Tower

Consequences of the Exchange of Notes Concerning The Alaska-Canada Provisional Boundary

The Provisional Boundary Agreement was a temporary expedient that was designed to maintain a structure for the administration of law and order in the somewhat chaotic environment spawned by outbreak of gold fever in the Klondike Region. The intention was to stabilize the border until a final resolution of the boundary location issue could be worked out between Great Britain (on behalf of Canada) and the United States. Meanwhile, the border continued to grow tense, as uncertainty prevailed with respect to the end of the sovereignty of one country, and the beginning of the sovereignty of the other country. Canadian gold-rush miners complained of discriminatory treatment at the hands of American officials. As a result, the Alaska-Canada border increasingly became a political issue in Canada as a jingoistic press in Canada nurtured the imagery of an American threat to the Yukon. In addition, the Liberal government of Prime Minister Sir Wilfrid Laurier was not above wrapping itself in the flag to maintain its popularity with the electorate. The stage was being set for a potentially very serious diplomatic confrontation between Canada and the United States.

The Hay-Herbert Treaty, 1903

Canada under Prime Minister Laurier had advanced an assertive interpretation of the Anglo-Russian Convention, 1825, to establish a location of the border with Alaska that would extend Canadian territory to include the Alaskan communities of Skagway and Dyea. Possession of those communities would have given Canada port facilities on the Pacific Ocean to serve the newly established Yukon Territory. The Yukon was experiencing explosive growth due to the gold rush, which may partially explain the maximizing claims advanced by Canada. However, Canada had no historic settlements, or presence, on the Pacific coastline at the locations which it now claimed the treaty of 1825 assigned to Canada.

The United States, under the presidency of Theodore Roosevelt, was taken aback by the audacity of the territorial claims made by Prime Minister Laurier's government, and the US vigorously opposed those claims. Roosevelt determined to send US troops to Alaska to underscore the American resolve. However, the gold rush in the Klondike region petered out and whatever economic impetus there had originally been for Canada in asserting its maximalist territorial claims was undermined. Laurier began looking for a politically expedient way out of a political morass. Ultimately, the three countries involved, Canada, Great Britain, and the United States agreed to submit the dispute to international arbitration in order to resolve the issue. Negotiations between them led to the Hay-Herbert Treaty between Great Britain (on behalf of Canada) and the United States in 1903.

Hay-Herbert Treaty

January 24, 1903

His Majesty the King of the United Kingdom of Great Britain and Ireland and of the British Dominions beyond the Seas, Emperor of India, and the United States of America, equally desirous for the friendly and final adjustment of the differences which exist between them in respect to the true meaning and application of certain clauses of the Convention between Great Britain and Russia, signed under date of the 28th (16th February), A.D. 1825, which clauses relate to the delimitation of the boundary line between the territory of Alaska, now in possession of the United States, and the British possessions in North America, have resolved to provide for the submission of the questions as hereinafter stated to a Tribunal and to that end have appointed their respective Plenipotentiaries, as follows:–

His Britannic Majesty, the Right Honourable Sir Michael H. Herbert, K.C.M.G., C.B., His Britannic Majesty's Ambassador Extraordinary and Plenipotentiary; and

The President of the United States of America, John Hay, Secretary of State of the United States;

Who, after an exchange of their full powers, which were found to be in good and due form, have agreed upon the following Articles:

I. A Tribunal shall be immediately appointed to consider and decide the questions set forth in Article IV of this Convention. The Tribunal shall consist of six impartial jurists of repute, who shall consider judicially the questions submitted to them, each of whom shall first subscribe an oath that he will impartially consider the arguments and evidence presented to the Tribunal, and will decide thereupon according to his true judgment. Three members of the Tribunal shall be appointed by His Britannic Majesty and three by the President of the United States. All questions considered by the

Tribunal, including the final award, shall be decided by a majority of all the members thereof.

In case of the refusal to act, or of the death, incapacity, or abstention from service of any of the persons so appointed, another impartial jurist of repute shall be forthwith appointed in his place by the same authority which appointed his predecessor.

The Tribunal may appoint a Secretary and a Bailiff to perform such duties as they may prescribe, and may employ scientific experts if found to be necessary, and may fix a reasonable compensation for such officers. The Tribunal shall keep an accurate record of all its proceedings.

Each of the High Contracting Parties shall make compensation for the services of the members of the Tribunal of its own appointment and of any agent, counsel, or other person employed in its behalf, and shall pay all costs incurred in the preparation of its Case. All expenses reasonably incurred by the Tribunal in the performance of its duties shall be paid by the respective Governments in equal moieties.

The Tribunal may, subject to the provisions of this Convention, establish all proper rules for the regulation of its proceedings.

II. Each of the High Contracting Parties shall also name one person to attend the Tribunal as its Agent.

The written or printed case of each of the two parties, accompanied by the documents, the official correspondence, and all other evidence in writing or print on which each Party relies, shall be delivered in duplicate to each member of the Tribunal and to the Agent of the other Party as soon as may be after the organization of the Tribunal but within a period not exceeding two months from the date of the exchange of ratifications of this Convention.

Within two months after the delivery on both sides of the written or printed Case, either Party may, in like manner, deliver in duplicate to each member of the Tribunal, and to the Agent of the other Party, a Counter-Case, and additional documents, correspondence and evidence, in reply to the Case, documents. correspondence and evidence so presented by the other Party. The Tribunal may however, extend this last mentioned period when in their judgment it becomes necessary, by reason of special difficulties which may arise in the procuring of such additional papers and evidence.

If in the Case submitted to the Tribunal either Party shall have specified or referred to any report or document in its own exclusive possession without Annexing a copy, such Party shall be bound, if the other Party shall demand it, within thirty days after the delivery of the Case, to furnish to the Party applying for it a duly certified copy thereof: and either Party may call upon the other, through the Tribunal, to produce the original or certified copies of any papers adduced as evidence, giving in each instance such reasonable notice as the Tribunal may require; and the original or copy so requested shall be delivered as soon as may be and within a period not exceeding forty days after receipt of notice.

Each Party may present to the Tribunal all pertinent evidence, documentary, historical, geographical, or topographical, including maps and charts, in its possession or control and applicable to the rightful decision of the questions submitted; and if it appears to the Tribunal that there is evidence pertinent to the case in the possession of either Party, and which has not been produced, the Tribunal may in its discretion order the production of the same by the Party having control thereof.

It shall be the duty of each Party, through its Agent, or Counsel, within two months from the expiration of the time limited for the delivery of the Counter-Case on both sides, to deliver in duplicate to each member of the said Tribunal and to the Agent of the other Party a written or printed argument showing the points and referring to the evidence upon which his Government relies, and either Party may also support the same before the Tribunal by oral argument of Counsel. The Tribunal may, if they shall deem further elucidation with regard to any point necessary, require from either Party a written, printed, or oral statement or argument upon the point; but in such case the other Party shall have the right to reply thereto.

III. It is agreed by the High Contracting Parties that the Tribunal shall consider in the settlement of the questions submitted to its decisions the Treaties respectively concluded between His Britannic Majesty and the Emperor of All the Russias under date of the 28th (16th) February, A.D. 1825, and between the United States of America and the Emperor of All the Russias, concluded under date of the 18th (30th) March, A.D. 1867, and particularly the Articles III, IV and V of the first-mentioned Treaty, which in the original text are, word for word, as follows:–

" III. La ligne de démarcation entre les possessions des Hautes Parties Contractantes sur la côte du Continent et les Iles de l'Amérique Nord-ouest, sera tracée ainsi qu'il suit:–

" A partir du point le plus méridional de l'île dite Prince of Wales, lequel point se trouve sous la parallèle du 54° 40' de latitude nord, et entre le 131e et le 133e degré de longitude ouest (méridien de Greenwich), la dite ligne remontera au nord le long de la passe dite Portland Channel, jusqu'au point de la terre ferme où elle atteint le 56e degré de latitude nord; de ce dernier point la ligne de démarcation suivra la crête des montagnes situées parallèlement à la côte, jusqu'au point d'intersection du 141e degré de longitude ouest (même méridien); et, finalement, du dit point d'intersection, la même ligne méridienne du 141e degré formera, dans son prolongement jusqu'à la mer glaciale, la limice entre les possessions Russes et Britanniques sur le Continent de l'Amérique Nord-ouest.

" IV. Il est entendu par rapport à la ligne de démarcation déterminée dans l'Article précédent:–

" 1. *Que l'île dite Prince of Wales appartiendra tout entière à la Russie.*

" 2. *Que partout où la crête des montagnes qui s'étendent dans une direction parallèle à la côte depuis le 56e degré de latitude nord au point d'intersection du 141e degré de longitude ouest se trouverait à la distance de plus de dix lieues, marines de l'Océan, la limite entre les possessions Britanniques et la lisière de côte mentionnée ci-dessus comme devant appartenir à la Russie sera formée par une ligne parallèle aux sinuosités de la côte, et qui ne pourra jamais en être éloignée que de dix lieues marines.*

" V. *Il est convenu, en outre, que nul établissement ne sera formé par l'une, des deux Parties dans les limites que les deux Articles précédents assignent aux possessions de l'autre. En conséquence, les sujets britanniques ne formeront aucun établissement soit sur la côte, soit sur la lisière de terre ferme comprise dans les limites des possessions Russes, telles qu'elles sont désignées dans les deux articles précédents; et, de même, nul établissement ne sera formé par des sujets Russes au delà des dites limites."*

The Tribunal shall also take into consideration any action of the several Governments or of their respective Representatives preliminary or subsequent to the conclusion of said Treaties, so far as the same tends to show the original and effective understanding of the Parties in respect to the limits of their several territorial jurisdictions under and by virtue of the provisions of said Treaties".

IV. Referring to Articles III, IV, and V of the said Treaty of 1826, the said Tribunal shall answer and decide the following questions:–

1. What is intended as the point of commencement of the line?

2. What channel is the Portland channel?

3. *What course should the line take from the point of commencement to the entrance to Portland Channel?*

4. *To what point on the 56th parallel is the line to be drawn from the head of the Portland Channel, and what course should it follow between these points?*

5. *In extending the line of demarcation northward from said point on the parallel of the 56th degree of north latitude, following the crest of the mountains situated parallel to the coast until its intersection with the 141st degree of longitude west of Greenwich, subject to the condition that if such line should anywhere exceed the distance of 10 marine leagues from the ocean then the boundary between the British and the Russian territory should be formed by a line parallel to the sinuosities of the coast and distant therefrom not more than 10 marine leagues, was it the intention and meaning of said Convention of 1825 that there should remain in the exclusive possession of Russia a continuous fringe or strip of coast on the mainland, not exceeding 10 marine leagues in width, separating the British possessions from the bays, ports, inlets, havens, and waters of the ocean, and extending from the said point on the 56th degree of latitude north to a point where such line of demarcation should intersect the 141st degree of longitude west of the meridian of Greenwich?*

6. *If the foregoing question should be answered in the negative, and in the event of the summit of such mountains proving to be in places more than 10 marine leagues from the coast, should the width of the lisière which was to belong to Russia be measured (1) from the mainland coast of the Ocean, strictly so-called, along a line perpendicular thereto, or (2) was it the intention and meaning of the said Convention that where the mainland coast is indented by deep inlets forming part of the territorial waters of Russia, the width of the lisière was to be measured (a) from the line of the general direction of the mainland coast or (b) from the line separating the waters of the Ocean from the territorial waters of Russia, or (e) from the heads of the aforesaid inlets?*

7. What, if any exist, are the mountains referred to as situated parallel, to the coast, which mountains, when within ten marine leagues from the coast, are declared to form the eastern boundary?The Tribunal shall assemble for their first meeting at London as soon as practicable after receiving their commissions, and shall themselves fix the times and places of all subsequent meetings.

The decision of the Tribunal shall be made so soon as possible after the conclusion of the arguments in the Case, and within three months thereafter, unless His Britannic Majesty and the President of the United States shall by common accord extend the time therefor. The decision shall be made in writing and dated, and shall be signed by the members of the Tribunal assenting to the same. It shall be signed in duplicate, one copy whereof shall be given to the Agent of His Britannic Majesty for his Government, and the other to the Agent of the United States of America for his Government.

VI. When the High Contracting Parties shall have received the decision of the Tribunal upon the questions submitted as provided in the foregoing Articles, which decision shall be final and binding upon all Parties, they will at once appoint, each on its own behalf, one or more scientific experts, who, shall with all convenient speed, proceed together to lay down the boundary-line in conformity with such decision.

Should there be, unfortunately, a failure by a majority of the Tribunal to agree upon any of the points submitted for their decision, it shall be their duty to so report in writing to the respective Governments through their respective Agents. Should there be an agreement by a majority upon a part of the questions submitted, it shall be their duty to sign and report their decision upon the points of such agreement in the manner hereinbefore prescribed.

VII. The present Convention shall be ratified by His Britannic

Majesty, and by the President of the United States, by and with the advice, and consent of the Senate, and the ratifications shall be exchanged in London or in Washington so soon as the same may be effected.

In faith whereof we, the respective Plenipotentiaries, have signed this Convention, and have hereunto affixed our seals.

Done at Washington, in duplicate, this 24th day of January, A.D. 1903.

(L.S.) MICHAEL H. HERBERT.

(L.S.) JOHN HAY

The Arbitral Award for the Alaska Boundary, 1903

The Arbitral tribunal for the Alaska Boundary Case consisted of six members with three appointed by the United States and three appointed by the British Empire. To reflect his irritation at the Canadian claim (which he personally thought was without merit) President Theodore Roosevelt appointed as American representatives the Secretary of War in his own cabinet, Elihu Root, and two sitting United States Senators, Henry Cabot Lodge, and George Turner, all of whom were regarded (at least in Canada) as non-jurists who were likely to be partial to the American position. Canada named two lawyers, the Lieutenant Governor of Quebec, Sir Louis Jetté, and a prominent barrister and solicitor from Toronto, Allen Aylesworth. Great Britain appointed Lord Alverstone, the Lord Chief Justice of England and Wales.

The arbitral panel convened at London and heard the respective cases of both parties to the dispute. Although the case was to be determined on the principles of law, and, in particular, to answer the points set out in Article IV of the Hay-Herbert Treaty, Britain was increasingly worried about the challenge posed to its naval dominance in Europe by the rising power of Imperial Germany, and the consequential necessity for Great Britain to retain its cordial relations with the United States. Whether Lord Alverstone was influenced in his approach to the Alaskan Boundary Case by those concerns is impossible to say with certainty. However, in the arbitral award issued in the autumn of 1903 Lord Alverstone agreed with the position advanced by the American members of the arbitral tribunal. In the result, Canada did not acquire Skagway or Dyea or any other location that could allow for the establishment of a Canadian port to directly serve the Yukon Territory.

Award of the Alaska Boundary Tribunal

October 20, 1903

Whereas by a Convention signed at Washington on the 24th day of January, 1903, by Plenipotentiaries of and on behalf of His Majesty the King of the United Kingdom of Great Britain and Ireland and of the British Dominions beyond the Seas, Emperor of India, and of and on behalf of the United States of America, it was agreed that a Tribunal should be appointed to consider and decide the questions hereinafter set forth, such Tribunal to consist of six impartial Jurists of repute, who should consider judicially the questions submitted to them, each of whom should first subscribe an oath that he would impartially consider the arguments and evidence presented to the said Tribunal, and would decide thereupon according to his true judgment, and that three members of the said Tribunal should be appointed by His Britannic Majesty and three by the President of the United States;

And Whereas it was further agreed by the said Convention that the said Tribunal should consider, in the settlement of the said questions submitted to its decision, the Treaties respectively concluded between His Britannic Majesty and the Emperor of All the Russias, under date of the 28th (16th) February, A.D. 1825, and between the United States of America and the Emperor of All the Russias, concluded under date of the 18th (30th) March, A.D. 1867, and particularly the Articles III, IV, and V of the first-mentioned Treaty, and should also take into consideration any action of the several Governments or of their respective representatives, preliminary or subsequent to the conclusion of the said Treaties, so far as the same tended to show the original and effective understanding of the parties in respect to the limits of their several territorial jurisdictions under and by virtue of the provisions of the said Treaties;

And Whereas it was further agreed by the said Convention, referring to Articles III, IV, and V of the said Treaty of 1825, that the said Tribunal should answer and decide the following questions:–

1. *What is intended as the point of commencement of the line?*

2. *What channel is the Portland Channel?*

3. *What course should the line take from the point of commencement to, the entrance to the Portland Channel?*

4. *To what point on the 56th parallel is the line to be drawn from the head of the Portland Channel, and what course should it follow between these points?*

5. *In extending the line Of demarcation northward from said point on the parallel of the 56th degree of north latitude, following the crest of the mountains situated parallel to the coast until its intersection with the 141st degree of longitude west of Greenwich, subject to the conditions that if such line should anywhere exceed the distance of 10 marine leagues from the ocean, then the boundary between the British and the Russian territory should be formed by a line parallel to the sinuosities of the coast and distant therefrom not more than 10 marine leagues, was it the intention and meaning of the said Convention of 1825 that there should remain in the*

> exclusive possession of Russia a continuous fringe, or
> strip, of coast on the mainland, not exceeding 10
> marine leagues in width, separating the British
> Possessions from the bays, ports, inlets, havens, and
> waters of the ocean, and extending from the said point
> on the 56th degree of latitude north to a Point where
> such line of demarcation should intersect the 141st
> degree of longitude west of the meridian of Greenwich?

6. If the foregoing question should be answered in the
    negative, and in the event of the summit of such
    mountains proving to be in places more than 10 marine
    leagues from the coast, should the width of the lisière,
    which was to belong to Russia, be measured (1) from
    the mainland coast of the ocean, strictly so-called,
    along a line perpendicular thereto, or (2) was it the
    intention and meaning of the said Convention that
    where the mainland coast is indented by deep inlets
    forming part of the territorial waters of Russia, the
    width of the lisière was to be measured (a) from the line
    of the general direction of the mainland coast, or (b)
    from the line separating the waters of the ocean from
    the territorial waters of Russia, or © from the heads of
    the aforesaid inlets?

7. What, if any exist, are the mountains referred to as
    situated parallel to the coast, which mountains, when
    within 10 marine leagues from the coast, are declared
    to form the eastern boundary?

And whereas His Britannic Majesty duly appointed Richard
Everard, Baron Alverstone, G.C.M.G., Lord Chief Justice of
England, Sir Louis Amable Jetté, K.C.M.G., Lieutenant-Governor
of the Province of Quebec, and Allen Bristol Aylesworth, one of
His Majesty's Counsel; and the President of the United States of
America duly appointed the Honourable Elihu Root, Secretary Of
War of the United States, the Honourable Henry Cabot Lodge,

*Senator of the United States from the State of Massachusetts, and
the Honourable George Turner, of the State of Washington, to be
members of the said Tribunal:*

*Now, therefore, we, the Undersigned, having each of us first
subscribed an oath, as provided by the said Convention, and
having taken into consideration the matters directed by the said
Convention to be considered by us, and having Judicially
considered the said questions submitted to us, do hereby make
Answer and Award as follows:–*

In answer to the 1st question–

*The Tribunal unanimously agrees that the point of commencement
of the line is Cape Muzon.*

In answer to the 2nd question–

*The Tribunal unanimously agrees that the Portland Channel is the
channel which runs from about 55° 56' north latitude, and passes
to the north of Pearse and Wales Islands.*

*A majority of the Tribunal, that is to say, Lord Alverstone, Mr.
Root, Mr. Lodge, and Mr. Turner, decides that the Portland
Channel, after passing to the north of Wales Island, is the channel
between Wales Island and Sitklan Island, called Tongass Channel.
The Portland Channel above mentioned is marked throughout its
length by a dotted red line from the point B to the point marked C
on the map signed in duplicate by the members of the Tribunal at
the time of signing their decision.*

In answer to the 3rd question–

*A majority of the Tribunal, that is to say, Lord Alverstone, Mr.
Root, Mr. Lodge, and Mr. Turner, decides that the course of the
line from the point of commencement to the entrance to Portland
Channel is the line marked A B in red on the aforesaid map.*

In answer to the 4th question–

A majority of the Tribunal, that is to say, Lord Alverstone, Mr. Root, Mr. Lodge, and Mr. Turner, decides that, the point to which the line is to be drawn from the head of the Portland Channel is the point on the 56th parallel of latitude marked D on the aforesaid map, and the course which the line should follow is drawn from C to D on the aforesaid map.

In answer to the 5th question–

A majority of the Tribunal, that is to say, Lord Alverstone, Mr. Root, Mr. Lodge, and Mr. Turner, decides that the answer to the above question is in the affirmative.

Question 5 having been answered in the affirmative, question 6 requires no answer.

In answer to the 7th question–

A majority of the Tribunal, that is to say, Lord Alverstone, Mr. Root, Mr. Lodge, and Mr. Turner, decides that the mountains marked S on the aforesaid map are the mountains referred to as situated parallel to the coast on that part of the coast where such mountains marked S are situated, and that between the points marked P (mountain marked S, 8,000) on the north, and the point marked T (mountain marked S, 7,950) in the absence of further survey, the evidence is not sufficient to enable the Tribunal to say which are the mountains parallel to the coast within the meaning of the Treaty.

In witness whereof we have signed the above-written decision upon the questions submitted to us.

Signed in duplicate this 20th day of October, 1903.

ALVERSTONE.

ELIHU ROOT.

HENRY CABOT LODGE.

GEORGE TURNER.

Witness:

REGINALD TOWER, Secretary

Consequences of the Hay-Herbert Treaty, and the Alaska-Canada Boundary Arbitration Award

Once again, Great Britain, Canada, and the United States opted for a process of international arbitration to resolve differences between them, although in this instance the substance of the dispute was between Canada and the United States alone. Canada, while autonomous, was still subject to the sovereignty of Great Britain and was therefore required to involve Great Britain in the outcome.

In the arbitration award Lord Alverstone, the British nominee to the panel, sided with the view of the three American arbitrators which set the boundary inland from the coast depriving Canada of any possibility of obtaining a port in northwestern British Columbia adjacent to the Yukon Territory. The two Canadian nominees to the arbitration panel refused to sign the award.

The Alaska Boundary Award settled the boundary but caused great controversy in Canada. Canadian politicians and the media probably misled the country about the strength of the Canadian position in the dispute. In hindsight, many scholars who have examined the issue have concluded that the Canadian case was weak, and the more conservative interpretation placed upon the Anglo-Russian Convention of 1825 by the United States was the better view in law. Nevertheless, many Canadians had anticipated that Canada would succeed and they were bitterly disappointed by the result. Lord Alverstone came in for much opprobrium from Canadians because it was believed that he had sided with the Americans out of concern for the interests of Great Britain, rather than making a principled decision in law. It is true that the award was a compromise award, and although the Canadian position was rejected the maximum American position was not chosen either. Rather, a middle position was taken, although it essentially deprived Canada of what it had sought.

While there is no evidence that Lord Alverstone was motivated by any larger diplomatic issues in the award the fact remains that the challenge posed by Imperial Germany, a major threat to British naval power, was alive in the minds of anyone who was a member of the British political and social elite. To the extent that Lord Alverstone did take into account of the diplomatic and military realities facing the British Empire at this juncture in history, he could hardly be faulted for doing so. The subsequent alliance between the British Empire and the United States prevented Germany's ascendency to world domination in the two world wars of the twentieth century.

Nevertheless, for a brief time there was a breach in Anglo-Canadian sentiments, and one important consequence flowing from the Alaska Boundary arbitration was Prime Minister Laurier's establishment of a small External Affairs department attached to the Prime Minister's Office. That office would eventually grow into the Department of Foreign Affairs, as Canada began to increasingly take the reins of its own foreign diplomacy commensurate with its movement toward *de jure* independence from Great Britain.

As for the Alaska Boundary arbitral award it was final, and it completed Canada's western land boundary.

ENDNOTES

[1] Gough, *Fortune's A River*, p.337.

[2] Gough, p. 339

[3] The land beyond Rupert's Land under the control of the Hudson's Bay Company was formally organized in 1859 as the North-Western territory, with responsibility for its governance vested in the Hudson's Bay Company.

[4] However, Royal Navy vessels which used the Esquimalt naval base on Vancouver Island did participate in hostile actions in the western Pacific Ocean, against the Russian mainland.

[5] Gough, p. 513

[6] Stuart, p. 220

[7] Canada at this point in time was still subject to the sovereignty of Great Britain of course but it had achieved internal autonomy, and it would obtain increasing control of its own foreign affairs until formal *de jure* independence in 1931 conferred full sovereignty upon Canada.

[8] Shelagh D. Grant, *Polar Imperative, A History of Arctic Sovereignty in North America*, Douglas & McIntyre, Vancouver, 2010, p.184.

[9] Grant, p. 184

[10] Pierre Berton, *Klondike*, McClelland and Stewart, Toronto, 1972, p. 248.

[11] Berton, pp. 157-58

6.

THE ARCTIC ARCHIPELAGO

Introduction

The growth of Canada in the years immediately after Confederation in 1867, was exponential. From a small eastern country clinging to the St. Lawrence River and the maritime Atlantic littoral, the country quickly expanded to become one of the largest single state territories in the world. The National Dream, as it has been described in popular history,[1] was essentially a reaction to American Manifest Destiny which popularized the American initiative to secure the entire North American continent north of the Rio Grande River for the American flag. As a reaction to American expansion, Canada's National Dream was essentially based on a fear of American annexation and that fear drove the young country not only to secure the other British territories lying to the north and west of the original four provinces but also compelled it to build transcontinental railways to link the country from the Atlantic Ocean to the Pacific Ocean, and later to James Bay and Hudson Bay.

Foremost on the mind of Prime Minister Sir John A. Macdonald in the early years of his first ministry was to acquire the vast western territories controlled by the Hudson's Bay Company. For two hundred years the company had ruled the western wilderness but the era of the great trading companies as a vehicle of empire was now ending.[2] In 1859 the Hudson's Bay Company's licence to trade over the whole of British North America was not renewed but the company remained in control of both Rupert's Land, which contained the lands drained by Hudson Bay that were given to the company by its original Royal Charter, and the North Western Territory, which consisted of the lands lying northwest of Rupert's Land and extending to the borders of Russian America (from October, 1867, that became the American territory of Alaska).

The Imperial Government in London agreed with Canadian political opinion that the western territories should form part of the new political entity of Canada. The *Rupert's Land Act* was therefore enacted by the British Parliament in 1868 to facilitate the transfer of Rupert's Land to Canada. Intensive negotiations were conducted between the Imperial Government, the Federal Government, and the Hudson's Bay Company in 1869, which resulted in the execution of a Deed of Surrender by the Hudson's Bay Company for the transfer of Rupert's Land to Canada. On December 1, 1869 Canada agreed to pay the company £300,000, and to give the Company 1/20 of the lands in the area contained by the Rocky Mountains in west, the North Saskatchewan River in the north, the Lake of the Woods/Winnipeg River in the east, and the boundary with the United States in the south, as well as the lands held by the company around its existing trading posts.

However, none of the parties consulted with the people who actually lived in Rupert's Land about the transfer. In particular, no one had discussed the transfer with the Métis and Scottish settlers who lived in the Red River Colony which had been established by Lord Selkirk earlier in the nineteenth century. Now, apprised of the pending transfer of their territory to Canada, the inhabitants proclaimed a Provisional Government with Métis leader Louis Riel at its head. The Provisional Government denied Canadian officials entry to the territory, prompting the dispatch of a military expedition by the Federal Government. At the same time, the Federal Government entered into negotiations with the inhabitants which were brokered by Donald Smith, an executive of the Hudson's Bay Company. As a result of those negotiations and subsequent negotiations in Ottawa between a delegation from the Red River colony and the Federal Government an agreement was reached whereby the settled part of Assiniboia (as the Red River colony was formally described) would enter Canada as the province of Manitoba and the remainder of Rupert's Land would become a territory of Canada.

The rest was a denouement. On May 7, 1870, the Deed of Surrender executed by the Hudson's Bay Company was formally transmitted to the Colonial Office by the company and on May 11, 1870, the agent of the Federal Government in London released the purchase funds to the company. Then, on June 22, 1870, Queen Victoria formally accepted the Deed of Surrender which transferred the company's property rights in Rupert's Land to the Crown. The next day an Imperial Order-in-Council was approved under section 146 of the *British North America Act, 1867*, which provided for the transfer of Rupert's Land and the North Western Territory to Canada with effect from July 15, 1870. On the same date the *Manitoba Act* came into effect admitting Manitoba into Confederation, although initially the newest Canadian province was much smaller than its ultimate territorial extent.

Subsequently, the westernmost colony of British North America, British Columbia, entered Confederation in 1871, with the firm promise that a transcontinental railway would be completed to the Pacific to allow for communications between the west coast and the eastern provinces of Canada. In 1885, the Canadian Pacific Railway was completed in satisfaction of that Confederation promise. And in 1873 the small east-coast island of Prince Edward Island entered Confederation after securing funding for a railway and ferries to the mainland, as well as the offloading of its colonial debt onto the Federal Government.[3]

The entry of Manitoba, British Columbia, and Prince Edward Island into Confederation was effected through negotiations between the Federal Government and the three colonial governments (a provisional government in the case of Manitoba). There were no international implications associated with these acquisitions because the southern and western borders of British

North America had been previously created through multiple treaty processes with other established sovereign states. Therefore, the transfer of the remaining British North American colonies to Canada was a matter that was internal to the British Empire and did not involve any other state. By the mid-1870's mainland Canada essentially possessed the shape that it possesses today, with the exception of Newfoundland and its Labrador Dependency. The eastern boundary with Labrador remained uncertain until the 1920's. There was, however, one other British territory remaining under London's rule which now began to engage the attention of the Imperial Government.

The Arctic Archipelago Order-in-Council, 1880

Beginning in the 1500's, with the early explorations of Martin Frobisher and John Davis, Great Britain asserted territorial claims to the various islands in the Arctic Archipelago north of mainland Canada. The archipelago then, as now, is a vast land with sparsely inhabited or uninhabited islands possessing an inhospitable climate. In the first half of the nineteenth century the popular imagination of the British public was captivated by the Admiralty's desire to prove the existence of the Northwest Passage. Multiple expeditions were sent out to find the elusive path through the ice-choked polar seas to establish a much shortened line of communication between Europe and Asia. All of those expeditions failed, sometimes, as with Sir John Franklin's expedition in 1845, disastrously so. Nevertheless, successive expeditions had the effect of filling in the map with a number of islands under the British flag. But Great Britain was not the only state active in the Arctic. By the middle of the nineteenth century Denmark was well established in western Greenland and the United States had begun sending expeditions to the Arctic although the American expeditions were not sent out in an official capacity or with the intention of claiming new territories for the United States.

For a time the Imperial Government largely forgot about its claims to the Arctic Archipelago until, in 1874, two inquiries were received from entrepreneurs (one of them an American) concerning the establishment of a whaling station and a mica mine.[4] Although published maps showed the Arctic Archipelago as British territory the British Admiralty also had in its possession unpublished maps showing potential American claims to the northern part of Ellesmere Island as a result of earlier American expeditions. Here was the nub of a problem facing the British government. As a result of previous American exploratory expeditions American maps used names such as Grant Land and Grinnell Land to describe portions of northern Ellesmere Island. The Imperial Government was concerned that any overt assertion of British sovereignty by granting or refusing requests from entrepreneurs would result in a diplomatic dispute with the United States. Since Great Britain had only a short time before resolved its diplomatic tensions with the United States by the Treaty of Washington, 1871, there was no desire in London for a new diplomatic spat with Washington over the sovereignty of uninhabited Arctic islands. At the same time, the British government had to protect itself from charges by the parliamentary opposition of not asserting British claims to territory that Britain had discovered. The Imperial Government sought and devised a clever approach to resolve the conundrum that it faced.

After first ascertaining from the Hudson's Bay Company that the Arctic islands had never belonged to the company, and therefore had not been passed to Canada by the earlier transfer of the company's property in North America to Canada, the Imperial Government decided to offer the islands to Canada provided that Canada accepted responsibility for their administration and policing. Accordingly, the Colonial Secretary, Lord Carnarvon, wrote to the Governor General of Canada, Lord Dufferin, proposing to transfer the Arctic Archipelago to Canada. Prime Minister Alexander Mackenzie was interested in obtaining the archipelago for Canada but his ministry requested more information about the territorial extent of the islands to be transferred to Canada.[5] The Canadian Government was also of the view that such a transfer should be effected by the passage of imperial legislation through the British Parliament.

The Imperial Government provided a series of maps to the Federal Government in Ottawa but did not provide Canada with copies of any of the maps held by the Admiralty that showed potential American claims on Ellesmere Island.[6] The matter of the transfer to Canada continued to drift since there did not appear to be any urgency for it but when it became known that a new American expedition to Ellesmere Island was planned for 1878 more urgent attention was focused on the subject. In May 1878, the Canadian Parliament passed an Address to the Throne that provided Canada's consent to the transfer of the Arctic Archipelago to Canada but it still sought that the transfer be implemented by imperial legislation. This time the Admiralty intervened and stated quite clearly that neither imperial legislation nor a statutory instrument would be able to transfer sovereignty over Ellesmere Island above 78 degrees north because of potential prior American claims.[7] Obviously, however, imperial legislation would elevate the issue and bring it to the attention of the American government, a course that the Imperial Government wished to avoid. Therefore, the Imperial Government decided that an Order-in-Council under section 146 of the *British North America Act, 1867,* transferring the islands to Canada, would be the only legal instrument acceptable to it. The Imperial Government pressed Canada to proceed with the transfer and ultimately the Federal Government agreed to the transfer by way of an Imperial Order-in-Council. Accordingly, on July 31, 1880, at Osborne House, Queen Victoria approved an Imperial Order-in-Council for the transfer of the Arctic Archipelago to Canada.

The Arctic Archipelago Order-in-Council

July 31, 1880

WHEREAS it is expedient that all British Territories and Possessions in North America, and the Islands adjacent to such

Territories and Possessions which are not already included in the Dominion of Canada, should (with the exception of the Colony of Newfoundland and its dependencies) be annexed to and form part of the said Dominion.

AND WHEREAS, the Senate and Commons of Canada in Parliament assembled, have, in and by an Address, dated the 3rd day of May, 1878, represented to Her Majesty "That it is desirable that the Parliament of Canada, on the transfer of the before-mentioned Territories being completed, should have authority to legislate for their future welfare and good government, and the power to make all needful rules and regulations respecting them, the same as in the case of the other territories (of the Dominion): and that the Parliament of Canada expressed its willingness to assume the duties and obligations consequent thereon:"

AND WEHREAS, Her Majesty is graciously pleased to accede to the desire expressed in and by the said Address:

NOW, therefore, it is hereby ordered and declared by Her Majesty, by and with the advice of Her Most Honourable Privy Council, as follows: –

From and after the first day of September, 1880, all British Territories and Possessions in North America, not already included within the Dominion of Canada, and all Islands adjacent to any of such Territories or Possessions, shall (with the exception of the Colony of Newfoundland and its dependencies) become and be annexed to and form part of the said Dominion of Canada; and become and be subject to the laws for the time being in force in the said Dominion, in so far as such laws may be applicable thereto.

Consequences of the Arctic Archipelago Order-in-Council

As the historian Shelagh Grant has pointed out in her work on arctic sovereignty, *Polar Imperative*, the title that Canada received to the Arctic Archipelago in 1880 was defective, in that Great Britain could not transfer the title to the whole of the known Arctic

Archipelago in 1880 because of the potential American claims to northern Ellesmere Island. The British claim was also vulnerable because adequate steps to occupy the claimed islands following discovery had not been made and therefore it was open to other countries to assert that Britain's title to the islands had remained inchoate, and subject to lapse. It is interesting to note that Canada was not given the complete dossier on the defectiveness of the British title to the Arctic Archipelago for many years.[8] As a result, Canada was compelled to assert sovereignty according to the broad principles of international law in order to complete its title to the whole of the Arctic Archipelago.

Very slowly Canada began to take control of its northern territories. The Arctic Archipelago was administratively incorporated into Canada by a Federal Order-in-Council in 1895, which established the District of Franklin of the Northwest Territories. Following concerns about violations of Canadian law by miners in the Klondike gold rush, and by whaling crews in Hudson Bay and the Beaufort Sea, the government began to establish North West Mounted Police posts in the isolated Canadian high arctic.

A more dynamic approach occurred under the ministry of Prime Minister Sir Wilfrid Laurier, who held office from 1896 to 1911. Members of Laurier's Cabinet such as Interior Minister Clifford Sifton and Justice Minister David Mills remained very much concerned about the promotion of Canadian sovereignty in the high arctic. The Federal Government therefore purchased a research vessel, the CGS Arctic, which it engaged in several voyages to the far north under the command of Captain Joseph Elzéar Bernier in order to assert Canadian control. Additional Arctic posts were also established by the North West Mounted Police to assert the primacy of Canadian law in the north. Arctic exploration continued under the Ministry of Prime Minster Sir Robert Borden, which held office from 1911 to 1920. A major expedition authorized by the Federal Government in 1913-16 under the command of Vilhjalmur Stefansson led to the discovery of several new islands in the archipelago, including the Brock, Mackenzie King, Borden, Meighen, and Lougheed Islands.

In 1925 Canada asserted a general claim to all of the Arctic islands north of its mainland through the application of the Sector Principle. Under that principle, Canada defined its territory geographically to encompass:

> ... the area bounded on the east by a line passing midway between Greenland and Baffin, Devon and Ellesmere islands and thence northward to the Pole. On the west Canada claims as the boundary the 141st meridian from the mainland of North America indefinitely northward without limitation.[9]

Essentially, Canada claimed all lands lying within the boundaries of this pie-shaped area in the frozen polar region. The Sector Principle was based on the concept of contiguity – the islands in the north being in proximity to the Canadian mainland – in place of the more formal theory that actual occupation was necessary to perfect a sovereign title. The Federal Government followed up on the assertion of the Sector Principle the following year by declaring the whole of the Arctic Archipelago to be a game preserve, thus using domestic environmental legislation to assert sovereignty – not the last time that it would resort to environmental laws to bolster Canadian sovereignty in the Arctic. Although the Sector Principle conflicted with the understanding of international law held by other foreign powers, including the United States, it was accepted by states with their own Arctic territories, such as the Soviet Union.

Canada was assisted in establishing its claims to the Arctic Archipelago by a decision of the Permanent Court of International Justice in 1933, which adjudicated conflicting claims between Denmark and Norway to portions of the island of Greenland. Eastern Greenland had then recently been claimed by Norway upon the grounds that the territory was *terra nullius* but the Norwegian claim was contested by Denmark, which asserted that the entire island, and not just the settled western coast, was subject to Danish sovereignty. Danish authority in eastern Greenland had been perfunctory, at best, with no real administrative system put in place. However, Denmark had routinely legislated for the entire island between 1814 and 1915 and that fact allowed the Court to determine that Denmark had the " . . . intention and will to exercise such sovereignty and the manifestations of state activity."[10] The decision of the Permanent Court of International Justice gave some relief against the strictures of the Occupation Principle and allowed a wider role for state intention in the administration of unsettled territories.

Canadian geographers and map-makers worked to subsume some of the American nomenclature, such as Grant Land and Grinnell Land, in revisions to maps of the Arctic Archipelago. The American descriptions were not removed entirely, but were geographically restricted, and have since been largely forgotten by the increased use of more recent Canadian nomenclature.[11] Canada's claim to the whole of Ellesmere Island was assisted by the fact that the potential American claims to the northern part of the island were never taken up by the US Government and thus those potential US claims lapsed with the passage of time, in the face of continued Canadian assertions of sovereignty. By 1933, the official geographer for the US State Department acknowledged that Canada had perfected its territorial claims to the Arctic Archipelago.[12]

Norway and Denmark

Canadian efforts to establish and maintain its sovereignty in the Arctic Archipelago also required that Canada assert its territorial sovereignty against both Denmark and Norway. Although there had been no overt claims by the Danes to Canadian territory, the northernmost part of Greenland, the lands of the so-called Polar Eskimos, or Greenland Inughuit, was administered through a Danish trader, Knud Rasmussen, rather than directly by the Danish Crown. Rasmussen claimed that Ellesmere Island was *terra nullius,* and that he provided the only administration in the northern area of Ellesmere Island where the Inughuit commonly undertook hunting expeditions. The Danish Government was cautious about providing any support to Rasmussen's claims, although Denmark did not initially reject them outright. The Federal Government naturally contested Rasmussen's claims, which, in any event, were not made on behalf of the Danish state. Eventually the matter was amicably resolved in 1949, when a diplomatic exchange of notes between Canada and Denmark provided for the right of the Inughuit to apply for hunting licences on Ellesmere Island, thus acknowledging Canada's sovereignty and satisfying the Inughuit's desire to hunt Musk-Ox on the island.[13]

The claims of Norway were more serious. Explorations in the high arctic by Norwegian explorer Otto Sverdrup aboard his arctic exploration vessel *Fram* between 1898 and 1902 resulted in his discovery of a number of islands in the Arctic Archipelago, including Axel Heiberg, and the Ringes Islands, as well as explorations of western Ellesmere Island. In total Sverdrup explored approximately 250,000 square kilometers of the Arctic Archipelago.[14] More important, Sverdrup made territorial claims for his discoveries on behalf of Norway. Neither the Kingdom of Sweden and Norway (as it then was) nor the subsequent successor state, the independent Kingdom of Norway, had ratified those territorial claims. Nevertheless, in the inter-war years Canada became concerned about the possibility of a Norwegian claim to islands in the Arctic Archipelago and it embarked upon a diplomatic solution to forestall that possibility.

The Exchange of Notes Regarding the Sverdrup Islands, 1930

In 1930 Canada approached Norway through Great Britain, which was still the *de jure* sovereign power in Canada under international law.[15] Otto Sverdrup was in retirement and the Canadian approach was to "purchase" his documents and the maps he made on his explorations in return for Norway foregoing any claims to the Arctic islands that Sverdrup had discovered. Sverdrup had been forced to wait until the age of seventy-two before obtaining a pension from Norway and it was thought that a payment by Canada for his documents and maps could provide him with a more comfortable retirement.[16] Norway was amenable, although in the end most of Sverdrup's documents were no longer available, and Canada received only several notebooks, documents and photographs in return for the sum of $67,000.00 that was settled upon as the final sum to be paid to Sverdrup.[17] Some authorities have suggested that Great Britain may have also sweetened the deal by agreeing to acknowledge Norwegian sovereignty over the North-Atlantic island of Jan Mayen.[18]

The matter of Norway's potential sovereignty claim was thus resolved diplomatically by an exchange of notes and, as the text below indicates, the Norwegian embassy had no sooner tendered its waiver of claims to any islands in the Arctic Archipelago then it sent a further letter attempting to maintain hunting and fishing rights for Norwegians on the islands. On the advice of the Canadian Government however, the British Foreign Office persuaded that Norwegians that the islands were designated as a game preserve and that exploitation of the living resources in the archipelago would be restricted to the aboriginal people residing in the area. Norway subsequently acquiesced to the Canadian viewpoint and did not advance its request for resource exploitation rights any further.

Otto Sverdrup died only a very short time after receiving the funds.

Exchange of Notes Regarding the Sverdrup Islands

August 8, 1930 and November 5, 1930

The Norwegian Chargé d'Affaires, London, to the Secretary of State for Foreign Affairs, London

Royal Norwegian Legation

LONDON, August 8th, 1930

No. 95/1930

The Right Honourable Arthur Henderson, P.C., M.P.,
etc., etc., etc.

Sir,

Acting on instructions from my Government I have the honour to request you to be good enough to inform His Majesty's Government in Canada that the Norwegian Government, who do not as far as they are concerned claim sovereignty over the Sverdrup Islands, formally recognise the sovereignty of His Britannic Majesty over these islands.

At the same time my Government is anxious to emphasize that their recognizance of the sovereignty of His Britannic Majesty over these islands is in no way based on any sanction whatever of what is named "the sector principle".

I have the honour to be, etc.,

Daniel Steen
Chargé d'Affaires a. I.

2.

The Norwegian Chargé d'*Affaires, London, to the Secretary of State for Foreign Affairs, London*

ROYAL NORWEGIAN LEGATION

LONDON, August 8th, 1930

No. 96/1930

The Right Honourable Arthur Henderson, P.C., M.P.,
etc., etc., etc.

Sir,

With reference to my note of to-day in regard to my Government's recognition of the sovereignty of His Britannic Majesty over the Sverdrup Islands, I have the honour, under instructions from my Government, to inform you that the said note has been despatched on the assumption on the part of the Norwegian Government that His Britannic Majesty's Government in Canada will declare themselves willing not to interpose any obstacles to Norwegian fishing, hunting or industrial and trading activities in the areas which the recognition comprises.

I have the honour to be, etc.,

Daniel Steen
Chargé d'Affaires a. I.

3.

The British Chargé d'*Affaires, Oslo, to the Norwegian Minister for Foreign Affairs, Oslo*

BRITISH LEGATION

OSLO, 5th November, 1930

No. 122

Son Excellence Monsieur J. L. Mowinckel,
etc., etc., etc.

Monsieur le Ministre d'État,

At the instance of His Majesty's Government in Canada and under the instructions of His Majesty's Principal Secretary of State for Foreign Affairs, I have the honour to invite reference to the two notes addressed to His Majesty's Secretary of State for Foreign Affairs by the Norwegian Chargé d'Affaires in London on August 8th last, in regard to the recognition by the Norwegian Government of the sovereignty of His Britannic Majesty over the

Otto Sverdrup Islands, and to inform you that His Majesty's Government in Canada has noted the desire on the part of the Norwegian Government that no obstacles should be interposed to Norwegian fishing, hunting, or industrial and trading activities in the area which the recognition comprises, and wishes to assure the Norwegian Government that it would have pleasure in according any possible facilities. It wishes, however, to draw attention to the fact that it is the established policy of the Government of Canada, as set forth in an Order in Council of July 19, 1926, and subsequent Orders, to protect the Arctic areas as hunting and trapping preserves for the sole use of the aboriginal population of the Northwest Territories, in order to avert the danger of want and starvation through the exploitation of the wild life by white hunters and traders. Except with the permission of the Commissioner of the Northwest Territories, no person other than native Indians or Eskimos is allowed to hunt, trap, trade, or traffic for any purpose whatsoever in a large area of the mainland and in the whole Arctic island area, with the exception of the southern portion of Baffin Island. It is further provided that no person may hunt or kill or traffic in the skins of the musk-ox, buffalo, wapiti, or elk. These prohibitions apply to all persons, including Canadian nationals. Should, however, the regulations be altered at any time in the future, His Majesty's Government in Canada would treat with the most friendly consideration any application by Norwegians to share in any fishing, hunting, industrial, or trading activities in the areas which the recognition comprises.

I avail myself of this opportunity to assure you, Monsieur le Ministre d'État, of my highest consideration.

Kenneth Johnstone

4.

The Norwegian Minister for Foreign Affairs, Oslo to the British Chargé d'*Affaires, Oslo*

(Translation)

ROYAL NORWEGIAN MINISTRY FOR FOREIGN AFFAIRS

OSLO, 5th November, 1930

Mr. Kenneth Johnstone, Esq.,
The British Government's Chargé d'Affaires,
etc., etc.

Monsieur le Chargé d' Affaires,

I have the honour to acknowledge the receipt of your note of the 5th instant in reply to the two notes from the Norwegian Chargé d'Affaires in London to the British Foreign Minister of the 8th August last regarding Norway's recognition of His Britannic Majesty's sovereignty over the Otto Sverdrup Islands.

The Norwegian Government has noted that the Canadian Government would willingly have granted every possible facility to Norwegian fishing, hunting or industrial and trading activities in these regions, but that it is a leading principle in the policy of the Canadian Government to preserve the Arctic regions as hunting and trapping preserves for the sole use of the Aboriginal population of the Northwest Territories, in order to prevent their being in want as a consequence of the exploitation of the wild life by white hunters and trappers, and that they have drawn up more definite regulations to this end by means of several Orders in Council.

The Norwegian Government has further noted that should these regulations be altered in the future, the Canadian Government will treat in the most friendly manner any application from Norwegians for facilities to carry on fishing, hunting, industrial or trading activities in the areas which the Norwegian Government's recognition comprises.

I beg to inform you that in these circumstances the Norwegian

Government find themselves able to concur in this reply to the above-mentioned notes of 8th August last.

I avail myself, etc.

(for the Minister for Foreign Affairs)
Aug. Esmarch

Consequences of the Exchange of Notes Regarding the Sverdrup Islands

With this Exchange of Notes Norway conclusively waived any territorial claims to portions of the Arctic Archipelago. The result was of considerable importance for the future, as the islands that were the subject of Sverdrup's claim have hydrocarbon resources with an estimated potential value of approximately one trillion dollars.[19] It also prevented the establishment of new European colonial possessions in the high arctic region adjacent to Canada.

Canada would continue to assert its territorial jurisdiction over the Arctic Archipelago in ensuring decades through marine and air patrols (the latter considerably assisted by the construction of new airfields in World War II). Police posts were established and maintained and legislation enacted concerning resource development in the north, as well as measures to protect the environment. Administrative structures would evolve to the point where elected territorial governments would be established in each of the three northern territories to govern the far northern regions of Canada.[20]

Summary

Canada's claims to the Arctic Archipelago were based on the original British grant of 1880 but as we have seen the British grant, which was based on discovery alone, was insufficient in that it provided Canada with only an inchoate claim that required active steps to implement occupation – a more difficult task in the Arctic than in the more temperate southern climes. Slowly,

Canada moved to assert its legislative and governing authority in the far north, erasing earlier unofficial American claims, and subsequently dealing with the potential Norwegian claims to the Sverdrup Islands, and Danish (Greenlandic) hunting claims in the north of Ellesmere Island, by exchanges of diplomatic notes.

Effective occupation in Arctic lands is determined by a different standard than that which prevails in more temperate climatic zones. The Permanent Court of International Justice ruled in 1933, in the Eastern Greenland Case that a legislative and administrative intent would be sufficient to support an assertion of sovereignty, and that standard suited Canada, which lacked the resources to provide for full-scale occupation in the early years of the twentieth century. Nevertheless, by the mid-thirties, and certainly by 1950, Canadian territorial claims to the islands of the Arctic Archipelago were undisputed, and have remained so. In the twenty-first century the territorial sovereignty of Canada over the Arctic Archipelago is undisputed, and the arctic archipelago forms the northern land boundary of the country.

ENDNOTES

[1] Pierre Berton, *The National Dream: The Great Railway 1871-1881*, McClelland and Stewart, Toronto, 1974.

[2] The East India Company which had long ruled British India was forced to transfer its control of Great Britain's possessions on the sub-continent to the Crown in 1858.

[3] Brown, *Illustrated History* , p. 333.

[4] Shelagh D. Grant, *Polar Imperative: A History of Arctic Sovereignty in North America*, Douglas & McIntyre, Vancouver, 2010, p. 155

[5] Grant, p. 157

[6] Grant, p. 161

[7] Grant, p. 166

[8] Grant, p. 167

[9] Quoted in Grant, p. 231.

[10] Quoted in Hill, p. 149

[11] For example, the area of Grinnell Land is now within Quttinirpaaq National Park and since 1953 Ellesmere Island itself is a part of the Queen Elizabeth Islands, a subset of the Arctic Archipelago.

[12] Grant, p. 245

[13] Grant, p. 236.

[14] Richard Sale and Eugen Potapov, *The Scramble for the Arctic: Ownership, Exploitation and Conflict in the Far North*, Frances Lincoln, London, 2010, p. 86

[15] Formal Canadian independence from Great Britain under international law took place the following year with the enactment of the *Statute of Westminster, 1931*.

[16] Sale and Potapov, p. 86

[17] Grant, p. 238

[18] Michael Byers, *International Law and the Arctic*, Cambridge University Press, Cambridge (UK), 2014, p. 25, n. 55, p. 37

[19] Michael Byers, *Who Owns the Arctic?; Understanding Sovereignty Disputes in the North*, Douglas & McIntyre, Vancouver, 2009, p. 34.

[20] The Northwest Territories were split in 1999 into the Northwest Territories in the west, and a new Inuit-dominated territory in the east named Nunavut.

7.

NEWFOUNDLAND AND THE EASTERN BOUNDARY

Introduction

Newfoundland and Labrador has a unique history in the Canadian Confederation owing to the fact that for some time the province followed an independent political track, and even became a separate country – recognized as an autonomous dominion in its own right within the British Commonwealth by the Balfour Declaration that was issued following the 1926 Imperial Conference. However, Newfoundland failed to claim the new status that was available to it following the Balfour Declaration, and in the subsequent Statute of Westminster, 1931, and the strains of the financial crisis in the Great Depression resulted in the loss of both its status as an autonomous dominion and its system of responsible government. It was only after a post-war National Convention that Newfoundland decided by a popular referendum to confederate with Canada.

The previous status of Newfoundland as a separate state also gives rise to a consideration of the eastern boundary of Canada. To Canadians of the present time the concept of an eastern boundary seems somewhat bizarre: What eastern boundary one may ask? Nevertheless, for the first eighty-two years following Confederation in 1867 Canada did possess an eastern boundary with a separate state – the colony and dominion of Newfoundland. And the location of that boundary was less clear than any other Canadian boundary, ultimately requiring an adjudication between the conflicting claims of both Canada and Newfoundland by the

Judicial Committee of the Privy Council, then (as now) the highest judicial tribunal in the Commonwealth of Nations.

Newfoundland had a dual presence by both the British and the French empires during the historic period of imperial competition that ended (for Newfoundland) with the Treaty of Utrecht, 1713. Under the terms of that treaty France was forced to surrender its colony in Newfoundland to Great Britain although the French were able to retain the right to fish in Newfoundland waters and to dry their fish upon a portion of the Newfoundland coast named the French Shore. In the Treaty of Paris, 1763, all of New France was lost but France was still able to maintain its fishing rights on the Grand Banks and to retain the right to dry fish caught by its fishers on the coast of Newfoundland. As part of the imperial settlements by which France was stripped of its empire in North America, the British Crown also agreed to cede two small islands, St. Pierre and Miquelon, to France to assist the French with their efforts in the fishery. However, there were conditions placed upon that cession including the restriction that France only use the islands: ". . . as a shelter to the French fishermen; and . . . not to fortify the said islands; to erect no buildings upon them [unless] for the conveniency of the fishery; and to keep upon them a guard of fifty men only for the police." Those restrictions remained an onerous burden on the quality of the French title to the islands.

The Treaty of Versailles, 1783

Twenty years later the diplomatic representatives of Great Britain and France found themselves in Paris once again to negotiate the end of a war in North America, this time concerning the war of the American Revolution, which was as much a world war as it was a war for the independence of Great Britain's American colonies. The Treaty of Versailles, 1783, ended the war between Great Britain and France and was a companion treaty to the Treaty of Paris, 1783, between Great Britain and the United States of America in which Great Britain conceded the independence of the United States.

In its negotiations with France to end the war between the two European states Great Britain was in a considerably weaker position in 1783, than it had been in the negotiations that led up to the Treaty of Paris, 1763, although not so weak that it had to negotiate a return of Newfoundland to France. The restrictions on the use by France of the islands of St. Pierre and Miquelon were no longer maintainable in light of the British need to extricate itself from a North American war that it had now lost. Britain was also compelled to adjust the location of the French Shore, an area along the Newfoundland coast that French fishers could access for the purpose of drying their catch. Under the Treaty of Paris the French Shore had been defined to run from Point Riche on the west coast to Cape Bonavista on the east coast. However, an influx of British settlers following the Seven Years War into the coastal lands between Cape Bonavista and Cape St. John resulted in recurring conflicts between the French fishers and the British settlers. To adjust to French demands for easier access to the Newfoundland coast Great Britain conceded the coast from Cape St. John to Cape Ray as the new French Shore, thus giving France fishing rights ranging from Cape St. John then north along the east coast and stretching around to the west coast and extending southwards all the way to the bottom of the west coast.

Treaty of Versailles, 1783 (Extracts)

September 3, 1783

4. His Majesty the king of Great Britain is maintained in his right to the island of Newfoundland, and to the adjacent islands, as the whole were assured to him by the thirteenth Article of the treaty of Utrecht; excepting the islands of St. Pierre and Miquelon, which are ceded in full right, by the present treaty, to his most Christian Majesty.

5. His Majesty the most Christian King, in order to prevent the quarrels which have hitherto arisen between the two nations of England and France, consents to renounce the right of fishing, which belongs to him in virtue of the aforesaid article of the treaty of Utrecht, from Cape Bonavista to Cape St. John, situated in the eastern coast of Newfoundland, in fifty degrees north latitude; and his Majesty the King of Great Britain consents on his part, that the fishery assigned to the subjects of his most Christian Majesty, beginning at the said Cape St. John, passing to the north, and descending by the western coast of the island of Newfoundland, shall extend to the place called Cape Raye, situated in forty-seven degrees, fifty minutes Latitude. The French fishermen shall enjoy the fishery which is assigned to them by the present article, as they had the right to enjoy that which was assigned to them by the treaty of Utrecht.

6. With regard to the fishery in the gulf of St. Laurence, the French shall continue to exercise it conformably to the fifth article of the treaty of Paris.

Declaration by the King of Great Britain and Ireland

The King having entirely agreed with his most Christian Majesty, upon the articles of the definitive treaty, will seek every means which shall not only ensure the execution thereof, with his accustomed good faith and punctuality, but will besides give, on his part, all possible efficacy to the principles which shall prevent even the least foundation of dispute for the future.

To this end, and in order that the fisherman of the two nations may not give cause for daily quarrels, his Britannic Majesty will take the most positive measures for preventing his subjects from interrupting, in any manner, by their competition, the fishery of the French, during temporary exercise of it which is granted to them upon the coasts of the island of Newfoundland; and he will, for this purpose, cause the fixed settlements, which shall be formed their, to be removed. His Britannic Majesty will give orders that the French fishermen be not incommoded, in cutting the wood necessary for the repair of their scaffolds, huts, and fishing vessels.

The thirteenth article of the treaty of Utrecht, and the method of carrying on the fishery, which has at all times been acknowledged, shall be the plan upon which the fishery shall be carried on their; it shall not be deviated from by either party the French fishermen building only their scaffolds, confining themselves to the repair of their fishing vessels, and not wintering there; the subjects of his Britannic Majesty, on their part, not molesting in any manner the French fishermen during their fishing, nor injuring their scaffolds during their absence.

The King of Great Britain, in ceding the islands of St. Pierre and Miquelon to France, regards them as ceded for the purpose of serving as a real shelter to the French fishermen, and in full confidence that their possession will not become an object of jealousy between the two nations and that the fishery between the said islands and that of Newfoundland shall be limited to the middle of the channel.

Counter declaration by the King of France and Navarre

The principles which have guided the King in the whole course of the negotiations which preceded the re-establishment of peace must have convinced the King of Great Britain that His Majesty has had no other design than to render it solid and lasting by preventing, as much as possible, in the four quarters of the world, every subject of discussion and quarrel.

The King of Great Britain undoubtedly places too much confidence in the uprightness of his Majesty's intentions, not to rely upon his constant attention prevent the islands of St. Pierre and Miquelon from becoming an object of jealousy between the two nations.

As to the fishery on the coast of Newfoundland, which has been the object of the new arrangements set by the two Sovereigns on this matter, it is sufficiently ascertained by the fifth article of the treaty of peace signed this day, and by that declaration likewise delivered today by his Britannic Majesty's Ambassador Extraordinary and

Plenipotentiary; and his Majesty declares that he is fully satisfied on this head.

In regard to the fishery between the island of Newfoundland, and those of St. Pierre and Miquelon, it is not to be carried on, by either party, but to the middle of the channel; and his Majesty will give the most positive orders, that the French fishermen shall not go beyond this. His Majesty is for me personally that the King of great Britain will give like orders to the English fishermen.

Consequences of the Treaty of Versailles

As a result of the Treaty of Versailles, 1783, the British conceded the full sovereignty of France over the islands of St. Pierre and Miquelon, thus removing the restrictions on French sovereignty that were imposed by the Treaty of Paris, 1763. In addition, the French acquired a longer French Shore in Newfoundland and were better able to engage in a greater exploitation of the fishery. Indeed, the French were left largely to themselves for the following decade in relation to their usage of the west coast of Newfoundland. This treaty was rather unique in the annals of the British Empire, as it allowed a foreign fishery to exist within the boundaries of an imperial British possession. However, the Napoleonic wars between 1793 – 1815 temporarily ended the French fishery in Newfoundland.

In the Gulf of St. Lawrence the French were maintained in their rights to fish at a distance beyond three leagues (about nine nautical miles) from the adjacent British-owned coastlines.

The Settlement of the Napoleonic Wars

Beginning in 1793, Great Britain found itself at war with France again, which was soon to become Napoleonic France, and for more than twenty years, with little interruption, those two European powers contested the posture advanced by the other. The wars ended with Napoleon's abdications, firstly in 1814, and then his subsequent, final, abdication in 1815. During the period of the

Napoleonic Wars the position of France on the French Shore of Newfoundland was abandoned but after Napoleon's defeat France was anxious to obtain a restoration of its fishery rights in Newfoundland.

In 1814, an initial peace treaty was entered into between Great Britain and France and in that treaty Great Britain found it desirable to promote the restoration of Bourbon-ruled France as much as possible. Consequently, France was restored to its historic rights with respect to the French Shore. That restoration of French rights to the Newfoundland Shore became part of the overall settlement of the Napoleonic Wars that was embodied in Congress of Vienna, and its related treaties, and specifically in the Treaty of Paris, 1814, and in the Treaty of Paris, 1815. The 1815 treaty followed the renewal of the war that occurred when Napoleon escaped from the island of Elba and ended with his subsequent final defeat at the Battle of Waterloo, his second abdication, and his exile to the south Atlantic island of St. Helena. Although the terms of the 1815 treaty were harsher on France than those in the earlier treaty of peace, the arrangements made in the 1814 treaty with respect to the French Shore were left undisturbed in the 1815 treaty of peace.

Treaty of Paris, 1814 (Extract)

May 30, 1814

XIII. The French right of fishery upon the bank of Newfoundland, upon the coasts of the island of that name, and of the adjacent islands in the Gulf of St. Lawrence, shall be replaced upon the footing in which it stood in 1792.

Treaty of Paris, 1815 (Extract)

November 20, 1815

XI. The Treaty of Paris of the 30th of May, 1814, and the final Act of the Congress of Vienna, of the 9th of June 1815, are confirmed, and shall be maintained in all such of their Enactments which shall not have been modified by the Articles of the present Treaty.

Consequences of the Settlement of the Napoleonic Wars

With the settlement of the Napoleonic Wars France returned to the French Shore, although in the interim period some coastal settlement by British settlers had occurred along that coast. France maintained that it possessed exclusive rights to the French Shore and it refused Newfoundland ships permission to fish adjacent to it. France also sought to compel the British settlers to depart from the coast, allowing only those who were useful to the French fishery to remain.[1]

In subsequent years the profitability of the French fishery declined although France maintained its presence on the French Shore throughout the nineteenth century. The Government of Newfoundland remained concerned throughout the nineteenth century about the competition from the French fishery. The presence of the French Shore affected the development of Newfoundland because government services were not extended to the French Shore until a date that was later than elsewhere in the colony, which suppressed economic development on the French Shore.

The Anglo-French *Entente Cordiale*, 1904

At the dawn of the twentieth century Great Britain's century of 'splendid isolation' drew to a close. The rapid economic expansion of other powers, particularly Germany, which embarked upon a major naval building program that threatened Britain's command of the seas made it imperative that Great Britain obtain allies in the event of an outbreak of a general war in Europe. The *Entente Cordiale* between Britain and France came to fruition in 1904, and addressed a number of outstanding irritants between the two countries, one of which was the continued presence of the French Shore in Newfoundland. Under the terms of an Anglo-

French Convention that formed part of the *Entente Cordiale*, France agreed to surrender its rights to the French Shore although not the right of its citizens to fish in Newfoundland waters.

The Anglo-French Convention of 1904 (Newfoundland and West and Central Africa)

(Part of the Entente Cordiale)

April 8, 1904

I. France renounces the privileges established to her advantage by Article X111 of the, Treaty of Utrecht , and confirmed or modified by subsequent provisions.

II. France retains for her citizens, on a footing of equality with British subjects, the right of fishing in the territorial waters on that portion of the coast of Newfoundland comprised between Cape St. John and Cape Ray, passing by the north; this right shall be exercised during the usual fishing season closing for all persons on the 20th October of each year.

The French may therefore fish there for every kind of fish, including bait and also shell fish. They may enter any port or harbour on the said coast and may there obtain supplies or bait and shelter on the same conditions as the inhabitants of Newfoundland, but they will remain subject to the local Regulations in force ; they may also fish at the mouths of the rivers, but without going beyond a straight line drawn between the two extremities of the banks, where the river enters the sea.

They shall not make use of stake-nets or fixed engines without permission of the local authorities. On the above-mentioned portion of the coast, British subjects and French citizens shall be subject alike to the laws and Regulations now in force, or which may hereafter be passed for the establishment of a close time in regard to any particular kind of fish, or for the improvement of the fisheries. Notice of any fresh laws or Regulations shall be given to the Government of the French Republic three months before they come into operation.

The policing of the fishing on the above-mentioned portion of the coast, and for prevention of illicit liquor traffic and smuggling of spirits, shall form the subject of Regulations drawn up in agreement by the two Governments.

III. A pecuniary indemnity shall be awarded by His Britannic Majesty's Government to the French citizens engaged in fishing or the preparation of fish on the "Treaty Shore," who are obliged, either to abandon the establishments they possess there, or to give up their occupation, in consequence of the modification introduced by the present Convention into the existing state of affairs.

This indemnity cannot be claimed by the parties interested unless they have been engaged in their business prior to the closing of the fishing season of 1903. Claims for indemnity shall be submitted to an Arbitral Tribunal, composed of an officer of each nation, and, in the event of disagreement, of an Umpire appointed in accordance with the procedure laid down by Article XXXII of The Hague Convention. The details regulating the constitution of the Tribunal and the conditions of the inquiries to be instituted for the purpose of substantiating the claims, shall form the subject of a special Agreement between the two Governments.

IV. His Britannic Majesty's Government, recognizing that, in addition to the indemnity referred to in the preceding Article, some territorial compensation is due to France in return for the surrender of her privilege in that part of the Island of Newfoundland referred to in Article 11, agree with the Government of the French Republic to the provisions embodied in the following Articles:

V. The present frontier between Senegambia and the English Colony of the Gambia shall be modified so as to give to France

Yarbutenda and the lands and landing places belonging to that locality.

VI. The group known as the Iles do Los, and situated opposite Konakry, is ceded by His Britannic Majesty to France.

Consequences of the *Entente Cordiale*

For Newfoundland, the consequence of the *Entente Cordiale* was the final removal of France from the island with the surrender of its rights to the French Shore. A major irritant in the relations between Newfoundland, France, and Britain was thus removed. Although France retained the rights of its citizens to fish in Newfoundland waters there was no longer the potential for foreign interference with the economic development of western Newfoundland. France finally surrendered its remaining fishing rights in 1972, in the Canada-France Fishing Agreement of that year, in which both the rights to fish in the Atlantic fishery and France's rights to fish in the Gulf of St. Lawrence, were extinguished.

The Dependency of Labrador

Labrador has a unique position in the Canadian confederation. It is a geographically distinct and recognized territorial entity but has never been a separate colony, territory, or province. Rather, its history is linked to that Newfoundland, to which Labrador was long appended as a dependency. In the early colonial period Labrador was under the sovereignty of the Crown of France, although French rule in northern Labrador was nominal at best. There were, however, French settlements in the southern regions adjacent to the Gulf of St. Lawrence.

Labrador passed into British sovereignty following the conclusion of the Seven Years War, under the terms of the Treaty of Paris, 1763. Following its transfer to British sovereignty the British Crown transferred Labrador from Quebec to Newfoundland in the Royal Proclamation, 1763, which defined the boundaries of the

British province of Quebec. However, during the period following 1763, Newfoundland was not considered to be a settled colony but rather it was considered to be more of a temporary way-station for British fishers, and an incubator of seaman for the Royal Navy. Overwintering in Newfoundland was discouraged and permanent settlements were not promoted by the government. That caused difficulties for the French settlers in southern Labrador who lived adjacent to the Gulf of St. Lawrence. Those inhabitants had settled upon the southern reaches of Labrador during the primacy of the French Crown in Canada and they could not accept that under the Newfoundland regime they were deprived of their rights to permanent settlement upon the lands that they had historically occupied. Representations were made to the Imperial Government in London concerning their situation, with the result that, in 1774, the Imperial Parliament enacted the Quebec Act,[2] which had the effect of substantially changing the borders of Quebec by extending Quebec deep into what later became the United States and by re-annexing Labrador to the province of Quebec. That result satisfied the original French settlers in the southern parts of Labrador.

However, the coast of Labrador was utilized by British fishers from Newfoundland and the government of Quebec (and after 1791, the government of Lower Canada, the successor colonial province to Quebec) had little interest in the coastal fishery, or in providing any government services to such a remote region. That caused disgruntlement among the fishers of Newfoundland and, as a result of representations they made to the Imperial Government, it led to an imperial decision to re-annex Labrador to Newfoundland. By an Imperial Statute enacted in 1809[3] the Coast of Labrador was removed from the Province of Lower Canada and was once again placed under the jurisdiction of the Governor of Newfoundland. By that time Newfoundland was considered a settled colony and emigration from the British Isles was contributing to a growing settled population. However, there continued to be dissatisfaction with rule from Newfoundland in the southern reaches of Labrador, where the settled population was largely French. To alleviate that dissatisfaction the Imperial Government, in 1825, enacted another statute[4] that separated the southern part of Labrador, and re-annexed it to Lower Canada. That transfer ultimately solved the dissension exhibited by the local populations and established an approximate boundary in the south. However, the western limits of Labrador remained unfixed throughout the nineteenth century.

Although the western limits of Labrador were uncertain in the nineteenth century, several maps, including the maps created by the Federal Government of the Dominion of Canada after Confederation in 1867, as well as maps created by the post-Confederation Province of Quebec, tended to show that the western limits of Newfoundland extended far into the interior, as far west as the height of land measured from the coastline. Such displays were consistent with the use of the heights of land dividing separate watersheds as a common feature for determining colonial boundaries in North America. Nevertheless, in the absence of a fixed western boundary for Labrador uncertainty continued to prevail over the location of the eastern border of Canada, as Newfoundland had opted to remain outside of Confederation after the results of a general election held in Newfoundland in 1869, which was fought in part on the issue of Confederation.

After 1869, Rupert's Land was transferred to Canada including the lands abutting central and northern Labrador. In 1895, the District of Ungava was created as an administrative sub-jurisdiction of the Northwest Territories to include all of the Canadian territory abutting Labrador. In 1898, the southern portion of the District of Ungava was transferred to the Province of Quebec and around the same time lumber interests sought licences for timber extraction in Labrador, raising the question of whether Canada, or Newfoundland, had jurisdiction over the lands in question.

The Reference to the Judicial Committee of the Privy Council

While Newfoundland maintained that the borders of Labrador extended westward from the ocean as far as the height of land dividing the watersheds between Hudson Bay and the Atlantic Ocean Canada maintained that the historic descriptive expression of the Coast of Labrador meant that the jurisdiction of Newfoundland extended inland from the Atlantic Ocean only for a distance of one statute mile. In the early twentieth century both Canada and Newfoundland agreed that the difference of views between the two countries should be submitted to adjudication. At that time both countries continued to be constituent parts of the British Empire and, as such, the ultimate sovereignty within both countries continued to be the King in Right of the United Kingdom. Imperial statutes and the powers of the Royal Prerogative allowed for disputes of this nature to be referred to the Judicial Committee of the Privy Council in London for adjudication and that forum was selected as the appropriate method to resolve the territorial dispute between Canada and Newfoundland over the Labrador Coast.

Although the effort to bring forward the case for adjudication began in the first decade of the twentieth century there were substantial delays and ultimately the matter was deferred until after the conclusion of World War One, in which both countries participated as elements of the British Empire. After the war a renewed effort was made to bring the matter forward for resolution and finally the case was heard in 1926, and decided in 1927.

In the long period leading up to the judicial determination of the dispute there were two significant developments. Firstly, the District of Ungava in the Northwest Territories disappeared after its mainland territory was transferred to Quebec by the Federal Government in 1912. Secondly, the Balfour Declaration, issued after the Imperial Conference of 1926, recognized that the self-governing dominions of the British Empire were equal to each other and to the United Kingdom within what subsequently came to be called the Commonwealth of Nations. As such, the dominions were no longer politically subordinate to the United

Kingdom, and the Governors General of the dominions (Governor, in the case of Newfoundland) henceforth acted only on the advice of local ministers. That development separated the various realms over which the British Monarch reigned and essentially meant that the dominions were independent of Great Britain as far as the Imperial Government was concerned. Initially however, that did not change the role of the Judicial Committee of the Privy Council as the highest judicial tribunal in what was now referred to as the British Commonwealth. Further refinements concerning the status of the dominions at the subsequent Imperial Conference of 1930 led to the Statue of Westminster, 1931, which provided for the *de jure* independence of each of the dominions as sovereign states in international law, although Newfoundland remained reluctant to claim its international sovereignty and voluntarily refrained from claiming an international legal personality separate and apart from the United Kingdom after 1931.[5]

In the case presented to the Judicial Committee of the Privy Council Canada placed great stress on the descriptive term 'Coast of Labrador' and maintained that:

> . . . the "coast," so described, is a strip of maritime territory, extending from Cape Chidley, at the entrance to Hudson Strait, to the eastern headland of the bay or harbour of Blanc Sablon on the Strait of Belle Isle, and comprising, in its depth inland, only so much of the land immediately abutting on the sea, above low-water mark, as was accessible and useful to the British fishermen annually resorting to that coast . . .

Canada concluded that:

> . . . the true boundary between Canada and Newfoundland in the Labrador peninsula is a line demarking the area of the coast accessible and useful for the fishery . . . the boundary [should] be located and defined as a line to be drawn from the eastern headland of the bay or harbour of Blanc Sablon, on the south, to Cape Chidley, on the north, at a distance from high-water mark on the sea-coast of the peninsula of Labrador of one mile.

Newfoundland countered that:

> . . . that the Judicial Committee should define as the boundary north
> of the 52nd degree of north latitude the line of the crest of the
> watershed, which is the height of land . . . [b]ecause the expression
> "coast" at all times material for the purposes of the present inquiry
> was understood to include and connote the whole area between the
> sea and the height of land . . . [and] [b]ecause in the law of nations
> at the times material to be considered for the purposes of the present
> inquiry, the occupation of a "coast" conferred a right to the hinterland
> as far as the height of land.[6]

Ultimately, the Judicial Committee of the Privy Council[7] ruled in
favour of Newfoundland and against Canada. The Privy Council
found that the word "coast" or "coasts" (for both are used in the
documents) is a word of undefined meaning; and while it is usually
to be understood in the sense of " . . . meaning the edge or margin
of the land next the sea" or "the shore," there are many examples
of its being used to denote a considerable tract of land bounded by
and looking towards the sea . . . ".[8] Furthermore, according to
the Privy Council:

> where that term is used in the wider sense, it is argued that the
> natural limit is to be found (in the absence of special circumstances)
> in the watershed which is the source of the rivers falling into the sea
> at that place; and there is much to be said in favour of that view.
> It is consistent with the doctrine of international law by which the
> occupation of a seacoast carries with it a right to the whole territory
> drained by the rivers which empty their water into its line (see Hall's
> International Law, 5th edition, page 104; Westlake's International
> Law, Part 1, page 112; and Lawrence's Principles of International
> Law, 3rd edition, page 151); and it is certainly difficult, in the
> absence of any specified boundary or of any special feature (such as
> a political frontier), which could be taken as a boundary, to suggest
> any [other] point between the seashore and the watershed at which a
> line could be drawn.[9]

Thus, according to the Privy Council:

> . . . the boundary between Canada and Newfoundland in the Labrador

Peninsula is a line drawn due north from the eastern boundary of the bay or harbour of Ance Sablon as far as the fifty-second degree of north latitude, and from thence westward along that parallel until it reaches the Romaine river, and then northward along the left or east bank of that river and its head waters to their source and from thence due north to the crest of the watershed or height of land there, and from thence westward and northward along the crest of the watershed of the rivers flowing into the Atlantic Ocean until it reaches Cape Chidley . . . [10]

Consequences of the Privy Council Reference

The decision of the Privy Council confirmed that Labrador possessed a substantial geographic extent consistent with the historical evidence that was derived from both Newfoundland and Canadian sources. Furthermore, the principle of the hinterland extension inland to the heights of land that divided watersheds was a principle commonly employed in the resolution of other territorial disputes in North America. The use of the height of lands principle was rational, and in conformity with the principles of international law.

If the Canadian position had prevailed it would have been a daunting prospect for Newfoundland to effectively govern a coastal strip of one mile in width and extending many hundreds of miles along the eastern seaboard of North America. As the judgment of the Privy Council showed, the effect of the Canadian position in some places would have been to create Canadian exclaves surrounded by Newfoundland territory, and Canada may have then had to rely upon the Newfoundland authorities for the efficient extraction of Canadian customs duties.

The decision of the Privy Council was considered both at the time it was rendered, and subsequently, to be legally sound, although the result was disappointing to the Canadian Government, and to the government of the Province of Quebec. Nevertheless, the Judicial Committee of the Privy Council was the highest judicial tribunal in both Canada and Newfoundland and the effect of its decision was to establish the fixed eastern boundary of Canada with its neighboring dominion. The boundary between the two countries would remain undisturbed until the union of Canada and Newfoundland in 1949, and afterwards.

When Confederation with Newfoundland occurred in 1949, Newfoundland was still concerned about the previous dispute over the Labrador boundary and Newfoundland insisted that the boundary, as determined by the Privy Council, be entrenched in the Terms of Union between Canada and Newfoundland when Newfoundland finally entered Confederation. Therefore the 1948 Terms of Union do contain a reference to the boundaries as determined by the Privy Council and those terms of union were implemented by the Newfoundland Act[11]as an amendment to the British North America Act, 1867. The Newfoundland Act was subsequently entrenched in the Constitution of Canada 1867-1982 by the Constitution Act, 1982, which was enacted by the Imperial Parliament as Schedule B to the Canada Act.[12] The legal effect of the entrenchment within the Constitution of Canada was to constitutionalise the boundary between Canada and Labrador as the provincial boundary of the province of Newfoundland.[13]

The boundary of Labrador is therefore now beyond legal dispute, although political claims to the Labrador hinterland have sometimes been raised by Quebec politicians. To underscore the territorial integrity of the province as a territorial unit, Newfoundland undertook to obtain a formal constitutional change to its name from the Province of Newfoundland to the Province of Newfoundland and Labrador on December 6, 2001. The effect of that change was to formally acknowledge the incorporation of Labrador into the Province of Newfoundland as a constituent part of the province, and to end any suggestion that Labrador remained a dependency of Newfoundland.

The Terms of Union of Newfoundland and Canada, 1948

Canada and Newfoundland remained separate countries joined by their mutual allegiance to the King throughout the 1930's and 1940's. In the early years both were autonomous dominions for the purposes of British Commonwealth relations but Newfoundland, unlike Canada, did not claim its sovereignty to establish an international legal personality, and it continued to be considered by the international community as a territorial possession of Great Britain for the purposes of international law. That suited Newfoundland and in the depths of the Great Depression, which began in 1929 and extended throughout the 1930's, Newfoundland found that it was unable to sustain itself financially, and its political elites agreed to surrender its status as a dominion and accordingly it reverted to the status of a British colony. Newfoundland abandoned responsible government in favour of a Commission of Government, established by Great Britain, that consisted of appointees of the Imperial Government chaired by the British Governor who exercised legislative and administrative powers over the colony. The Governor reverted to his former position as an officer and agent of the Imperial Government from the autonomous representative of the Sovereign that had been created by the Balfour Declaration in 1926. The effect of those changes, which took place in 1934, meant that the boundary between the two dominions of Canada and Newfoundland now became, in both intra-Commonwealth relations, as well as in international relations, a boundary between Canada and the United Kingdom.

The outbreak of World War Two in 1939 abruptly brought to the fore in Canada concerns about the security of its eastern boundary and the protection of Newfoundland. Surprisingly, no formal diplomatic relations existed between Canada and Newfoundland at the outbreak of the war and it was not until July 1941, that diplomatic relations were established. A Canadian High Commission was opened in St. Johns, Newfoundland, in September 1941.[14] Previously, in 1940, Canadian troops had been sent to Newfoundland for the defence of the country and by the end of the war Canada maintained a considerable number of its home defense troops in Newfoundland. Canadian forces in Newfoundland were also reinforced by American troops, who obtained base rights under the wartime Lend-Lease Agreement between Great Britain and the United States.

By the end of the second world war in 1945, the Newfoundland economy had recovered sufficiently to permit the reestablishment of constitutional government in Newfoundland although Newfoundland remained economically deprived, and a rather hardscrabble place. A National Convention was summoned to define a political way forward for the colony. On June 21, 1946, elections were held for delegates to the National Convention and among those who were elected was Joseph Smallwood of Gander, Newfoundland, who soon became the leading exponent of the proposition that Newfoundland should enter the Canadian Confederation. The National Convention decided to send delegations to Britain and to Canada to help it determine what future political course should be charted for Newfoundland. The formal options that the convention embraced were a continuation of the British-led Commission of Government, the restoration of responsible government as an autonomous dominion, or confederation with Canada. A fourth option, involving closer economic and political relations with the United States, was supported by some of the convention delegates but it was discouraged by the Imperial Government's Dominions Office.

Despite some hesitancy toward Confederation by Canadian Prime Minister, Mackenzie King, the Federal Government was disposed to bring Newfoundland into Confederation on generous terms. A number of joint committees were struck and the Newfoundland delegation met and negotiated with a Canadian team consisting of a cabinet committee chaired by future Prime Minister Louis St. Laurent, together with officials from various departments. Over the course of the summer months their fruitful negotiations facilitated a confederation between the two countries although no draft Terms of Union was completed before the Newfoundland delegation returned to their country in the autumn of 1947. A draft

Terms of Union offered by Canada was finally presented to the National Convention in Newfoundland on November 6, 1947.

There was substantial opposition to a union with Canada by many Newfoundlanders and the National Convention reflected a continuing reluctance to enter Confederation. Ultimately, it was proposed that a referendum be held in which two choices were to be presented to the people of Newfoundland. Option number one would be a continuation of the Commission of Government while Option number two would be a restoration of responsible government. However, the Imperial Government had decision-making authority on what such a referendum should consider and London insisted that any referendum should also provide the people of Newfoundland with the option of Confederation with Canada. Despite some support for closer relations with the United States, the British government remained unmoved, and no formal consideration was given to that option.

On June 3, 1948, the national referendum was held in Newfoundland and it resulted in 44.5% of the electorate favouring the restoration of responsible government, 41.1% favouring confederation with Canada and only 14.3% favouring a continuation of the Commission of Government for a further period of five years. The referendum turnout was approximately 88% of the electorate. As no option had received a majority of the votes cast, a second referendum was necessary in which the least favoured option (continuation of the Commission of Government) was dropped.

The second national referendum was held on July 22, 1948. This time, the confederation option prevailed but only narrowly. In a high turnout of the electorate, at 84% of the eligible voting population, the option of Confederation with Canada secured 52.3% of the votes while the restoration of responsible government option garnered 47.6% of the votes. The margin of success of the confederation option was deemed to be an acceptable expression of the popular will by both the British and Canadian governments.

A delegation from Newfoundland went to Ottawa to complete the negotiations around the Terms of Union and the final terms were thrashed out between October and December of 1948. The Terms of the Union between the two countries was signed in Ottawa on December 11, 1948, and Newfoundland (including Labrador) entered Confederation as the tenth Canadian province on March 31, 1949, in accordance with the Terms of Union between the two countries.[15] On the same date Canada closed its High Commission office in St. Johns.

The Terms of Union Between Newfoundland and Canada, 1948

December 11, 1948

Whereas a delegation appointed from its members by the National Convention of Newfoundland, a body elected by the people of Newfoundland, consulted in 1947 with the Government of Canada to ascertain what fair and equitable basis might exist for the union of Newfoundland with Canada;

Whereas, following discussions with the delegation, the Government of Canada sent to His Excellency the Governor of Newfoundland for submission to the National Convention a statement of terms which the Government of Canada would be prepared to recommend to the Parliament of Canada as a fair and equitable basis for union, should the people of Newfoundland desire to enter into confederation;

Whereas the proposed terms were debated in the National Convention in Newfoundland and were before the people of Newfoundland when, by a majority at a referendum held on the twenty-second day of July, 1948, they expressed their desire to enter into confederation with Canada;

Whereas the Governments of the United Kingdom, Canada and Newfoundland agreed after the referendum that representatives of

Canada and Newfoundland should meet and settle the final terms and arrangements for the union of Newfoundland with Canada;

And whereas authorized representatives of Canada and authorized representatives of Newfoundland have settled the terms hereinafter set forth as the Terms of Union of Newfoundland with Canada;

It is therefore agreed as follows:

TERMS OF UNION

UNION

1. On, from, and after the coming into force of these Terms (hereinafter referred to as the date of Union), Newfoundland shall form part of Canada and shall be a province thereof to be called and known as the Province of Newfoundland.

2. The Province of Newfoundland shall comprise the same territory as at the date of Union, that is to say, the island of Newfoundland and the islands adjacent thereto, the Coast of Labrador as delimited in the report delivered by the Judicial Committee of His Majesty's Privy Council on the first day of March, 1927, and approved by His Majesty in His Privy Council on the twenty-second day of March, 1927, and the islands adjacent to the said Coast of Labrador.

APPLICATION OF THE BRITISH NORTH AMERICA ACTS

3. The British North America Acts 1867 to 1946, shall apply to the Province of Newfoundland in the same way and to the like extent as they apply to the provinces heretofore comprised in Canada, as if the Province of Newfoundland had been one of the provinces originally united, except insofar as varied by these Terms and except such provisions as are in terms made or by reasonable intendment may be held to be specially applicable to or only to affect one or more and not all of the provinces originally united.

REPRESENTATION IN PARLIAMENT

4. *The Province of Newfoundland shall be entitled to be represented in the Senate by six members, and in the House of Commons by seven members out of a total membership of two hundred and sixty-two.*

5. *Representation in the Senate and in the House of Commons shall from time to time be altered or readjusted in accordance with the British North America Acts 1867 to 1946.*

6. *(1) Until the Parliament of Canada otherwise provides, the Province of Newfoundland shall for the purposes of the election of members to serve in the House of Commons, be divided into the electoral divisions named and delimited in the Schedule to these Terms, and each such division shall be entitled to return one member.*

(2) For the first election of members to serve in the House of Commons, if held otherwise than as part of a general election, the Governor General in Council may cause writs to be issued and may fix the day upon which the polls shall be held, and, subject to the foregoing, the laws of Canada relating to by-elections shall apply to an election held pursuant to any writ issued under this Term.

(3) The Chief Electoral Officer shall have authority to adapt the provisions of The Dominion Elections Act 1938, to conditions existing in the Province of Newfoundland so as to conduct effectually the first election of members to serve in the House of Commons.

PROVINCIAL CONSTITUTION

7. *The Constitution of Newfoundland as it existed immediately prior to the sixteenth day of February, 1934, is revived at the date of Union and shall, subject to these Terms and the British North America Acts, 1867 to 1946, continue as the Constitution of the*

Province of Newfoundland from and after the date of Union, until altered under the authority of the said Acts.

Executive

8. (1) For the Province of Newfoundland there shall be an officer styled the Lieutenant-Governor, appointed by the Governor General in Council by instrument under the Great Seal of Canada.

(2) Pending the first appointment of a Lieutenant-Governor for the Province of Newfoundland and the assumption of his duties as such, the Chief Justice, or if the office of Chief Justice is vacant, the senior judge, of the Supreme Court of Newfoundland, shall execute the office and functions of Lieutenant-Governor under his oath of office as such Chief Justice or senior judge.

9. The Constitution of the Executive Authority of Newfoundland as it existed immediately prior to the sixteenth day of February, 1934, shall, subject to these Terms and the British North America Acts 1867 to 1946, continue as the Constitution of the Executive Authority of the Province of Newfoundland from and after the date of Union, until altered under the authority of the said Acts.

10. The Lieutenant-Governor in Council shall as soon as may be after the date of Union adopt and provide a Great Seal of the Province of Newfoundland and may from time to time change such seal.

11. All powers, authorities, and functions that under any statute were at or immediately prior to the date of Union vested in or exercisable by the Governor of Newfoundland individually, or in Council, or in Commission,

(a) as far as they are capable of being exercised after the date of Union in relation to the Government of Canada, shall be vested in and shall or may be exercised by the Governor General, with the advice, or with the advice and consent, or in conjunction with, the King's Privy Council for Canada or any member or members

thereof, or by the Governor General individually, as the case requires, subject nevertheless to be abolished or altered by the Parliament of Canada under the authority of the British North America Acts 1867 to 1946; and

(b) as far as they are capable of being exercised after the date of Union in relation to the Government of the Province of Newfoundland, shall be vested in and shall or may be exercised by the Lieutenant-Governor of the Province of Newfoundland, with the advice, or with the advice and consent, or in conjunction with, the Executive Council of the Province of Newfoundland or any member or members thereof, or by the Lieutenant-Governor individually, as the case requires, subject nevertheless to be abolished or altered by the Legislature of the Province of Newfoundland under the authority of the British North America Acts 1867 to 1946.

12. Until the Parliament of Canada otherwise provides, the powers, authorities, and functions vested in or imposed on any member of the Commission of Government of Newfoundland, as such member or as a Commissioner charged with the administration of a Department of the Government of Newfoundland, at or immediately prior to the date of Union in relation to matters other than those coming within the classes of subjects by the British North America Acts 1867 to 1946, assigned exclusively to the Legislature of a province, shall in the Province of Newfoundland be vested in or imposed on such person or persons as the Governor General in Council may appoint or designate.

13. Until the Legislature of the Province of Newfoundland otherwise provides, the powers, authorities, and functions vested in or imposed on any member of the Commission of Government of Newfoundland, as such member or as a Commissioner charged with the administration of a Department of the Government of Newfoundland, at or immediately prior to the date of Union in relation to matters coming within the classes of subjects by the British North America Acts 1867 to 1946, assigned exclusively to the Legislature of a province, shall in the Province of Newfoundland be vested in or imposed on such person or persons as the Lieutenant-Governor in Council may appoint or designate.

Legislature

14. (1) Subject to paragraph two of this Term, the Constitution of the Legislature of Newfoundland as it existed immediately prior to the sixteenth day of February, 1934, shall, subject to these Terms and the British North America Acts 1867 to 1946, continue as the Constitution of the Legislature of the Province of Newfoundland from and after the date of Union, until altered under the authority of the said Acts.

(2) The Constitution of the Legislature of Newfoundland insofar as it relates to the Legislative Council shall not continue, but the Legislature of the Province of Newfoundland may at any time re-establish the Legislative Council or establish a new Legislative Council.

15. (1) Until the Legislature of the Province of Newfoundland otherwise provides, the powers, authorities, and functions vested in or imposed on a Minister or other public officer or functionary under any statute of Newfoundland relating to the Constitution of the Legislature of Newfoundland as it existed immediately prior to the sixteenth day of February, 1934, shall, subject to these Terms and the British North America Acts 1867 to 1946, be vested in or imposed on such person or persons as the Lieutenant-Governor in Council may appoint or designate.

(2) Until the Legislature of the Province of Newfoundland otherwise provides,

(a) the list of electors prepared pursuant to The List of Electors Act, 1947, shall be deemed to be the list of electors for the purposes of The Election Act 1913, subject to the provisions of The Election Act 1913 respecting supplementary lists of electors;

(b) the franchise shall be extended to female British subjects who have attained the full age of twenty-one years and are otherwise qualified as electors;

(c) the Coast of Labrador together with the islands adjacent thereto shall constitute an additional electoral district to be known as Labrador and to be represented by one member, and residents of the said district who are otherwise qualified as electors shall be entitled to vote; and

(d) the Lieutenant-Governor in Council may by proclamation defer any election in the electoral district of Labrador for such period as may be specified in the proclamation.

16. The Legislature of the Province of Newfoundland shall be called together not later than four months after the date of Union.

EDUCATION

17. In lieu of section ninety-three of the British North America Act 1867, the following Term shall apply in respect of the Province of Newfoundland:

In and for the Province of Newfoundland the Legislature shall have exclusive authority to make laws in relation to education, but the Legislature will not have authority to make laws prejudicially affecting any right or privilege with respect to denominational schools, common (amalgamated) schools, or denominational colleges, that any class or classes of persons have by law in Newfoundland at the date of Union, and out of public funds of the Province of Newfoundland provided for education,

(a) all such schools shall receive their share of such funds in accordance with scales determined on a non-discriminatory basis from time to time by the Legislature for all schools then being conducted under authority of the Legislature; and

(b) all such colleges shall receive their share of any grant from

time to time voted for all colleges then being conducted under authority of the Legislature, such grant being distributed on a non-discriminatory basis.

CONTINUATION OF LAWS

General

18. (1) Subject to these Terms, all laws in force in Newfoundland at or immediately prior to the date of Union shall continue therein as if the Union had not been made, subject nevertheless to be repealed, abolished, or altered by the Parliament of Canada or by the Legislature of the Province of Newfoundland according to the authority of the Parliament or of the Legislature under the British North America Acts 1867 to 1946, and all orders, rules, and regulations made under any such laws shall likewise continue, subject to be revoked or amended by the body or person that made such orders, rules, or regulations or the body or person that has power to make such orders, rules, or regulations after the date of Union, according to their respective authority under the British North America Acts 1867 to 1946.

(2) Statutes of the Parliament of Canada in force at the date of Union, or any part thereof, shall come into force in the Province of Newfoundland on a day or days to be fixed by Act of the Parliament of Canada or by proclamation of the Governor General in Council issued from time to time, and any such proclamation may provide for the repeal of any of the laws of Newfoundland that

(a) are of general application;

(b) relate to the same subject matter as the statute or part thereof so proclaimed; and

(c) could be repealed by the Parliament of Canada under paragraph one of this Term.

(3) Notwithstanding anything in these Terms, the Parliament of Canada may with the consent of the Legislature of the Province of Newfoundland repeal any law in force in Newfoundland at the date of Union.

(4) Except as otherwise provided by these Terms, all courts of civil and criminal jurisdiction and all legal commissions, powers, authorities, and functions, and all officers and functionaries, judicial, administrative, and ministerial, existing in Newfoundland at or immediately prior to the date of Union, shall continue in the Province of Newfoundland as if the Union had not been made, until altered, abolished, revoked, terminated, or dismissed by the appropriate authority under the British North America Acts 1867 to 1946.

Supply

19. Any statute of Newfoundland enacted prior to the date of Union for granting to His Majesty sums of money for defraying expenses of, and for other purposes relating to, the public service of Newfoundland, for the financial year ending the thirty-first day of March, one thousand nine hundred and fifty, shall have effect after the date of Union according to its terms, until otherwise provided by the Legislature of the Province of Newfoundland.

Patents

20. (1) Subject to this Term, Canada will provide that letters patent for inventions issued under the laws of Newfoundland prior to the date of Union shall be deemed to have been issued under the laws of Canada, as of the date and for the term thereof.

(2) Canada will provide further that in the event of conflict between letters patent for an invention issued under the laws of Newfoundland prior to the date of Union and letters patent for an invention issued under the laws of Canada prior to the date of Union

(a) the letters patent issued under the laws of Newfoundland shall have the same force and effect in the Province of Newfoundland as if the Union had not been made, and all rights and privileges acquired under or by virtue thereof may continue to be exercised or enjoyed in the Province of Newfoundland as if the Union had not been made; and

(b) the letters patent issued under the laws of Canada shall have the same force and effect in any part of Canada other than the Province of Newfoundland as if the Union had not been made, and all rights and privileges acquired under or by virtue thereof may continue to be exercised or enjoyed in any part of Canada other than the Province of Newfoundland as if the Union had not been made.

(3) The laws of Newfoundland existing at the date of Union shall continue to apply in respect of applications for the grant of letters patent for inventions under the laws of Newfoundland pending at the date of Union, and any letters patent for inventions issued upon such applications shall, for the purposes of this Term, be deemed to have been issued under the laws of Newfoundland prior to the date of Union; and letters patent for inventions issued under the laws of Canada upon applications pending at the date of Union shall, for the purposes of this Term, be deemed to have been issued under the laws of Canada prior to the date of Union.

(4) Nothing in this Term shall be construed to prevent the Parliament of Canada from providing that no claims for infringement of a patent issued in Canada prior to the date of Union shall be entertained by any court against any person for anything done in Newfoundland prior to the date of Union in respect of the invention protected by such patent, and that no claims for infringement of a patent issued in Newfoundland prior to the date of Union shall be entertained by any court against any person for anything done in Canada prior to the date of Union in respect of the invention protected by such patent.

Trade Marks

21. (1) Canada will provide that the registration of a trade mark under the laws of Newfoundland prior to the date of Union shall have the same force and effect in the Province of Newfoundland as if the Union had not been made, and all rights and privileges acquired under or by virtue thereof may continue to be exercised or enjoyed in the Province of Newfoundland as if the Union had not been made.

(2) The laws of Newfoundland existing at the date of Union shall continue to apply in respect of applications for the registration of trade marks under the laws of Newfoundland pending at the date of Union and any trade marks registered upon such applications shall, for the purposes of this Term, be deemed to have been registered under the laws of Newfoundland prior to the date of Union.

Fisheries

22. (1) In this Term, the expression "Fisheries Laws" means the Act No. 11 of 1936, entitled "An Act for the creation of the Newfoundland Fisheries Board", the Act No. 14 of 1936, entitled "An Act to Prevent the Export of Fish Without Licence", the Act No. 32 of 1936, entitled "An Act to Amend the Newfoundland Fisheries Board Act (No. 11 of 1936)", the Act No. 37 of 1938, entitled "An Act further to Amend the Newfoundland Fisheries Board Act 1936", the Act No. 10 of 1942, entitled "An Act Respecting Permits for the Exportation of Salt Fish", the Act No. 39 of 1943, entitled "An Act Further to Amend the Newfoundland Fisheries Board Act 1936", the Act No. 16 of 1944, entitled "An Act Further to Amend the Newfoundland Fisheries Board Acts 1936-38," and the Act No. 42 of 1944, entitled "An Act Further to Amend the Newfoundland Fisheries Board Act 1936," insofar as they relate to the export marketing of salted fish from Newfoundland to other countries or to any provinces of Canada.

(2) Subject to this Term, all Fisheries Laws and all orders, rules, and regulations made thereunder shall continue in force in the Province of Newfoundland as if the Union had not been made, for a period of five years from the date of Union and thereafter until the Parliament of Canada otherwise provides, and shall continue to be administered by the Newfoundland Fisheries Board; and the costs involved in the maintenance of the Board and the administration of the Fisheries Laws shall be borne by the Government of Canada.

(3) The powers, authorities, and functions vested in or imposed on the Governor in Commission or the Commissioner for Natural Resources under any of the Fisheries Laws shall after the date of Union respectively be vested in or imposed on the Governor General in Council and the Minister of Fisheries of Canada or such other Minister as the Governor General in Council may designate.

(4) Any of the Fisheries Laws may be repealed or altered at any time within the period of five years from the date of Union by the Parliament of Canada with the consent of the Lieutenant-Governor in Council of the Province of Newfoundland and all orders, rules, and regulations made under the authority of any Fisheries Laws may be revoked or altered by the body or person that made them or, in relation to matters to which paragraph three of this Term applies, by the body or person that under the said paragraph three has power to make such orders, rules, or regulations under the Fisheries Laws after the date of Union.

(5) The Chairman of the Newfoundland Fisheries Board or such other member of the Newfoundland Fisheries Board as the Governor General in Council may designate shall perform in the Province of Newfoundland the duties of Chief Supervisor and Chief Inspector of the Department of Fisheries of the Government of Canada, and employees of the Newfoundland Fisheries Board shall become employees in that Department in positions

comparable to those of the employees in that Department in other parts of Canada.

(6) Terms eleven, twelve, thirteen and eighteen are subject to this Term.

FINANCIAL TERMS

Debt

23. *Canada will assume and provide for the servicing and retirement of the stock issued or to be issued on the security of Newfoundland pursuant to The Loan Act 1933, of Newfoundland and will take over the Sinking Fund established under that Act.*

Financial Surplus

24 (1) *In this Term the expression "financial surplus" means the balances standing to the credit of the Newfoundland Exchequer at the date of Union (less such sums as may be required to discharge accounts payable at the date of Union in respect of appropriations for the public services) and any public moneys or public revenue (including loans and advances referred to in Term twenty-five) in respect of any matter, thing, or period prior to the date of Union recovered by the Government of the Province of Newfoundland subsequent to the date of Union.*

(2) Newfoundland will retain its financial surplus subject to the following conditions:

(a) one-third of the surplus shall be set aside during the first eight years from the date of Union, on deposit with the Government of Canada, to be withdrawn by the Government of the Province of Newfoundland only for expenditures on current account to facilitate the maintenance and improvement of Newfoundland public services, and any portion of this one-third of the surplus remaining unspent at the end of the eight-year period shall become

available to the Province of Newfoundland without the foregoing restriction;

(b) the remaining two-thirds of the surplus shall be available to the Government of the Province of Newfoundland for the development of resources and for the establishment or extension of public services within the Province of Newfoundland; and

(c) no part of the surplus shall be used to subsidize the production or sale of products of the Province of Newfoundland in unfair competition with similar products of other provinces of Canada, but nothing in this paragraph shall preclude the Province of Newfoundland from assisting industry by developmental loans on reasonable conditions or by ordinary provincial administrative services.

(3) The Government of the Province of Newfoundland will have the right within one year from the date of Union to deposit with the Government of Canada all or any part of its financial surplus held in dollars and on the thirty-first day of March and the thirtieth day of September in each year to receive with respect thereto interest at the rate of two and five-eighths per centum per annum during a maximum period of ten years from the date of Union on the minimum balance outstanding at any time during the six-month period preceding payment of interest.

Loans

25. (1) The Province of Newfoundland will retain its interest in, and any securities arising from or attaching to, any loans or advances of public funds made by the Government of Newfoundland prior to the date of Union.

(2) Unless otherwise agreed by the Government of Canada, paragraph one of this Term shall not apply to any loans or advances relating to any works, property, or services taken over by Canada pursuant to Term thirty-one or Term thirty-three.

Subsidies

26   Canada will pay to the Province of Newfoundland the following subsidies:

(a) an annual subsidy of $180,000 and an annual subsidy equal to 80 cents per head of the population of the Province of Newfoundland (being taken at 325,000 until the first decennial census after the date of Union), subject to be increased to conform to the scale of grants authorised by the British North America Act 1907, for the local purposes of the Province and the support of its Government and Legislature, but in no year shall sums payable under this paragraph be less than those payable in the first year after the date of Union; and

(b) an additional annual subsidy of $1,100,000 payable for the like purposes as the various fixed annual allowances and subsidies provided by statutes of the Parliament of Canada from time to time for the Provinces of Nova Scotia, New Brunswick, and Prince Edward Island or any of them and in recognition of the special problems of the Province of Newfoundland by reason of geography and its sparse and scattered population.

Tax Agreement

27. (1) The Government of Canada will forthwith after the date of Union make an offer to the Government of the Province of Newfoundland to enter into a tax agreement for the rental to the Government of Canada of the income, corporation income, and corporation tax fields, and the succession duties tax field.

(2) The offer to be made under this Term will be similar to the offers to enter into tax agreements made to other provinces, necessary changes being made to adapt the offer to circumstances arising out of the Union, except that the offer will provide that the agreement may be entered into either for a number of fiscal years expiring at the end of the fiscal year in 1952, as in the case of other provinces, or for a number of fiscal years expiring at the

end of the fiscal year in 1957, at the option of the Government of the Province of Newfoundland, but if the Government of the Province of Newfoundland accepts the latter option the agreement will provide that the subsequent entry into a tax agreement by the Government of Canada with any other province will not entitle the Government of the Province of Newfoundland to any alteration in the terms of its agreement.

(3) The offer of the Government of Canada to be made under this Term may be accepted by the Government of the Province of Newfoundland within nine months after the date of the offer but if it is not so accepted will thereupon expire.

(4) The Government of the Province of Newfoundland shall not by any agreement entered into pursuant to this Term be required to impose on any person or corporation taxation repugnant to the provisions of any contract entered into with such person or corporation before the date of the agreement and subsisting at the date of the agreement.

(5) If the Province of Newfoundland enters into a tax agreement pursuant to this Term the subsidies payable under Term twenty-six will, as in the case of similar subsidies to other provinces, be included in the computation of tax agreement payments.

Transitional Grants

28. (1) In order to facilitate the adjustment of Newfoundland to the status of a province of Canada and the development by the Province of Newfoundland of revenue-producing services, Canada will pay to the Province of Newfoundland each year during the first twelve years after the date of Union a transitional grant as follows, payment in each year to be made in equal quarterly instalments commencing on the first day of April, namely,

$

First year 6,500,000

Second year 6,500,000

Third year 6,500,000

Fourth year 5,650,000

Fifth year 4,800,000

Sixth year 3,950,000

Seventh year 3,100,000

Eighth year 2,250,000

Ninth year 1,400,000

Tenth year 1,050,000

Eleventh year 700,000

Twelfth year350,000.

(2) The Government of the Province of Newfoundland will have the right to leave on deposit with the Government of Canada any portion of the transitional grant for the first eight years with the right to withdraw all or any portion thereof in any subsequent year and on the thirty-first day of March and the thirtieth day of September in each year to receive in respect of any amounts so left on deposit interest at the rate of two and five-eighths per centum per annum up to a maximum period of ten years from the date of Union on the minimum balance outstanding at any time during the six-month period preceding payment of interest.

Review of Financial Position

29. In view of the difficulty of predicting with sufficient accuracy the financial consequences to Newfoundland of becoming a province of Canada, The Government of Canada will appoint a Royal Commission within eight years from the date of Union to review the financial position of the Province of Newfoundland and to recommend the form and scale of additional financial assistance, if any, that may be required by the Government of the Province of Newfoundland to enable it to continue public services at the levels and standards reached subsequent to the date of Union, without resorting to taxation more burdensome, having regard to capacity to pay, than that obtaining generally in the region comprising the Maritime Provinces of Nova Scotia, New Brunswick, and Prince Edward Island.

Miscellaneous Provisions

Salaries of Lieutenant-Governor and Judges

30. The salary of the Lieutenant-Governor and the salaries, allowances, and pensions of the judges of such superior, district, and county courts as are now or may hereafter be constituted in the Province of Newfoundland shall be fixed and provided by the Parliament of Canada.

Public Services, Works and Property

31. At the date of Union, or as soon thereafter as practicable, Canada will take over the following services and will as from the date of Union relieve the Province of Newfoundland of the public costs incurred in respect of each service taken over, namely,

(a) the Newfoundland Railway, including steamship and other marine services;

(b) the Newfoundland Hotel, if requested by the Government of the Province of Newfoundland within six months from the date of Union;

(c) postal and publicly-owned telecommunication services;

(d) civil aviation, including Gander Airport;

(e) customs and excise;

(f) defence;

(g) protection and encouragement of fisheries and operation of bait services;

(h) geological, topographical, geodetic, and hydrographic surveys;

(i) lighthouses, fog alarms, buoys, beacons, and other public works and services in aid of navigation and shipping;

(j) marine hospitals, quarantine, and the care of ship-wrecked crews;

(k) the public radio broadcasting system; and

(l) other public services similar in kind to those provided at the date of Union for the people of Canada generally.

32. (1) Canada will maintain in accordance with the traffic offering a freight and passenger steamship service between North Sydney and Port aux Basques, which, on completion of a motor highway between Corner Brook and Port aux Basques, will include suitable provision for the carriage of motor vehicles.

(2) For the purpose of railway rate regulation the Island of Newfoundland will be included in the Maritime region of Canada, and through-traffic moving between North Sydney and Port aux Basques will be treated as all-rail traffic.

(3) All legislation of the Parliament of Canada providing for special rates on traffic moving within, into, or out of, the Maritime region will, as far as appropriate, be made applicable to the Island of Newfoundland.

33. The following public works and property of Newfoundland shall become the property of Canada when the service concerned is taken over by Canada, subject to any trusts existing in respect thereof, and to any interest other than that of Newfoundland in the same, namely,

(a) the Newfoundland Railway, including rights of way, wharves, dry docks, and other real property, rolling stock, equipment, ships, and other personal property;

(b) the Newfoundland Airport at Gander, including buildings and equipment, together with any other property used for the operation of the Airport;

(c) the Newfoundland Hotel and equipment;

(d) public harbours, wharves, break-waters, and aids to navigation;

(e) bait depots and the motor vessel Malakoff;

(f) military and naval property, stores, and equipment;

(g) public dredges and vessels except those used for services that remain the responsibility of Newfoundland and except the nine motor vessels known as the Clarenville boats;

(h) the public telecommunication system, including rights of way, land lines, cables, telephones, radio stations, and other real and personal property;

(i) real and personal property of the Broadcasting Corporation of Newfoundland; and

(j) subject to the provisions of Term thirty-four, customs houses, and post-offices and generally all public works and property, real and personal, used primarily for services taken over by Canada.

34. Where at the date of Union any public buildings of

Newfoundland included in paragraph (j) of Term thirty-three are used partly for services taken over by Canada and partly for services of the Province of Newfoundland the following provisions shall apply:

(a) where more than half the floor space of a building is used for services taken over by Canada the building shall become the property of Canada and where more than half the floor space of a building is used for services of the Province of Newfoundland the building shall remain the property of the Province of Newfoundland;

(b) Canada shall be entitled to rent from the Province of Newfoundland on terms to be mutually agreed such space in the buildings owned by the Province of Newfoundland as is used for the services taken over by Canada and the Province of Newfoundland shall be entitled to rent from Canada on terms to be mutually agreed such space in the buildings owned by Canada as is used for the services of the Province of Newfoundland;

(c) the division of buildings for the purposes of this Term shall be made by agreement between the Government of Canada and the Government of the Province of Newfoundland as soon as practicable after the date of Union; and

(d) if the division in accordance with the foregoing provisions results in either Canada or the Province of Newfoundland having a total ownership that is substantially out of proportion to the total floor space used for its services an adjustment of the division will be made by mutual agreement between the two Governments.

35. Newfoundland public works and property not transferred to Canada by or under these Terms will remain the property of the Province of Newfoundland.

36. Without prejudice to the legislative authority of the Parliament of Canada under the British North America Acts 1867 to 1946, any works, property, or services taken over by Canada pursuant to these Terms shall thereupon be subject to the legislative authority of the Parliament of Canada.

Natural Resources

37. All lands, mines, minerals, and royalties belonging to Newfoundland at the date of Union, and all sums then due or payable for such lands, mines, minerals, or royalties, shall belong to the Province of Newfoundland, subject to any trusts existing in respect thereof, and to any interest other than that of the Province in the same.

Veterans

38. Canada will make available to Newfoundland veterans the following benefits, on the same basis as they are from time to time available to Canadian veterans, as if the Newfoundland veterans had served in His Majesty's Canadian forces, namely,

(a) The War Veterans Allowance Act 1946, free hospitalization and treatment, and civil service preference will be extended to Newfoundland veterans who served in the First World War or the Second World War or both;

(b) Canada will assume as from the date of Union the Newfoundland pension liability in respect of the First World War, and in respect of the Second World War Canada will assume as from the date of Union the cost of supplementing disability and dependants' pensions paid by the Government of the United Kingdom or an Allied country to Newfoundland veterans up to the level of the Canadian rates of pensions, and, in addition, Canada will pay pensions arising from disabilities that are pensionable under Canadian law but not pensionable either under the laws of the United Kingdom or under the laws of an Allied country;

(c) The Veterans' Land Act 1942, Part IV of the Unemployment Insurance Act 1940, The Veterans' Business and Professional

Loans Act, and The Veterans Insurance Act will be extended to Newfoundland veterans who served in the Second World War;

(d) a re-establishment credit will be made available to Newfoundland veterans who served in the Second World War equal to the re-establishment credit that might have been made available to them under The War Service Grants Act 1944, if their service in the Second World War had been service in the Canadian forces, less the amount of any pecuniary benefits of the same nature granted or paid by the Government of any country other than Canada;

(e) Canada will assume, as from the date of Union, the cost of vocational and educational training of Newfoundland veterans of the Second World War on the same basis as if they had served in His Majesty's Canadian forces; and

(f) sections six, seven, and eight of The Veterans Rehabilitation Act will be extended to Newfoundland veterans of the Second World War who have not received similar benefits from the Government of any country other than Canada.

Public Servants

39. (1) Employees of the Government of Newfoundland in the services taken over by Canada pursuant to these Terms will be offered employment in these services or in similar Canadian services under the terms and conditions from time to time governing employment in those services, but without reduction in salary or loss of pension rights acquired by reason of service in Newfoundland.

(2) Canada will provide the pensions for such employees so that the employees will not be prejudiced, and the Government of the Province of Newfoundland will reimburse Canada for the pensions for, or at its option make to Canada contributions in respect of, the service of these employees with the Government of Newfoundland prior to the date of Union, but these payments or contributions

will be such that the burden on the Government of the Province of Newfoundland in respect of pension rights acquired by reason of service in Newfoundland will not be increased by reason of the transfer.

(3) Pensions of employees of the Government of Newfoundland who were retired on pension before the service concerned is taken over by Canada will remain the responsibility of the Province of Newfoundland.

Welfare and Other Public Services

40. Subject to these Terms, Canada will extend to the Province of Newfoundland, on the same basis and subject to the same terms and conditions as in the case of other provinces of Canada, the welfare and other public services provided from time to time by Canada for the people of Canada generally, which, in addition to the veterans' benefits, unemployment insurance benefits, and merchant seamen benefits set out in Terms thirty-eight, forty-one, and forty-two respectively, include family allowances under The Family Allowances Act 1944, unemployment insurance under The Unemployment Insurance Act 1940, sick mariners' benefits for merchant seamen and fishermen under the Canada Shipping Act 1934, assistance for housing under The National Housing Act 1944, and, subject to the Province of Newfoundland entering into the necessary agreements or making the necessary contributions, financial assistance under The National Physical Fitness Act for carrying out plans of physical fitness, health grants, and contributions under the Old Age Pensions Act for old age pensions and pensions for the blind.

Unemployment Insurance

41. (1) Subject to this Term, Canada will provide that residents of the Province of Newfoundland in insurable employment who lose their employment within six months prior to the date of Union and are still unemployed at that date, or who lose their employment

within a two-year period after that date, will be entitled for a period of six months from the date of Union or six months from the date of unemployment, whichever is the later, to assistance on the same scale and under the same conditions as unemployment insurance benefits.

(2) The rates of payment will be based on the individual's wage record for the three months preceding his loss of employment, and to qualify for assistance a person must have been employed in insurable employment for at least thirty per centum of the working days within the period of three months preceding his loss of employment or thirty per centum of the working days within the period since the date of Union, whichever period is the longer.

Merchant Seamen

42. (1) Canada will make available to Newfoundland merchant seamen who served in the Second World War on British ships or on ships of Allied countries employed in service essential to the prosecution of the war, the following benefits, on the same basis as they are from time to time available to Canadian merchant seamen, as if they had served on Canadian ships, namely,

(a) disability and dependants' pensions will be paid, if disability occurred as a result of enemy action or counter-action, including extraordinary marine hazards occasioned by the war, and a Newfoundland merchant seaman in receipt of a pension from the Government of the United Kingdom or an Allied country will be entitled, during residence in Canada, to have his pension raised to the Canadian level; and

(b) free hospitalization and treatment, vocational training, The Veterans' Land Act 1942, and The Veterans Insurance Act will be extended to disability pensioners.

(2) Vocational training, Part IV of The Unemployment Insurance Act 1940, and The Veterans Insurance Act will be extended to Newfoundland merchant seamen who were eligible for a Special

Bonus or a War Service Bonus, on the same basis as if they were Canadian merchant seamen.

(3) The Unemployment Insurance Act 1940, and The Merchant Seamen Compensation Act will be applied to Newfoundland merchant seamen as they are applied to other Canadian merchant seamen.

Citizenship

43. Suitable provision will be made for the extension of the Canadian citizenship laws to the Province of Newfoundland.

Defence Establishments

44. Canada will provide for the maintenance in the Province of Newfoundland of appropriate reserve units of the Canadian defence forces, which will include the Newfoundland Regiment.

Economic Survey

45. (1) Should the Government of the Province of Newfoundland institute an economic survey of the Province of Newfoundland with a view to determining what resources may profitably be developed and what new industries may be established or existing industries expanded, the Government of Canada will make available the services of its technical employees and agencies to assist in the work.

(2) As soon as may be practicable after the date of Union, the Government of Canada will make a special effort to collect and make available statistical and scientific data about the natural resources and economy of the Province of Newfoundland, in order to bring such information up to the standard attained for the other provinces of Canada.

Oleomargarine

46. (1) Oleomargarine or margarine may be manufactured or sold in the Province of Newfoundland after the date of the Union and the Parliament of Canada shall not prohibit or restrict such manufacture or sale except at the request of the Legislature of the Province of Newfoundland, but nothing in this Term shall affect the power of the Parliament of Canada to require compliance with standards of quality applicable throughout Canada.

(2) Unless the Parliament of Canada otherwise provides or unless the sale and manufacture in, and the interprovincial movement between, all provinces of Canada other than Newfoundland, of oleomargarine and margarine, is lawful under the laws of Canada, oleomargarine or margarine shall not be sent, shipped, brought, or carried from the Province of Newfoundland into any other province of Canada.

Income Taxes

47. In order to assist in the transition to payment of income tax on a current basis Canada will provide in respect of persons (including corporations) resident in Newfoundland at the date of Union, who were not resident in Canada in 1949 prior to the date of Union, and in respect of income that under the laws of Canada in force immediately prior to the date of Union was not liable to taxation, as follows:

(a) that prior to the first day of July, 1949, no payment will be required or deduction made from such income on account of income tax;

(b) that for income tax purposes no person shall be required to report such income for any period prior to the date of Union;

(c) that no person shall be liable to Canada for income tax in respect of such income for any period prior to the date of Union; and

(d) that for individuals an amount of income tax for the 1949

taxation year on income for the period after the date of Union shall be forgiven so that the tax on all earned income and on investment income of not more than $2,250 will be reduced to one-half the tax that would have been payable for the whole year if the income for the period prior to the date of Union were at the same rate as that subsequent to such date.

Statute of Westminster

48. From and after the date of Union the Statute of Westminster 1931, shall apply to the Province of Newfoundland as it applies to the other Provinces of Canada.

Saving

49. Nothing in these Terms shall be construed as relieving any person from any obligation with respect to the employment of Newfoundland labour incurred or assumed in return for any concession or privilege granted or conferred by the Government of Newfoundland prior to the date of Union.

Coming into Force

50. These Terms are agreed to subject to their being approved by the Parliament of Canada and the Government of Newfoundland; shall take effect notwithstanding the Newfoundland Act 1933, or any instrument issued pursuant thereto; and shall come into force immediately before the expiration of the thirty-first day of March 1949, if His Majesty has theretofore given His Assent to an Act of the Parliament of the United Kingdom of Great Britain and Northern Ireland confirming the same.

Signed in duplicate at Ottawa this eleventh day of December 1948.

Consequences of the Terms of Union of Newfoundland and Canada

From the perspective of territorial sovereignty the effect of the union of Newfoundland and Canada was to terminate the eastern international boundary between Canada and the United Kingdom (Newfoundland) and to expand the territory of Canada by 156,649.3 square miles (405,720 square kilometers). Although the boundary between Canada and Labrador remained exactly as it had been prescribed by the Judicial Committee of the Privy Council in 1927, it no longer existed as an international boundary between Canada and a separate state. Newfoundland and Labrador were now part of Canada and the Labrador border now became a provincial boundary between the Province of Quebec and the Province of Newfoundland (now the Province of Newfoundland and Labrador).

From a historical perspective the entry of Newfoundland and Labrador into Confederation completed the dream of Sir John A. Macdonald and the other fathers of Confederation for the creation of a country that would extend from sea to sea.

ENDNOTES

[1] *The French Treaty Shore*, J.K. Hiller, Heritage Newfoundland and Labrador, (http://www.heritage.nf.ca/articles/exploration/french-shore.php) (Accessed April 27, 2018)

[2] 14 Geo. III., c. 83

[3] Newfoundland Act, 1809, 49. Geo. III., c. 27

[4] British North America (Seigniorial Rights) Act, 1825, 6 Geo. IV., c. 59.

[5] For a discussion of Newfoundland's status in international law following the Balfour Declaration of 1926 see William C. Gilmore, *Newfoundland and Dominion Status: The External Affairs*

Competence and International Law Status of Newfoundland, 1855 – 1934, Carswell, Toronto, 1988.

[6] www.heritage.nf.ca/articles/politics/pdf/labrador-boundary-dispute-documents.pdf (accessed April 29, 2018)

[7] The Committee consisted of several distinguished British jurists (Viscount Cave, L.C., Viscount Haldane, Viscount Finlay, Lord Sumner, and Lord Warrington),

[8] I*n Re Labrador Boundary* https://www.heritage.nf.ca/articles/politics/pdf/labrador-boundary-dispute-documents.pdf. Judgement, p. 1014

[9] Ibid, p. 1015

[10] Ibid, p. 1026

[11] 12-13 Geo. VI, c. 22 (UK)

[12] 1982 (U.K.) 1982, c. 11, s. 52

[13] Section 43 of the Constitution Act, 1982 further provides that no alteration of the boundaries of a province in Confederation can be made without the legislative assent of the province in respect of which the boundary alteration is proposed to be made.

[14] A High Commission is the descriptive term for an embassy between two countries that are part of the Commonwealth of Nations (formerly the British Commonwealth). The word embassy is not used in such circumstances because historically the relations between Commonwealth countries were not considered to be relations between foreign states.

[15] The formal admission of Newfoundland into Confederation was made in accordance with the British North America (No. 1) Act, 1949 12-12 Geo. VI, c. 22.

8.

THE OCEANIC AND ATMOSPHERIC BOUNDARIES OF CANADA

General Principles Concerning Maritime Boundaries

Although Canada is a continental country, in the sense that it possesses an immense territory, geography has also endowed the country with the longest coastline in the world bordering on three oceans, the Atlantic, Pacific and Arctic Oceans. The presence of three adjacent states, the United States of America, France, and Denmark, requires that attention be given by Canada to establishment of maritime boundaries with its three neighbouring states.

Maritime boundaries are established by the application of the principles of maritime law. In the modern period the customary international law in relation to maritime boundaries has been largely, though not wholly, codified in the United Nations Convention on the Law of the Sea (UNCLOS), which was adopted in 1982, and which came into force as part of international law in 1994. Canada is a signatory to the Convention. In a nutshell, under the Convention the boundaries established in the oceans are an emanation of a country's terrestrial sovereignty. However, the sovereignty rights available to a littoral state over adjacent maritime areas vary from complete state sovereignty to restricted state sovereignty, depending upon what part of the ocean is involved.

The key element in the process of creating a maritime boundary is the establishment of a baseline adjacent to the shoreline of a country. Such baselines normally follow the low water mark of the tidal shores along a country's coastline. Straight baselines may, however, be adopted where the coastline involves deeply indented bays, or a fringe of islands and islets. Such straight baselines must still generally follow the coastline of the state that establishes them.

All waters that lie inward of the baselines (i.e., waters that lie in direction of the land) are described as Internal Waters and are subject to the absolute sovereignty of the state which has established the baselines. That includes sovereignty over the water column, the seabed and the subsoil as well as the atmosphere above the waters to the edge of outer space. Nevertheless, UNCLOS provides that the enclosure of waters within Internal Waters that were previously not so regarded cannot have the effect of extinguishing an existing right of innocent passage for foreign ships. Canada has established baselines along its coasts and has used straight baselines to enclose the waters (free and ice-covered) within the Arctic Archipelago.

Customary international law also provides recognition of a category of historic bays for which a coastal state may claim absolute sovereignty. This category applies where it can be shown that a state has exercised control over a certain bay for a long period of time and the international community has acquiesced to the coastal state's claim. As early as 1906, Canada claimed Hudson Bay as part of Canada's historic waters and although a protest to that claim was lodged by the United States the international community appears to have acquiesced to the Canadian claim.[1] A straight baseline has been established across Hudson Strait, which is at the entrance to the bay.

A state may also claim a Territorial Sea of up to 12 nautical miles projecting outward from the standard or straight baselines that it has established. Formerly, a three-mile limit was provided for a Territorial Sea under customary international law but now almost all littoral states have extended their Territorial Sea claim to 12 nautical miles. Canada claims a 12-mile Territorial Sea that is seaward from its baselines. Within its Territorial Sea, a coastal state is sovereign but its sovereignty is restricted. A coastal state has sovereignty over the sea and the water column, seabed, and subsoil, as well as the atmosphere above the Territorial Sea to the edge of outer space but the coastal state must permit the right of innocent passage for maritime traffic, and innocent passage for aeronautical overflights. The coastal state cannot levy charges for transiting its Territorial Sea but it can charge fees for certain services that it provides in relation to the Territorial Sea, such as air traffic control. Ships and airplanes exercising the right of innocent passage must not undertake any actions that would endanger the peace, or be disruptive to the coastal state.

Beyond the Territorial Sea there is a zone described as the Contiguous Zone. The Contiguous Zone is measured for a distance of 24 nautical miles from the coastal baselines and is described as the oceanic zone that lies outward from the 12-mile limit of the Territorial Sea to the limit of 24 nautical miles measured from the coastal baselines. In effect it provides a further 12 nautical miles of jurisdiction to the coastal state. Within the Contiguous Zone the coastal state may enforce its immigration, customs, fiscal, and sanitary laws, as if the zone was within the sovereign territory of the coastal state. Otherwise, the sea within the Contiguous Zone and the airspace above it are international waters, or international airspace, and the coastal state cannot exercise any sovereign rights beyond those four categories of laws previously mentioned. Canada has both claimed and exercised its rights under international law with respect to its Contiguous Zone.

Beyond the Territorial Sea for a distance of 200 nautical miles measured from the normal or straight baselines coastal states may claim an Exclusive Economic Zone (EEZ) in which the coastal state may exercise sovereign rights for the management, exploitation, and conservation of the natural resources lying within that zone. EEZ jurisdiction extends to the natural resources (both living and non-living) in the water column, the seabed, and in the subsoil beneath the seabed. However, the waters of the EEZ are otherwise considered to be international waters and both the rights of free navigation, and overflight, exist in relation to the EEZ of a coastal state.

Beyond the EEZ, a coastal state may claim the right to exploit the natural prolongation of the continental shelf beyond the 200 nautical mile limit to a distance of 350 nautical miles from the coastal baselines, or 100 nautical miles beyond the 2,500-metre isobath.[2] What constitutes a natural prolongation of the continental shelf however, can be difficult to determine and therefore the Convention prescribes a process that is administered by the UNCLOS Law of the Sea Tribunal. While the coastal state that receives recognition of the prolongation of its continental shelf beyond the 200 nautical mile EEZ has the exclusive right to exploit the non-living resources of the prolonged continental shelf, it must nevertheless pay royalties to the International Seabed Authority with respect to its exploitative activities. The sea column and the airspace above the prolongation of the continental shelf remain international waters, and international airspace, and are not subject to the sovereign rights of the littoral state. Canada is currently researching and preparing a submission to the UNCLOS Law of the Sea Tribunal to obtain recognition for the prolongation of its continental shelf in the Arctic Ocean.

The Southeastern Maritime Boundary

The boundary between Canada and the United States through Passamaquoddy Bay remained uncertain well into the early twentieth century. In order to resolve the uncertainties, a series of treaties were entered into by Great Britain (on behalf of Canada) and the United States of America, to resolve the uncertainties present along the southeastern maritime boundary between the two states. The first attempt to address the uncertainties was contained in the Anglo-American Convention of 1892 (Alaska and Passamaquoddy Bay).

The Anglo-American Convention of 1892 (Alaska and Passamaquoddy Bay)

This convention established a commission to demarcate the border between the two countries in Passamaquoddy Bay adjacent to the municipality of Eastport, Maine.

The Anglo-American Convention of 1892 (Alaska and Passamaquoddy Bay) (Extract)

July 22, 1892

Article II

The High Contracting Parties agree that the Governments of Her Britannic Majesty in behalf of the Dominion of Canada and of the United States shall, with as little delay as possible, appoint two Commissioners, one to be named by each party, to determine upon a method of more accurately marking the boundary-line between the two countries in the waters of Passamaquoddy Bay in front of and adjacent to Eastport, in the State of Maine, and to place buoys or fix such other boundary marks as they may determine to be necessary.

Consequences of The Anglo-American Convention of 1892 (Alaska and Passamaquoddy Bay)

The commissioners appointed under the 1892 convention were given additional time to complete their work by a subsequent treaty (The Anglo-American Convention of 1894 (Alaska and Passamaquoddy Bay), February 3, 1894) which extended the time for the completion of the work of the commissioners until December 31, 1895. The commissioners were able to ascertain portions of the boundary but there was disagreement with respect to one section, which was left for resolution to another day.

The Treaty to Demarcate the International Boundary between the United States and Canada, 1908

In 1908, as part of a general effort to demarcate the entire border between Canada and the United States of America, a renewed effort was made to establish the boundary between the two countries through Passamaquoddy Bay.

Treaty between the United Kingdom and the United States of America respecting the Demarcation of the International Boundary between the United States and the Dominion of Canada (Extracts)

April 11, 1908

ARTICLE 1

The High Contracting Parties agree that each shall appoint, without delay, an expert geographer or surveyor to serve as Commissioners for the purpose of more accurately defining and marking the international. boundary line between the United States and the Dominion of Canada in the waters of Passamaquoddy Bay from the mouth of the St. Croix River to the Bay of Fundy, and that in defining and marking said boundary line the Commissioners shall adopt and follow, as closely as may be, the line surveyed and laid down by the Commissioners appointed under Article II of the Treaty of July 22, 1892, between Great Britain and the United States, so far as said Commissioners agreed upon the location of said line, namely:

(1.) From a point at the mouth of the St. Croix River defined by the ranges established by them, by a connected series of six straight lines defined by ranges and cross ranges, to a point between Treat Island-and Friar head, likewise defined by ranges and cross ranges established by them; and also

(2.) From it point in Quoddy Roads, defined by the intersection of the range passing through the position of the Beacon of 1886 and Lubec Channel Light, with a range established by them on the west shore of Quoddy Roads along the course of this latter range, which is about 8U° 35' east of true south, into the Bay of Fundy.

In ascertaining the location of the above-described line, the Commissioners shall be controlled by the indications of the range marks and monuments established along its course by said former Commissioners and by the charts upon which the said Commissioners marked the line as tentatively agreed upon by them.

The remaining portion of the line, lying between the two above-described sections, and upon the location of which said former Commissioners did not agree, shall pass through the center of the Lubec Narrows Channel between Campobello Island and the mainland, and, subject to the provisions hereinafter stated, it shall follow on either side of the said Narrows such courses as will connect with the parts of the line agreed upon as aforesaid, and such boundary shall consist of a series of' straight lives defined by distances and courses; but inasmuch as differences have arisen in the past as to the location of the line with respect to Pope's Folly Island above Lubec Narrows and with respect to certain fishing grounds east of the dredged channel below Lubec

Narrows, it is agreed that each of the High Contracting Parties shall present to the other within six months after the ratification of this Treaty a full printed statement of the evidence, with certified copies of original documents referred to therein which are in its possession, and the' arguments upon which. it bases its contentions, with a view to arriving at an adjustment of the location of this portion of the line in accordance with the true intent and meaning of the provisions relating thereto of the Treaties of 1783 and 1814 between Great Britain and the United States, and the• award of the Commissioners appointed in that behalf under the Treaty of 1814; it being-understood that. any action by either or both Governments or their representatives authorized in that behalf or by the local governments on either side of the line, whether prior or subsequent to such Treaties and award, tending to aid in the interpretation thereof, shall be taken into consideration in determining their true intent and meaning.

Such agreement, if reached, shall be reduced to writing in the form of a protocol and shall be communicated to the said Commissioners, who shall lay down and mark this portion of the boundary in accordance therewith and as herein provided.

Consequences of the Treaty to Demarcate the International Boundary between the United States and Canada

The commissioners appointed to determine the boundary proceeded according to the treaty but were unable to resolve the outstanding issues in a timely manner. Nevertheless, a basis for agreement was reached and resulted in a subsequent, determinative treaty.

The Treaty Respecting the Boundary between Canada and the United States in Passamaquoddy Bay, 1910

Two years later, in 1910 the two states were able to arrive at a satisfactory accommodation with respect to the maritime boundary in Passamaquoddy Bay.

Treaty Respecting the Boundary between Canada and the United States in Passamaquoddy Bay (Extracts)

May 21, 1910

Article 1

Whereas, by Article 1 of the Treaty of April 11, 1908, between Great Britain and the United States, it was agreed that Commissioners should be appointed for the purpose of more accurately defining and marking the international boundary line between the United States and the Dominion of Canada in the waters of Passamaquoddy Bay from the mouth of the St. Croix River to the Bay of Fundy, the description of the location of certain portions of such line being set forth in the aforesaid Article, and it was agreed with respect to the remaining portion of the line that–

each of the High Contracting Parties shall present to the other within six months after the ratification of this Treaty a full printed statement of the evidence, with certified copies of original documents referred to therein which are in its possession, and the arguments upon which it bases its contentions, with a view to arriving at an adjustment of the location of this portion of the line in accordance with the true intent and meaning of the provisions relating thereto of the treaties of 1783 and 1814 between Great Britain and the United States, and the award of the Commissioners appointed in that behalf under the Treaty of 1814; it being understood that any action by either or both Governments or their representatives authorized in that behalf or by the local governments on either Side of the line, whether prior or subsequent to such treaties and award, tending to aid in the interpretation thereof, shall be taken into consideration in determining their true intent and meaning;

And it was further agreed that if such agreement was reached between the Parties the Commissioners aforesaid should lay down and mark this, portion of the boundary in accordance therewith and as provided in the said Article, but it was provided that in the event of a failure to agree within a set period, the location of such portion of the line should be determined by reference to arbitration ;

And whereas, the time for reaching an agreement under the provisions of the aforesaid Article expired before such agreement was reached but the High Contracting Parties are nevertheless desirous, of arriving at an adjustment of the location of this portion of the line by agreement without resort to arbitration, and have already, pursuant to the provisions above quoted of Article I of the Treaty aforesaid, presented each to the other a full printed statement of the evidence and of the arguments upon which the contentions of each, are based, with a view to arriving at an adjustment of the location of the portion of the line referred to, in accordance with the true intent and meaning of the provisions relating thereto in the Treaties of 1783 and 1814 between Great

Britain and the United States and the award of the Commissioners, appointed in that behalf under the Treaty of 1814;

Now, therefore, upon the evidence and arguments so presented, and after taking into consideration all actions, of the respective Governments and of their representatives authorized in that behalf and of the local governments on either side of the line, whether prior or subsequent to such treaties and award, tending to aid in the interpretation thereof, the High Contracting Parties hereby agree that the location of the international boundary line between the United States and the Dominion of Canada from a point in Passamaquoddy Bay accurately defined in the Treaty between Great Britain and the United State's of April 11, 1908, as, lying between Treat Island and Friar Head, and extending thence through Passamaquoddy Bay and to, the middle of Grand Manan Channel, shall run in a series of seven connected straight lines for the distances and in the directions as follows:

Beginning at the aforesaid point lying between Treat Island and Friar Head, thence

(1) South 8° 29' 57" West true, for a distance of 1152.6 meters; thence

(2) South 8° 29' 34" East, 759.7 meters; thence

(3) South 23° 56' 25" East, 1156.4 meters; thence

(4) South 0° 23' 14" West, 1040.0 meters; thence

(5) South 28° 04' 26" East, 1607.2 meters; thence

(6) South 81° 48' 45" East, 2616.8 meters to a point on the line which runs approximately North 40° East true, and which joins Sail Rock, off West Quoddy Head Light, and the southernmost rock lying off the southeastern point of the southern extremity of Campobello Island; thence

(7) South 47° East 5100 meters to the middle of Grand Manan Channel.

The description of the last two portions of the line thus defined, viz., those numbered (6) and (7), is intended to replace the description of the lowest portion of the line, viz., that numbered (2), as defined in Article 1 of the Treaty of April 11, 1908.

Article 2

The location of the boundary line as, defined in the foregoing Article shall be laid down and marked by the Commissioners under Article 1 of the aforesaid Treaty of April 11, 1908, in accordance with the provisions of such Article, and the line so defined and laid down shall be taken and deemed to be the international boundary extending between the points therein mentioned in Grand Manan Channel and Passamaquoddy Bay.

Consequences of The Treaty Respecting the Boundary between Canada and the United States in Passamaquoddy Bay

With the ratification of this treaty the maritime boundary between Canada and the United States within Passamaquoddy Bay was finally ascertained.

The Gulf of Maine

Later in the twentieth century a dispute over the placement of the southeastern maritime border between the province of Nova Scotia and the state of Maine engaged the attention of Canada and the United States. The importance of this dispute revolved around control of the Georges Bank, a rich fishery that was coveted by the fishers of both countries. Negotiations to resolve the issue were undertaken but proved fruitless.

The Gulf of Maine Arbitration Treaty, 1979

In recognition of the fact that the two countries were unable to negotiate an acceptable compromise with respect to their dispute over the Georges Bank, both states jointly decided to place the matter before the International Court of Justice for a determination of the dispute on its merits. Accordingly, a treaty was negotiated between Canada and the United States whereby the dispute would be given to a Chamber of the Court for a decision. The Chamber of the Court was to consist of five persons chosen in consultation with Canada and the United States who would be charged with answering the specific legal question posed by the litigants to the Court Chamber. Ultimately, it was decided that the court would consist of judges from Italy, France, West Germany, the United States, and Canada.

Treaty to Submit to Binding Dispute Settlement the Delimitation of the Maritime Boundary in the Gulf of Maine Area (Extracts)

March 29, 1979

The Government of Canada and the Government of the United States of America,

RECOGNIZING that they have been unable to resolve by negotiation the differences between them concerning the delimitation of the continental shelf and the fisheries zones of Canada and the United States of America in the Gulf of Maine area,

DESIRING to reach an early and amicable settlement of these differences,

HAVE AGREED as follows:

Article I

The Parties shall, pursuant to Article 40 of the Statute of the International Court of Justice, notify the Court of the Special Agreement between the Government of Canada and the

Government of the United States of America to Submit to a Chamber of the International Court of Justice the Delimitation of the Maritime Boundary in the Gulf of Maine Area annexed hereto. The Chamber of the International Court of Justice shall be deemed to have been constituted when the Registrar of the Court has been notified of the name or names of the judge or judges ad hoc.

. . . .

Annex

SPECIAL AGREEMENT BETWEEN THE GOVERNMENT OF CANADA AND THE GOVERNMENT OF THE UNITED STATES OF AMERICA TO SUBMIT TO A CHAMBER OF THE INTERNATIONAL COURT OF JUSTICE THE DELIMITATION OF THE MARITIME BOUNDARY IN THE GULF OF MAINE AREA

The Government of Canada and the Government of the United States of America,

RECOGNIZING that they have been unable to resolve by negotiation the differences between them concerning the delimitation of the continental shelf and the fisheries zones of Canada and the United States of America in the Gulf of Maine area,

DESIRING to reach an early and amicable settlement of these differences,

. . . .

Article II

The Chamber is requested to decide, in accordance with the principles and rules of international law applicable in the matter as between the Parties, the following question:

What is the course of the single maritime boundary that divides the continental shelf and fisheries zones of Canada and the United States of America from a point in latitude 44°11'12"N, longitude 67°16'46"W to a point to be determined by the Chamber within an area bounded by straight lines connecting the following sets of geographic coordinates: latitude 40°N, longitude 65°W; latitude 42°N, longitude 65°W?

. . . .

The Parties shall accept as final and binding upon them the decision of the Chamber rendered pursuant to this Article.

Consequences of the Gulf of Maine Arbitration Treaty

A Chamber of the International Court of Justice was subsequently empaneled and proceeded to hear and decide the case. The United States presented a maximilist claim suggesting that the entirety of the Georges Bank fell to the United States as part of its continental shelf while Canada maintained that it was entitled to one-half of the Georges Bank. The underlying issue was the division of the rich fishery that was centered on the Georges Bank, involving about 30,000 nautical square miles of continental shelf.

Ultimately, the International Court of Justice did not accept the case presented by either Canada or the United States. Rather, the Court decided to divide the disputed area between the two countries with the United States receiving approximately two-thirds and Canada receiving the remaining one-third. Of the Georges Bank proper the United States received approximately 75% and Canada received approximately 25% of the bank. However, the Canadian portion was particularly rich in terms of the fishery resources, which balanced out the differences in total area awarded to the two countries by the Court. This was a successful outcome from the Canadian perspective despite the fact that the country received less than its expressed claim.

Machias Island and North Rock

There is one remaining dispute over the location of the southeastern maritime boundary between Canada and the United States.

Machias Island is a small barren island near the boundary of the Gulf of Maine and the Bay of Fundy. The island has no permanent residents but has been continuously occupied by Great Britain, and subsequently by Canada, since 1832, when a lighthouse was first established on the island. Currently, the Canadian Coast Guard maintains the operations of the lighthouse on Machias Island. Canada maintains its assertion of sovereignty over the island as well as neighboring North Rock, which is uninhabited. Neither the island nor the rock has any natural resources although the fishery in the adjacent waters is important.

The United States claims Machias island (and North Rock) based on the language of the Treaty of Paris, 1783, but it has never occupied Machias Island, or attempted to assert sovereignty over it in any material way. Canada claims the island because the Treaty of Paris, 1783, created an exception for islands that were historically part of the colonial province of Nova Scotia, and an ancient land grant is said to support the Canadian position that the island and the rock were historically considered to be part of the colonial province of Nova Scotia.

Pending some ultimate resolution of the sovereignty dispute between Canada and the United States Machias Island and North Rock must be considered as, at a minimum, *de facto* sovereign territory of Canada.

The South-Western Maritime Boundary

The southwestern maritime boundary through the Strait of Juan de Fuca between the province of British Columbia is a settled border. However, the creation of the EEZs for Canada and the United States in this area has resulted in a small area of overlap concerning a total marine area of approximately twenty square miles. The discrepancy results from the creation of different baselines although both countries have adhered to the equidistant principle. The dispute is a relatively minor matter that will probably result in a negotiated solution when political conditions for a settlement are favourable.

The Western Maritime Boundary

There is a long-standing dispute over the western maritime border between Canada and the American state of Alaska. Actually, there are two separate disputes. The first dispute concerns the creation of the western marine border adjacent to the province of British Columbia at the southernmost limits of the state of Alaska. The marine feature described as the Dixon Entrance is the subject of two varying interpretations based on the Arbitral Award in the Alaska Boundary Dispute. In the 1903 award the arbitral panel drew a line from a point A at the northern tip of the Dixon Entrance eastward to a point B which appeared to leave almost the entire Dixon Entrance to Canada. However, the United States maintains that the so-called A-B line was merely meant to define the limits of the terrestrial sovereignties of the United States and Canada, and does not to define a maritime border between Alaska and Canada.

The second dispute involves the interpretation of the Anglo-Russian Convention of 1825 which defined the border between Russian America and British North America. Canada maintains that the language of the treaty which states "dans son prolongation jusqu'à la Mer Glaciale" is inclusive of the ocean and thus the 141st meridian of longitude which is the land border also serves as the maritime border between Alaska and the Yukon Territory. The United States however, disputes the Canadian interpretation and has proposed that the maritime border should be an emanation from the coastline, with the result that the United States claims some portion of the Beaufort Sea that Canada also claims under its interpretation of the 1825 treaty.[3]

The Arctic Archipelago and the Canadian Northwest Passage

In 1985 Canada drew straight baselines around its Arctic Archipelago and enclosed the waters of the archipelago as Internal Waters, prompting protests from the United States and the European Union. Despite that action however, Canada has maintained its position by promulgating regulations concerning the movement of marine traffic within the archipelago, and by and large the international shipping community has conformed to the Canadian requirements.

Nevertheless, an international legal dispute continues to exist over the status of the Northwest Passage. As internal and historic waters Canada asserts the right to prohibit or regulate the innocent passage of ships through the Northwest Passage. Other states however, especially the United States, assert that the Northwest Passage is an international strait and that Canada cannot prohibit transit passage, or innocent overflight, through the strait. The issue is important because a right of transit passage cannot be blocked by a coastal state and many of the restrictions that would otherwise apply to a vessel transiting territorial waters are inapplicable within an international strait. For example, a submarine can remain submerged while exercising the right to a transit passage within an international strait but it would have to surface if it was exercising a right of innocent passage within the Territorial Sea of a coastal state. Renewed interest in the use of the Northwest Passage has occurred as a result of global warming, which later in the twenty-first century may render the Northwest Passage ice-free, and economically viable for use the international shipping industry. The dispute over the status of the Canadian Northwest Passage has existed for many years however, and although it was brought to the fore of public diplomacy by the passage of the American oil tanker *Manhattan* through the Northwest Passage in 1969 without express Canadian permission, it has not, to date, significantly impacted Canadian-American relations.

The legal issue of whether the Northwest Passage constitutes an international strait within international law is a complicated question that is not capable of an easy answer. Different opinions have certainly been expressed by Canadian and American authorities.[4] The dispute largely concerns the two major North American states, as the European states have been relatively mute about the Northwest Passage, and China has not expressed a public opinion on the subject. Russia has a position with respect to the Northern Sea Route across the vast Russian land mass bordering the Arctic Ocean that is close to the Canadian position concerning the Canadian Northwest Passage.

The effects of global warming will have the most pronounced effect on the future usage of the Arctic Ocean both for shipping and for resource exploitation. The key strategic position of the Arctic Ocean has naturally motivated the United States to take cognizance of the area for defence purposes.[5] One writer on the subject implies that the United States Navy has already reserved a descriptive number for its future Arctic Fleet, to be mobilized as global warming trends increasingly open the Arctic Ocean to shipping.[6]

Canada has also sought to increase the military resources available to it in the Arctic Ocean in recent years, including the development of a new military training facility, and marine docks in the Arctic Archipelago, and the construction of ice-reinforced patrol vessels capable of Arctic operations. New capabilities for the monitoring of the Arctic region and the Arctic Ocean have also been created. New regulatory structures have also been implemented to assist the Canadian Coast Guard in the protection of the lives of mariners and passengers, as well as the protection of the environment and the enforcement of Canadian laws. Those efforts have had the effect of bolstering the implementation of Canadian sovereignty within the Arctic Archipelago and its adjacent waters. However some issues of sovereignty remain the high arctic, including the status of the Canadian Northwest Passage, the extent of the prolongation of the continental shelf that Canada may claim in the Arctic Ocean, as well as the settling of the marine boundary between Canada and Greenland.

The Prolongation of the Continental Shelf

Under UNCLOS, a coastal state may claim the part of its continental shelf extending beyond the 200 nautical mile limit of the EEZ belonging to the coastal state if the claim made by the coastal state is approved by the Law of the Sea Tribunal. In order to secure approval from the Tribunal a coastal state must prepare and submit a formal submission describing its claim and supported by evidence of the geomorphological features of the continental shelf that support its claim. In May 2008 the five countries bordering on the Arctic Ocean (United States, Canada, Denmark (Greenland), Norway and Russia met at Ilulissat in Greenland to discuss the process for determining claims for a prolonged continental shelf in the Arctic Ocean. In a declaration to which all of the Arctic Ocean states subscribed each of them professed their intention to follow the principles of international law, and more particularly the process described in Article 76 of the Convention, for the determination of state rights to extended continental shelves.[7]

United Nations Convention on the Law of the Sea, Article 76 (Extract)

December 10, 1982

Article76

Definition of the continental shelf

1. The continental shelf of a coastal State comprises the seabed and subsoil of the submarine areas that extend beyond its territorial sea throughout the natural prolongation of its land territory to the outer edge of the continental margin, or to a distance of 200 nautical miles from the baselines from which the breadth of the territorial sea is measured where the outer edge of the continental margin does not extend up to that distance.

2. The continental shelf of a coastal State shall not extend beyond the limits provided for in paragraphs 4 to 6.

3. The continental margin comprises the submerged prolongation of the land mass of the coastal State, and consists of the seabed and subsoil of the shelf, the slope and the rise. It does not include the deep ocean floor with its oceanic ridges or the subsoil thereof.

4. (a) For the purposes of this Convention, the coastal State shall establish the outer edge of the continental margin wherever the margin extends beyond 200 nautical miles from the baselines from which the breadth of the territorial sea is measured, by either:

(i) a line delineated in accordance with paragraph 7 by reference to the outermost fixed points at each of which the thickness of sedimentary rocks is at least 1 per cent of the shortest distance from such point to the foot of the continental slope; or

(ii) a line delineated in accordance with paragraph 7 by reference to fixed points not more than 60 nautical miles from the foot of the continental slope.

(b) In the absence of evidence to the contrary, the foot of the continental slope shall be determined as the point of maximum change in the gradient at its base.

5. The fixed points comprising the line of the outer limits of the continental shelf on the seabed, drawn in accordance with paragraph 4 (a)(i) and (ii), either shall not exceed 350 nautical miles from the baselines from which the breadth of the territorial sea is measured or shall not exceed 100 nautical miles from the 2,500 metre isobath, which is a line connecting the depth of 2,500 metres.

6. Notwithstanding the provisions of paragraph 5, on submarine ridges, the outer limit of the continental shelf shall not exceed 350 nautical miles from the baselines from which the breadth of the territorial sea is measured. This paragraph does not apply

to submarine elevations that are natural components of the continental margin, such as its plateaux, rises, caps, banks and spurs.

7. The coastal State shall delineate the outer limits of its continental shelf, where that shelf extends beyond 200 nautical miles from the baselines from which the breadth of the territorial sea is measured, by straight lines not exceeding 60 nautical miles in length, connecting fixed points, defined by coordinates of latitude and longitude.

8. Information on the limits of the continental shelf beyond 200 nautical miles from the baselines from which the breadth of the territorial sea is measured shall be submitted by the coastal State to the Commission on the Limits of the Continental Shelf set up under Annex II on the basis of equitable geographical representation. The Commission shall make recommendations to coastal States on matters related to the establishment of the outer limits of their continental shelf. The limits of the shelf established by a coastal State on the basis of these recommendations shall be final and binding.

9. The coastal State shall deposit with the Secretary-General of the United Nations charts and relevant information, including geodetic data, permanently describing the outer limits of its continental shelf. The Secretary-General shall give due publicity thereto.

10. The provisions of this article are without prejudice to the question of delimitation of the continental shelf between States with opposite or adjacent coasts.

Consequences of Article 76 of the United Nations Convention on the Law of the Sea

The Convention has sought to balance the interests of coastal states to the resources of the continental shelf lying offshore from its territory with the interests of the general international community in the resources that are or should be considered to be the common inheritance of all mankind.[8] The coastal states in the Arctic that are signatories to UNCLOS have embarked upon marine surveys to obtain the evidence necessary to support a formal submission by each of them to the Law of the Sea Tribunal. The work has been ongoing for a number of years and has been characterized by a high degree of cooperation amongst the Arctic states. Initial results suggest that there could be overlaps between the claims of various Arctic states and that determining overlapping claims will likely prove difficult and untimely unless the Arctic states exhibit and maintain a high degree of cooperation.[9] Canada's claim to a prolongation of its continental shelf in the Arctic is the most serious territorial sovereignty issue that it faces in the early part of the twenty-first century.

The North-Eastern Maritime Boundary

The North-Eastern Maritime boundary concerns the division of the seabed between Greenland, a territory subject to the sovereignty of the Kingdom of Denmark, and Canada's Nunavut Territory (formerly the Northwest Territories). The matter long remained a dormant issue but became important in the aftermath of the transit of the Northwest Passage by the *Manhattan* in 1969. Afterwards, Canada extended its Territorial Sea from three to twelve nautical miles and that affected the positioning of a median line between Ellesmere Island and Greenland. It therefore became necessary to enter into negotiations with Denmark to fix the marine boundary between the two countries.

The Canada-Denmark Boundary Agreement, 1973

Canada and Denmark entered into a treaty on the division of the seabed between the Arctic Archipelago and Greenland in 1973 using the equidistant principle. The treaty also subsequently became the basis for demarcating the fishery resources in the ocean between the two countries.

The Canada-Denmark Boundary Agreement, 1973 (Extracts)

December 17, 1973

The Government of the Kingdom of Denmark and the Government of Canada,

Having decided to establish in the area between Greenland and the Canadian Arctic Islands a dividing line beyond which neither Party exercising its rights under the Convention on the Continental Shelf of April 29, 1958, will extend its sovereign rights for the purpose of exploration and exploitation of the natural resources of the continental shelf,

Have agreed as follows:

Article I.

The dividing line in the area between Greenland and the Canadian Arctic Islands, established for the purpose of each Party's exploration and exploitation of the natural resources of that part of the continental shelf which in accordance with international law appertains to Denmark and to Canada respectively, is a median line which has been determined and adjusted by mutual agreement.

Article II.

1. In implementation of the principle set forth in article I, the dividing line in the area between latitude 61 00' N and latitude 75 00' N (Davis Strait and Baffin Bay) shall be a series of geodesic lines . . . [that] have been computed from straight baselines along the coast of the Canadian Arctic Islands and of Greenland . . .

2. In "Nares Strait" the dividing line shall be two series of geodesic lines joining . . . points . . . *defined by latitude and longitude on Canadian Hydrographic Service Charts 7071 of July 31, 1964 and 7072 of April 30, 1971.*

3. That portion of the dividing line joining point 113 to point 114 is a geodesic line.

4. For the time being the Parties have not deemed it necessary to draw the dividing line further north than point No. 127 or further south than point No. 1 . . . on the plan attached to this Agreement

Article III.

In view of the inadequacies of existing hydrographic charts for certain areas and failing a precise determination of the low-water line in all sectors along the coast of Greenland and the eastern coasts of the Canadian Arctic Islands, neither Party shall issue licences for exploitation of mineral resources in areas bordering the dividing line without the prior agreement of the other Party as to exact determination of the geographic co-ordinates of points of that part of the dividing line bordering upon the areas in question.

Article IV.

1. The Parties undertake to co-operate and to exchange all relevant data and measurements with a view to obtaining and improving
the hydrographic and geodetic knowledge necessary for more precise charting and mapping of the region covered by this Agreement. When knowledge is obtained enabling the Parties to estimate the datum shift between the 1927 North American Datum and the Qornoq Datum, the geographic coordinates of points listed in article II shall be adjusted and re-listed in relation to both the 1927 North American Datum and the Qornoq Datum.

2. If new surveys or resulting charts or maps should indicate that the dividing line requires adjustment, the Parties agree that an adjustment will be carried out on the basis of the same principles as those used in determining the dividing line, and such adjustment shall be provided for in a Protocol to this Agreement.

Article V.

If any single geological petroleum structure or field, or any single geological structure or field of any other mineral deposit, including sand and gravel, extends across the dividing line and the part of such structure or field which is situated on one side of the dividing line is exploitable, wholly or in part, from the other side of the dividing line, the Parties shall seek to reach an agreement as to the exploitation of such structure or field.

Article VI.

Should international law concerning the delimitation of national jurisdiction over the continental shelf be altered in a manner acceptable to both Parties which could have an effect upon the dividing line in the area between 67 and 69 North latitude, each of the Parties shall waive jurisdiction over any part of the continental shelf which appertains to the other Party on the basis of the new agreed rules of international law concerning the delimitation of national jurisdiction over the continental shelf.

Consequences of the Canada-Denmark Boundary Agreement

The treaty between Canada and Denmark resolved the uncertainty over most of the length of the maritime boundary between the two countries with three exceptions. The first point that remains unresolved concerns the ownership of Hans Island, a small island in the Kennedy Channel, over which both Canada and Denmark have claimed sovereignty. Although former Prime Minister Pierre Trudeau was once famously reported to have said on a European trip that the Danes could have the island, the dispute over the ownership of the tiny island has proved to be intractable. In this treaty Canada and Denmark placed the geodesic lines marking the division of the seabed at the north and south low water marks of the island, thus avoiding any presumed division of sovereignty over Hans Island.

The second area of uncertainty concerns the definition of the oceanic boundary in the Lincoln Sea north of Ellesmere Island and Greenland. At issue in that instance is the use by Denmark of a small island known as Beaumont Island as part of a baseline, which conflicts in two small areas of the Lincoln Sea with a projection by Canada from its own baseline around Ellesmere Island.

A third area of uncertainty concerned the exploitation of mineral resources close to the boundary line in circumstances where very precise locations of the low water line may not be available. In order to avoid any disputes arising concerning the exploitation of mineral resources adjacent to the boundary, both countries agreed to a moratorium on the issuance of exploration licences for areas close to the boundary line in the absence of the consent of the other country.

Otherwise, the 1973 treaty has effectively defined the seabed interests of both Canada and Denmark. The agreement also contemplated that technical differences between the Canadian and Danish geodetic coordinate systems would be resolved in the future.

The Canada-Denmark Boundary Amending Agreement, 2004

In 1982, Canada and Denmark agreed to work together on coordinating the use of the World Geodetic System used by Canada with the Qornoq Datum used by Denmark. The work on this re-computation continued over many years and resulted in the signing of an amending agreement to the 1973 treaty in 2004. That exchange of notes substituted revised geodetic datum in place of the coordinates in the 1973 agreement.

The Canada-Denmark Boundary Amending Agreement, 2004 (Extracts)

April 5/20, 2004

Exchange of Notes Constituting an Agreement to Amend the

Agreement Between the Government of Canada and the Government of the Kingdom of Denmark Relating to the Delimitation of the Continental Shelf Between Greenland and Canada

1.

The Minister of Foreign Affairs of the Kingdom of Denmark to the Counsellor and Consul of Canada

Copenhagen, 5 April 2004

Sir,

I have the honour to refer to the recommendations of Danish and Canadian experts made in April 2003 in their "Report on the Determination of the Boundary between Canada and Greenland in World Geodetic System 1984" and to the Agreement between the Government of the Kingdom of Denmark and the Government of Canada relating to the Delimitation of the Continental Shelf between Greenland and Canada done at Ottawa on 17 December 1973.

I further have the honour to propose that the recommended median line coordinates listed in Enclosure 5 of the above-mentioned Report, attached hereto, shall replace the coordinates in Article II of the 1973 Agreement defining the dividing line between latitude 61° N and latitude 75° N (points No.1 -109), at the same time keeping the "set-back" zone agreed in the Understanding of 17 December 1973 unchanged at a width of two nautical miles on either side of the dividing line.

If the foregoing proposal is acceptable to the Government of Canada, I have the honour to propose that the present Note, with its attachment, and Your Note in reply to that effect shall constitute an agreement between our two Governments, which shall enter into force on the date on which we have notified each other that all necessary internal requirements have been fulfilled.

I avail myself of this opportunity to renew to you, Sir, the assurance of my highest consideration.

Per Stig Møller

2.

The Counsellor and Consul of Canada to the Minister of Foreign Affairs of the Kingdom of Denmark

Copenhagen, April 20, 2004

His Excellency Mr. Per Stig Møller

Minister of Foreign Affairs

Copenghagen, Denmark

Sir:

I have the honour to refer to your Note of April 5, 2004 which reads as follows:

. . . [contents of the Danish Note omitted – see above]

I have the further honour to inform you that the Government of Canada accepts the proposal contained in Your Excellency's note and to confirm that your Note, with its attachment, and this Note in reply, which shall be equally authentic in English and French, shall constitute an agreement between our two Governments, which shall enter into force on the date on which we have notified each other that all necessary internal requirements have been fulfilled.

I avail myself of this opportunity to renew to you, Sir, the assurance of my highest consideration.

Brian Herman

Counsellor and Consul

Consequences of the Canada-Denmark Boundary Amending Agreement

The amending agreement updated the coordinates based on mutually acceptable geodetic data.

Outstanding Boundary Issues With Denmark

The two outstanding oceanic boundary issues that Canada has with Denmark remain the sovereignty over Hans Island, and the determination of the Lincoln Sea boundary. The Lincoln Sea is a body of water lying north of Greenland/Ellesmere Island. Canada and Denmark declined to address the definition of the maritime boundary in the Lincoln Sea when they negotiated the 1973 treaty defining the maritime boundary between Canada and Greenland. Later, Denmark promulgated straight baselines that were based in part on a small island known as Beaumont Island, which Canada has claimed is too far west to form part of a fringe of islands that would support an extended straight baseline at this location. The interaction of the Danish baselines with the Canadian baselines drawn around the Arctic Archipelago created two small disputed areas of the sea to which both countries advanced claims. The dispute involves a total area of approximately 65 square nautical miles. Despite that disagreement, which is based on differing technical positions,[10] both states have adhered to the equidistant principle for the purposes of establishing the maritime boundary in the Lincoln Sea.

Modifications to the Danish baselines in 2004 reduced the scope of the disagreement and thereafter the two countries resolved to deal with their disagreement amicably. In 2012 the Canadian Department of Foreign Affairs announced that the dispute over the Lincoln Sea boundary had been resolved in an *ad referenda* agreement, and that the agreement would subsequently be embodied in an international treaty between Canada and

Denmark. According to the announcement, "The boundary in the Lincoln Sea agreed *ad referendum* by [Danish and Canadian] negotiators is an equidistance line that extends to 200 nautical miles from the coasts of Ellesmere Island and northern Greenland."[11] To date however, no treaty has been signed by the two countries, and thus, in a formal sense, the dispute continues to exist.

The second dispute concerns tiny Hans Island in the Kennedy Channel, which is part of the Nares Strait between Ellesmere Island and Greenland. This tiny uninhabited islet has been the object of a dispute between Canada and Denmark for several decades. While the tiny island was originally discovered by an American exploratory expedition in the nineteenth century, it was subsequently claimed by both Denmark and Canada. The island lies close to the center of the channel although it is slightly closer to Greenland than to Ellesmere Island. The importance of the island revolves around the potential for hydrocarbon resources to exist in the vicinity of the island.[12]

The result of the Hans Island dispute has been a kind of diplomatic opera-bouffe, with alternating visits by personnel from the armed forces of both Canada and Denmark to assert national sovereignty over Hans Island. (Generally, the armed forces of both countries leave behind a good bottle of liquour!) There have also been staged visits by high state representatives, such as a Canadian Minister of National Defence, to reinforce territorial claims. Most Canadians, who are the citizens of the second largest country in the world by total land area, appear to be perplexed that successive Canadian ministries have been unable to resolve this minor irritant with Denmark and Greenland.

The Eastern Maritime Boundary

The Eastern Maritime Boundary consists of the boundary between Canada and France located between the Canadian island of Newfoundland and the French islands of St. Pierre and Miquelon.

The small French islands are the last remaining portion of the historical territory of New France that continued to remain under French sovereignty following the Treaty of Paris, 1763. France previously surrendered its coastal fishing rights in Newfoundland in 1904, in the *Entente Cordiale* with Great Britain. However, at the time of the *Entente Cordiale*, France retained its rights to conduct offshore fishing operations in Newfoundland waters from its St. Pierre and Miquelon territory. Canada inherited Newfoundland and Labrador's obligations after the union of that colony with Canada in 1949. Changing circumstances however, prompted a modernization of fishing rights in the early 1970's, and the two countries took advantage of that process to define the oceanic boundary between their respective sovereign territories.

The Canada-France Fishing Treaty, 1972

The Canada-France Fishing Agreement defined the maritime boundary between Canada and the French overseas territory of St. Pierre and Miquelon.

The Canada-France Fishing Treaty, 1972 (Extracts)

March 27, 1972

The Government of Canada and the Government of France, Having regard to the fact that the Canadian Government has deemed it necessary, notably with a view to ensuring the protection of Canadian fisheries, to adopt certain measures relating to the delimitation of the territorial sea and the fishing zones of Canada, Considering it desirable to adapt to present circumstances their mutual relations in fishery matters,

Have agreed as follows :

Article I

The Government of France renounces the privileges established to its advantage in fishery matters by the Convention signed at

London, on April 8, 1904, between the United Kingdom and France. The present Agreement supersedes all previous treaty provisions relating to fishing by French nationals off the Atlantic coast of Canada.

Article 2

In return, the Canadian Government undertakes in the event of a modification to the juridical regime relating to the waters situated beyond the present limits of the territorial sea and fishing zones of Canada on the Atlantic coast, to recognize the right of French nationals to fish in these waters subject to possible measures for the conservation of resources, including the establishment of quotas. The French Government undertakes for its part to grant reciprocity to Canadian nationals off the coast of Saint-Pierre and Miquelon.

. . . .

Article 8

The line defined in the annex to the present Agreement determines, in the area between Newfoundland and the islands of Saint-Pierre and Miquelon, the limit of the territorial waters of Canada and of the zones submitted to the fishery jurisdiction of France.

Article 9

No provision of the present Agreement shall be interpreted as prejudicing the views and future claims of either Party concerning internal waters, territorial waters or jurisdiction with respect to fisheries or the resources of the continental shelf, or the bilateral or multilateral agreements to which either Government is a party.

Article 10

1. The Contracting Parties shall establish a Commission to

consider all disputes concerning the application of this Agreement.

2. The Commission shall consist of one national expert nominated by each of the Parties for ten years. In -addition, the two Governments shall designate by mutual agreement a third expert who shall not be a national of either Party.

3. If, in connection with any dispute referred to the Commission by either of the Contracting Parties, the Commission has not within one month reached a decision acceptable to the Contracting Parties, reference shall be made to the third expert. The Commission shall then sit as an arbitral tribunal under the chairmanship of the third expert.

4. Decisions of the Commission sitting as an arbitral tribunal shall be taken by a majority, and shall be binding on the Contracting Parties.

. . . .

ANNEX TO THE AGREEMENT BETWEEN CANADA AND FRANCE

The line which determines the limit of the territorial waters of Canada and the zones submitted to the fishery jurisdiction of France extends northward and westward in a series of eight connected straight lines joining the following points:

Point (1) Equidistant 12 nautical miles from L'Enfant Perdu (France) and Lamaline Shag Rock (Canada). Latitude 46° 38' 46" N., Longitude 55° 54' 12" W. approximately.

Point (2) Equidistant from L'Enfant Perdu (France) and Lamaline Shag Rock and Otter Rock (Canada). Latitude 46° 41' 56" N., Longitude 55° 55' 28" W. approximately.

Point (3) Equidistant from L'Enfant Perdu (France) and Otter

Rock and Enfant Perdu (Canada). Latitude 46° 48' 10" N., Longitude 55° 58' 57" W. approximately.

Point (4) The low Vater mark on the south-westernmost point of Enfant Perdu (Canada). Latitude 46° 51' 20" N., Longitude 56° 05' 30" W. approximately.

Point (5) The low water mark on the west point of the south-westernmost island of the Little Green Island group. Latitude 46° 51' 36" N., Longitude 56° 05' 58" W. approximately.

Point (6) The intersection of the French mid-channel line of 1907 with a line parallel to, and 3 miles distant from a line joining Green Island to Dantzig Point, Latitude 46° 55' 52" N., Longitude 56° 07' 47" W. approximately.

Point (7) The intersection of the French mid-channel line of 1907 with the median line, equidistant from Bout du Nordet (France) and Little Plate Island (Canada) Latitude 47° 06' 02" N., Longitude 56° 06' 18" W. approximately.

Point (8) Equidistant from Cap du Nid à l'Aigle (France) and Little Plate Island and the southwest Wolf Rock (Canada). Latitude 47° 18' 19" N., Longitude 56° 15' 18" W. approximately.

Point (9) The intersection of the French mid-channel line of 1907 with the outer limit of Canada's 12-mile territorial Sea. Latitude 47° 21' 54" N., Longitude 56° 29' 40" W. approximately.

Consequences of the Canada-France Fishing Treaty

The Canada-France Fishing Treaty established the international maritime boundary between the island of Newfoundland and the French territory of St. Pierre and Miquelon. However, an outstanding disagreement remained concerning the extent of the EEZ that belonged to the French territory. Canada and France were unable to secure a satisfactory negotiated arrangement with respect to the French EEZ, and therefore the dispute was submitted to international arbitration.

The Canada-France Arbitration Agreement Concerning Delimitation of Maritime Areas, 1989

In 1989 Canada and France established an international arbitration panel to hear and decide the case respecting French claims to an EEZ around the French Overseas Territory of St. Pierre and Miquelon. This was an important issue because the rights of a coastal state to an EEZ confer exclusive fishery rights on the state which possesses an EEZ. Canada and France were far apart on the question of defining the EEZ in relation to their respective territories. The arbitration panel in this instance was an *ad hoc* panel created by the parties, rather than a chamber of the International Court of Justice as was created by Canada and the United States in the Gulf of Maine case.

The Canada-France Arbitration Agreement Concerning Delimitation of Maritime Areas (Extracts)

March 30, 1989

The Government of Canada and the Government of the Republic of France (hereinafter "the Parties");

Considering that by an agreement signed in Ottawa on March 27, 1972 the Parties partially delimited the maritime areas appertaining respectively to Canada and France;

Considering that, in view of the differences between them, the parties have been unable to complete the delimitation;

Considering that the Parties have expressed a common desire to resolve the dispute arising from these differences by submitting it to third-party binding arbitration;

Have agreed as follows:

Article 1

1. A Court of Arbitration (hereinafter "the Court") is hereby established, consisting of five members, namely:

> *a. M. Prosper Weil, appointed by the French Government,*

> *b. M. Allan E. Gotlieb, appointed by [Canada],*

> *c. Mr. Eduardo Jimenez De Arechaga,*

> *d. M. Gaetano Arangio-Juiz,*

> *e. M. Oskar Schachyer.*

The President of the court shall be Mr. Eduardo Jimenez De Arechaga.

2. If a member of the Court appointed by one of the Parties is unable to act, that Party shall name a replacement within a period of one month from the date on which the Court declares the existence of the vacancy.

3. a. If another member of the Court is unable to act, the Parties shall agree on a replacement within a period of two months from the date on which the court declares the existence of the vacancy.

b. In the absence of an agreement within the period mentioned in paragraph a) the Parties shall have recourse to the good offices of the President of the Court or, if the office of the president is vacant, the Secretary General of the United Nations.

Article 2

1. Ruling in accordance with the principles and rules of international law applicable in the matter, the court is requested to carry out the delimitation as between the Parties of the maritime areas appertaining to France and of those appertaining to

Canada. This delimitation shall be effected from point 1 and from point 9 of the delimitation referred to in Article 8 of the Agreement of March 27, 1972 and described in the Annex thereto. The Court shall establish a single delimitation which shall govern all rights and jurisdiction which the Parties may exercise under international law in these maritime areas.

2. The Court shall describe the course of this delimitation in a technically precise manner. To this end, the geometric nature of all the elements of the delimitation shall be indicated and the position of all the points mentioned shall be given by reference to their geographical coordinates in the North America Datum 1972 (NAD 27) geodesic system.

The Court shall also indicate for illustrative purposes only the course of the delimitation on an appropriate chart.

3. After consultation with the Parties, the court shall designate a technical expert to assist it in carrying out the duties specified in paragraph 2 above.

. . . .

Article 9

1. The Court's decision shall be fully reasoned. Each member shall be entitled to attach an individual or dissenting opinion.

2. The Court shall inform the Parties of its decision as soon as practicable.

3. Each Party may make public the text of the award or of any individual or dissenting opinion.

Article 10

1. The decision of the Court shall be final and binding.

2. Each Party may refer to the Court any dispute with the other Party as to the meaning and scope of the decision within three months of its notification.

3. The Court is empowered to correct any material error relating to its decision at the request of either Party, within three months of notification.

Consequences of the Canada-France Arbitration Agreement Concerning Delimitation of Maritime Areas

The arbitral panel held hearings in New York city beginning on July 29, 1991, and its decision, an unexpected and controversial decision, was rendered on June 10, 1992. While maintaining the equidistant principle between St. Pierre and Miquelon and the island of Newfoundland the arbitral tribunal decided that the French EEZ should be extended to the west. Even more controversially the arbitral panel decided to provide France with a southern EEZ corridor of approximately 10.5 nautical miles wide, and extending 188 nautical miles into the Grand Banks. All told, France obtained approximately 18% of its original claim. Nevertheless, the parties had agreed to abide by the decision and thus however irregularly shaped, the decision of the arbitral panel on the shape and extent of the French EEZ for St. Pierre and Miquelon was final.[13]   This decision has been particularly criticized because the extension of the Canadian EEZ would wholly encompass the French EEZ, a circumstance that the arbitral panel seemingly did not intend, or contemplate.

With the completion of the arbitration of the EEZ for St. Pierre and Miquelon in 1992, all of the outstanding sovereignty issues with respect to the eastern maritime boundary of Canada appear to have been resolved.

Atmospheric Boundary of Canada

There is no firmly established boundary in international law to differentiate between the sovereign airspace of a state on the Earth and outer space, over which no state can claim sovereignty. Various demarcation points have been proposed with several having a functional basis for establishing this division. However, none have been widely adopted. Perhaps the most commonly accepted definition is the Kármán line, named for the prominent twentieth century physicist who first proposed it. The Kármán line is 100 km (or 62 miles) above sea level.

Within the atmosphere above its sovereign territory a state may, subject to the principles of international law, and treaties, exercise its full sovereign rights over its national airspace.

ENDNOTES

[1] During the late nineteenth and early twentieth centuries the whaling industry was active in Hudson Bay, which may have prompted the American protest, as American whalers did penetrate Hudson Bay in search of whales to slaughter. However, the commercial whaling industry in Hudson Bay died out prior to World War One and commercial whaling is no longer permitted in any Canadian waters. It appears unlikely that the 1906 American protest would be sufficient to overturn the Canadian claim, given the passage of time without further protests, and the silence of the remainder of the world community, which may be sufficient to establish international acquiescence.

[2] An isobath is an imaginary line on a chart that connects all points having the same depth below the surface of an ocean.

[3] For a discussion of the various arguments see Michael Byers, *International Law and the Arctic*, Cambridge University Press, Cambridge (UK), 2014, pp. 56-91.

[4] For a discussion of the various Canadian arguments see Byers,

International Law and the Arctic, pp. 131-143. For the perspective of an American scholar see James C Kraska, *The Law of the Sea Convention and the Northwest Passage* in *Defence Requirements for Canada's Arctic*, Vimy Paper 2007, Brian MacDonald, ed., The Conference of Defence Associations Institute, Ottawa, 2007, pp. 36-59.

[5] For a recent perspective on the US strategic interest in the Arctic Ocean see Admiral (ret.) James Stavridis, *Sea Power, The History and Geoplitics of the World's Oceans*, Penguin Press, New York, 2017, pp. 237-267.

[6] Ibid, p. 332

[7] Byers, *International Law*, p. 93; Richard Sale and Eugene Potapov, *The Scramble for the Arctic, Ownership, Exploitation and Conflict in the Far North*, Frances Lincoln Ltd, London, 2010, p. 196

[8] Byers, *International Law*, p. 101.

[9] Byers, *International Law*, p. 127

[10] The substance of the dispute is discussed in Byers, *International Law*, pp. 46-54.

[11]https://www.canada.ca/en/news/archive/2012/11/canada-kingdom-denmark-reach-tentative-agreement-lincoln-sea-boundary.html [accessed May 15, 2018]

[12] Grant, *Polar Imperative*, p. 456

[13] It is perhaps interesting to note that the two panel members from Canada and France dissented from the decision, which was a 3-2 majority decision.

9.

CANADA-UNITED STATES BORDER MANAGEMENT TREATIES

Introduction

Canada and the United States of America share the longest international border on the planet. More than a century ago both countries acknowledged that an effective, marked boundary must be maintained and for that purpose they appointed commissioners to mark the boundaries between the two countries. The initial impetus for boundary demarcation was agreed-to in a 1908 treaty but over time the value of a permanent boundary commission became apparent to both countries and, in 1925, the boundary commission was made permanent.

Today, the International Boundary Commission is jointly administered by both countries and is charged with the task of maintaining the terrestrial and maritime boundaries between Canada and the United States. The activities of the Commission include inspections of the boundary monuments and the performance of any necessary maintenance on the monuments, as well as the installation of additional monuments, including more elaborate or decorated monuments at important border crossing points. The Commission also maintains a clear vista on both sides of the boundary through forested areas, conducts additional surveying to enhance the precision of the boundary location, files reports with governments, and communicates with the public in both countries.

The Commission is headed by two commissioners, one appointed by Canada, and one appointed by the United States. They are assisted by a staff that is drawn from both countries by their respective commissioners.

The Treaty to Demarcate the International Boundary between the United States and Canada, 1908 (Extracts)

April 11, 1908

The High Contracting Parties agree that each shall appoint, without delay, an expert geographer or surveyor to serve as Commissioners for the purpose of more accurately defining and marking the international. boundary line between the United States and the Dominion of Canada ....

ARTICLE IX.

The Commissioners appointed under the provisions of this Treaty shall proceed without delay to perform the duties assigned to them, but each Commissioner shall, before entering upon his duties, make oath in writing that he will impartially and faithfully perform his duties as such Commissioner. In case a vacancy occurs in any of the Commissions constituted by this Treaty, by reason of the death, resignation, or other disability of a Commissioner, before the work of such Commission is completed, the vacancy so caused shall be filled forthwith by the appointment of another Commissioner by the party on whose side the vacancy occurs, and the Commissioner so appointed shall have the same powers and be subject to the same duties and obligations as the Commissioner originally appointed.

If a dispute or difference should arise about the location or demarcation of any portion of the boundary covered by the provisions of this Treaty and an agreement with respect thereto is not reached by the Commissioners charged herein with locating and marking such portion of the line, they shall make a report in writing jointly to both Governments, or severally each to his own Government, setting out fully the questions in dispute and the differences between them, but such Commissioners shall, nevertheless, proceed to carry on and complete as far as possible the work herein assigned to them with respect to the remaining portions of the line.

In case of such a disagreement between the Commissioners, the two Governments shall endeavor to agree upon an adjustment of the questions in dispute, and if an agreement is reached between the two Governments it shall be reduced to writing in the forum of a protocol, and shall be communicated to the said Commissioners, who shall proceed to lay down and mark the boundary in accordance therewith, and as herein provided, but without prejudice to the special provisions contained in Articles I and 11 regarding arbitration.

It is understood that under the foregoing articles the same persons will be appointed to carry out the delimitation of boundaries in the several sections aforesaid, other than the section covered by Article IV, unless either of the Contracting Powers finds it expedient for some reason which it may think sufficient to appoint some other person to be Commissioner for any one of the above-mentioned sections.

Each Government shall pay the expenses of its own Commissioners and their assistants, and the cost of marking and monumenting the boundary shall be paid in equal moieties by the two Governments.

Subsequently, Canada and the United States perceived the need for certain technical adjustments to the international boundary between them and undertook to make a new treaty to implement improvements to border management. In light of the clear value of the services provided by the boundary commissioners, the governments of Canada and the United States also moved to make the International Boundary Commission a permanent organization for the joint management of border issues.

The Treaty Between Canada and the United States of America to define more accurately and to complete the International Boundary between the two Countries

February 24, 1925

The United States of America and His Majesty the King of the United Kingdom of Great Britain and Ireland and of the British Dominions beyond the Seas, Emperor of India, in respect of the Dominion of Canada, desiring to define more accurately at certain points and to complete the international boundary between the United States and Canada and to maintain the demarcation of that boundary, have resolved to conclude a treaty for these purposes, and to that end have appointed as their respective plenipotentiaries:

The President of the United States of America: Charles Evans Hughes, Secretary of State of the United States; and

His Britannic Majesty, in respect of the Dominion of Canada: The Honourable Ernest Lapointe, K.C., a member of His Majesty's Privy Council for Canada and Minister of Justice in the Government of that Dominion;

Who, after having communicated to each other their respective full powers, which were found to be in due and proper form, have agreed to and concluded the following articles:

Article I

Whereas Article V of the Treaty concerning the boundary between the Dominion of Canada and the United States concluded on April 11, 1908, between Great Britain and the United States, provided for the survey and demarcation of the international boundary line between the Dominion of Canada and the United States from the mouth of Pigeon River, at the western shore of Lake Superior, to the north-westernmost point of Lake of the Woods, as defined by the treaties concluded between Great Britain and the United States on September 3, 1783, and August 9, 1842;

And whereas Article VI of the said Treaty concluded on April 11, 1908, provided for the relocation and repair of lost or damaged monuments and for the establishment of additional monuments and boundary marks along the course of the international boundary between the Dominion of Canada and the United States from the north-westernmost point of Lake of the Woods to the summit of the Rocky Mountains, as established under existing treaties and surveyed, charted, and monumented by the Joint Commission appointed for that purpose by joint action of the Contracting Parties in 1872;

And whereas it has been found by surveys executed under the direction of the Commissioners appointed pursuant to the said Treaty of April 11, 1908, that the boundary line between the Dominion of Canada and the United States from the mouth of Pigeon River, at the western shore of Lake Superior, to the north-westernmost point of Lake of the Woods as defined by the treaties concluded on September 3, 1783, and August 9, 1842, is intersected by the boundary from the north-westernmost point of Lake, of the Woods to the summit of the Rocky Mountains as established under existing treaties and surveyed, charted, and monumented by the Joint Commission appointed for that purpose in 1872, at five points in Lake of the Woods adjacent to and directly south of the said north-westernmost point, and that there are two small areas of United States waters in Lake of the Woods, comprising a total area of two and one-half acres, entirely surrounded by Canadian waters;

And whereas no permanent monuments were ever erected on these boundary lines north of the most southerly of these points of intersection;

The Contracting Parties, in order to provide for a more practical definition of the boundary between the Dominion of Canada and the United States in Lake of the Woods, hereby agree that this most southerly point of intersection, being in latitude 49° 23' 04".49 north and longitude 95° 09' 11".61 west, shall be the terminus of the boundary line heretofore referred to as the international boundary line between the Dominion of Canada and the United States from the mouth of Pigeon River, at the western shore of Lake Superior, to the north-westernmost point of Lake of the Woods and the initial point of the boundary line heretofore referred to as the international boundary between the Dominion of Canada and the United States from the north-westernmost point of Lake of the Woods to the summit of the Rocky Mountains, in lieu of the said north-westernmost point.

The aforesaid most southerly point shall be located and monumented by the Commissioners appointed under the said Treaty of April 11, 1908, and shall be marked by them on the chart or charts prepared in accordance with the provisions of Articles V and VI of the said Treaty, and a detailed account of the work done by the Commissioners in locating said point, together with a description of the character and location of the several monuments erected, shall be included in the, report or reports prepared pursuant to the said Articles.

The point so defined and monumented shall be taken and deemed to be the terminus of the boundary line heretofore referred to as the international boundary line between the Dominion of Canada and the United States, from the mouth of Pigeon River, at the western shore of Lake Superior, to the north-westernmost point of Lake of the Woods and the initial point of the boundary line heretofore referred to as the international boundary between the Dominion of Canada and the United States from the north-westernmost point of Lake of the Woods to the summit of the Rocky Mountains.

Article II

Whereas Article VI of the Treaty concerning the boundary between the Dominion of Canada and the United States concluded on April

11, 1908, between Great Britain and the United States provided for the relocation and repair of lost or damaged monuments and for the establishment of additional monuments and boundary marks along the courses of the international boundary between the Dominion of Canada and the United States from the north-westernmost point of Lake of the Woods south to the 49th parallel of north latitude and thence westward along said parallel of latitude to the summit of the Rocky Mountains, as established under existing treaties and surveyed, charted, and monumented by the Joint Commission appointed for that purpose by joint action of the Contracting Parties in 1872;

And whereas Article VI of the said Treaty concluded on April 11, 1908, further provides that in carrying out the provisions of that article the agreement stated in the protocol of the final meeting of the said Joint Commission, dated May 29, 1876, should be observed, by which protocol it was agreed that in the intervals between the monuments along the 49th parallel of north latitude the boundary line has the curvature of a parallel of 49° north latitude;

And whereas the Commissioners appointed and acting under the provisions of Article VI of the said Treaty of 1908 have marked the boundary line wherever necessary in the intervals between the original monuments established by the said Joint Commission, appointed in 1872, in accordance with the agreement stated in the Protocol of the final meeting, dated May 29, 1876, of the Joint Commission aforesaid, and as set forth in Article VI of the Treaty of 1908, by placing intermediate monuments on lines joining the original monuments, which have in each case the curvature of a parallel of 49° north latitude;

And whereas the average distance between adjacent monuments as thus established or re-established along the 49th parallel of north latitude from Lake of the Woods to the summit of the Rocky Mountains by the Commissioners acting under Article VI of the Treaty of 1908 is one and one-third miles and therefore the deviation of the curve of the 49th parallel from a straight or right line joining adjacent monuments is, for this average distance between monuments, only one-third of a foot, and in no case does the actual deviation exceed one and eight-tenths feet;

And whereas it is impracticable to determine the course of a line having the curvature of a parallel of 49° north latitude on the ground between the adjacent monuments which have been established or re-established by the Commissioners and the demarcation of the boundary would be more thoroughly effective if the line between adjacent monuments be defined as a straight or right line; And whereas it is desirable that the boundary at any point between adjacent monuments may be conveniently ascertainable on the ground, the Contracting Parties, in order to complete and render thoroughly effective the demarcation of the boundary between the Dominion of Canada and the United States from the north-westernmost point of Lake of the Woods to the summit of the Rocky Mountains, hereby agree that the line heretofore referred to as the international boundary between the Dominion of Canada and the United States from the north-westernmost point of Lake of the Woods to the summit of the Rocky Mountains shall be defined as consisting of a series of right or straight lines joining adjacent monuments as now established or re-established and as now laid down on charts by the Commissioners acting under Article VI of the Treaty of 1908, in lieu of the definition set forth in the agreement of the aforesaid Joint Commissioners, dated May 29, 1876, and quoted in Article VI of the said Treaty of 1908, that in the intervals between the monuments the line has the curvature of the parallel of 49° north latitude.

Article III

Whereas the Treaty concluded on May 21, 1910, between Great Britain and the United States, defined the international boundary line between the Dominion of Canada and the United States from a point in Passamaquoddy Bay lying between Treat Island and

Friar Head to the middle of Grand Manan Channel and provided that the location of the line so defined should be laid down and marked by the Commissioners appointed under the Treaty of April 11, 1908.

And whereas it has been found by the surveys executed pursuant to the said Treaty of May 21, 1910, that the terminus of the boundary line defined by said Treaty at the middle of Grand Manan Channel is less than three nautical miles distant both from the shore line of Grand Manan Island in the Dominion of Canada and from the shore line of the State of Maine in the United States, and that there is a small zone of waters of controvertible jurisdiction in Grand Manan Channel between said terminus and the High Seas;

The Contracting Parties, in order completely to define the boundary line between the Dominion of Canada and the United States in the Grand Manan Channel, hereby agree that an additional course shall be extended from the terminus of the boundary line defined by the said Treaty of May 21, 1910, south 34° 42' west, for a distance of two thousand three hundred eighty-three (2,383) metres, through the middle of Grand Manan Channel, to the High Seas.

The course so defined shall be located and marked by the Commissioners appointed under the Treaty of April 11, 1908, and shall be laid down by them on the chart or charts adopted in accordance with the provisions of Article I of the said Treaty, and a detailed account of the work done by the Commissioners in locating and marking said line, together with a description of the Several monuments erected, shall be included in the report or reports prepared pursuant to Article I of the Treaty of April 11, 1908.

The course so defined and laid down shall be taken and deemed to be the boundary line between the Dominion of Canada and the United States in Grand Manan Channel from the terminus of the boundary line as defined by the Treaty of May 21, 1910, to the High Seas.

Article IV

Whereas, pursuant to existing treaties between Great Britain and the United States, a survey and effective demarcation of the boundary line between the Dominion of Canada and the United States through the Great Lakes and the St. Lawrence River and through the Straits of Georgia, Haro, and Juan de Fuca from the 49th parallel to the Pacific Ocean and between the Dominion of Canada and Alaska from the Arctic Ocean to Mount St. Elias have been made and the signed joint maps and reports in respect thereto have been filed with the two Governments;

And whereas a survey and effective demarcation of the boundary line between the Dominion of Canada and the United States from the Gulf of Georgia to Lake Superior and from the St. Lawrence River to the Atlantic Ocean and between the Dominion of Canada and Alaska from Mount St. Elias to Cape Muzon are nearing completion;

And whereas boundary monuments deteriorate and at times are destroyed or damaged; and boundary vistas become closed by the growth of timber;

And whereas changing conditions require from time to time that the boundary be marked more precisely and plainly by the establishment of additional monuments or the relocation of existing monuments;

The Contracting Parties, in order to provide for the maintenance of an effective boundary line between the Dominion of Canada and the United States and between the Dominion of Canada and Alaska, as established or to be established, and for the determination of the location of any point thereof, which may become necessary in the settlement of any question that may arise between the two Governments, hereby agree that the

Commissioners appointed under the provisions of the Treaty of April 11, 1908, are hereby jointly empowered and directed: to inspect the various sections of the boundary line between the Dominion of Canada and the United States and between the Dominion of Canada and Alaska at such times as they shall deem necessary; to repair all damaged monuments and buoys; to relocate and rebuild monument's which have been destroyed; to keep the boundary vistas open; to move boundary monuments to new sites and establish such additional monuments and buoys as they shall deem desirable; to maintain at all times an effective boundary line between the Dominion of Canada and the United States and between the Dominion of Canada and Alaska, as defined by the present treaty and treaties heretofore concluded, or hereafter to be concluded; and to determine the location of any point of the boundary line which may become necessary in the settlement of any question that may arise between the two Governments.

The said Commissioners shall submit to their respective Governments from time to time, at least once in every calendar year, a joint report containing a statement of the inspections made, the monuments and buoys repaired, relocated, rebuilt, moved, and established, and the mileage and location of vistas opened, and shall submit with their reports, plats and tables certified and signed by the Commissioners, giving the locations and geodetic positions of all monuments moved and all additional monuments established within the year, and such other information as may be necessary to keep the boundary maps and records accurately revised.

After the completion of the survey and demarcation of the boundary line between the Dominion of Canada and the United States from the Gulf of Georgia to Lake Superior and from the St. Lawrence River to the Atlantic Ocean, as provided for by the Treaty of April 11, 1908, the Commissioners appointed under the provisions of that Treaty shall continue to carry out the provisions of this Article, and, upon the death, resignation, or other disability of either of them, the Party on whose side the vacancy occurs shall appoint an Expert Geographer or Surveyor as Commissioner, who shall have the same powers and duties in respect to carrying out the provisions of this Article, as are conferred by this Article upon the Commissioner appointed under the provisions of the said Treaty of 1908.

The Contracting Parties further agree that each Government shall pay the salaries and expenses of its own commissioner and his assistants, and that the expenses jointly incurred by the Commissioners in maintaining the demarcation of the boundary line in accordance with the provisions of this Article shall be borne equally by the two Governments.

Article V

This treaty shall be ratified by the Contracting Parties and the ratifications shall be exchanged in Ottawa or Washington as soon as practicable. The treaty shall take effect on the date of the exchange of ratifications.

Upon the expiration of six years from the date of the exchange of ratifications of the present treaty, or any time thereafter, Article IV may be terminated upon twelve months' written notice given by either Contracting Party to the other, and following such termination the Commissioners therein mentioned and their successors shall cease to perform the functions thereby prescribed.

In faith whereof, the respective Plenipotentiaries have signed this treaty in duplicate and have hereunto affixed their seals.

Done at Washington the 24th day of February, A.D. 1925.

(L.S.) ERNEST LAPOINTE.

(L.S.) CHARLES EVANS HUGHES.

Consequences of the 1908 and 1925 Boundary Treaties

The main consequence of both of the treaties was to ensure the permanent demarcation of the international boundary line. Permanently maintained demarcation ensures that the longest boundary between two countries in the world is properly maintained, and provides certainty to the federal, provincial, state, and local authorities concerning the extent and scope of their national jurisdictions. The International Border Commission established by these treaties provides a model for other countries with respect to joint border management.

The treaty also dealt with three technical issues arising from boundary demarcation. Firstly, it was determined that in the Lake of the Woods two small water territories of approximately two-and-one-half acres in total within the lake was within United States territory but was completely surrounded by Canadian territory. In order to avoid this outcome, the United States freely gifted the water territories to Canada under Article 1 of the treaty.

Secondly, new monuments were added on the boundary line under the treaty of 1908, between the monuments set in 1872 in respect of that portion of the boundary between the Lake of the Woods and the Rocky Mountains but it was considered to be "impracticable to determine the course of a line having the curvature of a parallel of 49° north latitude on the ground between the adjacent monuments which have been established or reestablished by the Commissioners and the demarcation of the boundary would be more thoroughly effective if the line between adjacent monuments be defined as a straight or right line". Therefore, the parties to the treaty agreed that straight lines would be used between monuments in lieu of the formula that was provided for in 1872, which had also been followed in 1908.

Lastly, the treaty provided for a further demarcation effort in Passamaquoddy Bay on the east coast to avoid the possibility of a controversy over the international boundary within the Grand Manan Channel.

The International Joint Commission

Early in the twentieth century Canada and the United States also foresaw that the activities undertaken by one or the other country in proximity to the international boundary could have deleterious effects on the environment, particularly in relation to the waters that connected the two countries. In order to forestall such deleterious impacts from negatively affecting their cordial relationship the two countries agreed that an international commission ought to be established to study the impacts on water quality of developments in both countries and to report to the two governments on measures to protect the shared water boundary between Canada and the United States. Subsequently, the mandate was extended to encompass trans-border air quality issues as well. This Commission, known as the International Joint Commission, concerns itself with water flows and water levels that cross the border, and the air quality in the air-shed that connects both countries.

Each country appoints three commissioners to the International Joint Commission and the commissioners are served by an expert staff that is drawn from both countries.

The Boundary Waters Treaty, 1909

January 11, 1909

PRELIMINARY ARTICLE

For the purpose of this treaty boundary waters are defined as the waters from main shore to main shore of the lakes and rivers and connecting waterways, or the portions thereof, along which the international boundary between the United States and the Dominion of Canada passes, including all bays, arms, and inlets thereof, but not including tributary waters which in their natural channels would flow into such lakes, rivers, and waterways, or waters flowing from such lakes, rivers, and waterways, or the waters of rivers flowing across the boundary.

ARTICLE I

The High Contracting Parties agree that the navigation of all navigable boundary waters shall forever continue free and open for the purposes of commerce to the inhabitants and to the ships, vessels, and boats of both countries equally, subject, however, to any laws and regulations of either country, within its own territory, not inconsistent with such privilege of free navigation and applying equally and without discrimination to the inhabitants, ships, vessels, and boats of both countries.

It is further agreed that so long as this treaty shall remain in force, this same right of navigation shall extend to the waters of Lake Michigan and to all canals connecting boundary waters, and now existing or which may hereafter be constructed on either side of the line. Either of the High Contracting Parties may adopt rules and regulations governing the use of such canals within its own territory and may charge tolls for the use thereof, but all such rules and regulations and all tolls charged shall apply alike to the subjects or citizens of the High Contracting Parties and the ships, vessels, and boats of both of the High Contracting Parties, and they shall be placed on terms of equality in the use thereof.

ARTICLE II

Each of the High Contracting Parties reserves to itself or to the several State Governments on the one side and the Dominion or Provincial Governments on the other as the case may be, subject to any treaty provisions now existing with respect thereto, the exclusive jurisdiction and control over the use and diversion, whether temporary or permanent, of all waters on its own side of the line which in their natural channels would flow across the boundary or into boundary waters; but it is agreed that any interference with or diversion from their natural channel of such waters on either side of the boundary, resulting in any injury on the other side of the boundary, shall give rise to the same rights and entitle the injured parties to the same legal remedies as if *such injury took place in the country where such diversion or interference occurs; but this provision shall not apply to cases already existing or to cases expressly covered by special agreement between the parties hereto. It is understood however, that neither of the High Contracting Parties intends by the foregoing provision to surrender any right, which it may have, to object to any interference with or diversions of waters on the other side of the boundary the effect of which would be productive of material injury to the navigation interests on its own side of the boundary.*

ARTICLE III

It is agreed that, in addition to the uses, obstructions, and diversions heretofore permitted or hereafter provided for by special agreement between the Parties hereto, no further or other uses or obstructions or diversions, whether temporary or permanent, of boundary waters on either side of the line, affecting the natural level or flow of boundary waters on the other side of the line shall be made except by authority of the United States or the Dominion of Canada within their respective jurisdictions and with the approval, as hereinafter provided, of a joint commission, to be known as the International Joint Commission.

The foregoing provisions are not intended to limit or interfere with the existing rights of the Government of the United States on the one side and the Government of the Dominion of Canada on the other, to undertake and carry on governmental works in boundary waters for the deepening of channels, the construction of breakwaters, the improvement of harbours, and other governmental works for the benefit of commerce and navigation, provided that such works are wholly on its own side of the line and do not materially affect the level or flow of the boundary waters on the other, nor are such provisions intended to interfere with the ordinary use of such waters for domestic and sanitary purposes.

ARTICLE IV

The High Contracting Parties agree that, except in cases provided for by special agreement between them, they will not permit the construction or maintenance on their respective sides of the boundary of any remedial or protective works or any dams or other obstructions in waters flowing from boundary waters or in waters at a lower level than the boundary in rivers flowing across the boundary, the effect of which is to raise the natural level of waters on the other side of the boundary unless the construction or maintenance thereof is approved by the aforesaid International Joint Commission.

It is further agreed that the waters herein defined as boundary waters and waters flowing across the boundary shall not be polluted on either side to the injury of health or property on the other.

ARTICLE V

The High Contracting Parties agree that it is expedient to limit the diversion of waters from the Niagara River so that the level of Lake Erie and the flow of the stream shall not be appreciably affected. It is the desire of both Parties to accomplish this object with the least possible injury to investments which have already been made in the construction of power plants on the United States side of the river under grants of authority from State of New York, and on the Canadian side of the river under licences authorized by the Dominion of Canada and the Province of Ontario.

So long as this treaty shall remain in force, no diversion of the waters of the Niagara River above the Falls from the natural course and stream thereof shall be permitted except for the purposes and to the extent hereinafter provided.

. . . .

ARTICLE VI

The High Contracting Parties agree that the St. Mary and Milk

Rivers and their tributaries (in the State of Montana and the Provinces of Alberta and Saskatchewan) are to be treated as one stream for the purposes of irrigation and power, and the waters thereof shall be apportioned equally between the two countries, but in making such equal apportionment more than half may be taken from one river and less than half from the other by either country so as to afford a more beneficial use to each. It is further agreed that in the division of such waters during the irrigation season, between the 1st of April and 31st of October, inclusive, annually, the United States is entitled to a prior appropriation of 500 cubic feet per second of the waters of the Milk River, or so much of such amount as constitutes three-fourths of its natural flow, and that Canada is entitled to a prior appropriation of 500 cubic feet per second of the flow of St. Mary River, or so much of such amount as constitutes three-fourths of its natural flow.

The channel of the Milk River in Canada may be used at the convenience of the United States for the conveyance, while passing through Canadian territory, of waters diverted from the St. Mary River. The provisions of Article II of this treaty shall apply to any injury resulting to property in Canada from the conveyance of such waters through the Milk River.

The measurement and apportionment of the water to be used by each country shall from time to time be made jointly by the properly constituted reclamation officers of the United States and the properly constituted irrigation officers of His Majesty under the direction of the International Joint Commission.

ARTICLE VII

The High Contracting Parties agree to establish and maintain an International Joint Commission of the United States and Canada composed of six commissioners, three on the part of the United States appointed by the President thereof, and three on the part of the United Kingdom appointed by His Majesty on the recommendation of the Governor in Council of the Dominion of Canada.

ARTICLE VIII

This International Joint Commission shall have jurisdiction over and shall pass upon all cases involving the use or obstruction or diversion of the waters with respect to which under Article III or IV of this Treaty the approval shall be governed by the following rules and principles which are adopted by the High Contracting Parties for this purpose:

The High Contracting Parties shall have, each on its own side of the boundary, equal and similar rights in the use of the waters hereinbefore defined as boundary waters.

The following order of precedence shall be observed among the various uses enumerated hereinafter for these waters, and no use shall be permitted which tends materially to conflict with or restrain any other use which is given preference over it in this order of precedence:

1. Uses for domestic and sanitary purposes;

2. Uses for navigation, including the service of canals for the purposes of navigation;

3. Uses for power and for irrigation purposes.

The foregoing provisions shall not apply to or disturb any existing uses of boundary waters on either side of the boundary. The requirement for an equal division may in the discretion of the Commission be suspended in cases of temporary diversions along boundary waters at points where such equal division can not be made advantageously on account of local conditions, and where such diversion does not diminish elsewhere the amount available for use on the other side.

The Commission in its discretion may make its approval in any case conditional upon the construction of remedial or protective works to compensate so far as possible for the particular use or diversion proposed, and in such cases may require that suitable and adequate provision, approved by the Commission, be made for the protection and indemnity against injury of all interests on the other side of the boundary.

In cases involving the elevation of the natural level of waters on either side of the line as a result of the construction or maintenance on the other side of remedial or protective works or dams or other obstructions in boundary waters or in waters flowing therefrom or in waters below the boundary in rivers flowing across the boundary, the Commission shall require, as a condition of its approval thereof, that suitable and adequate provision, approved by it, be made for the protection and indemnity of all interests on the other side of the line which may be injured thereby.

The majority of the Commissioners shall have power to render a decision. In case the Commission is evenly divided upon any question or matter presented to it for decision, separate reports shall be made by the Commissioners on each side to their own Government. The High Contracting Parties shall thereupon endeavour to agree upon an adjustment of the question or matter of difference, and if an agreement is reached between them, it shall be reduced to writing in the form of a protocol, and shall be communicated to the Commissioners, who shall take such further proceedings as may be necessary to carry out such agreement.

ARTICLE IX

The High Contracting Parties further agree that any other questions or matters of difference arising between them involving the rights, obligations, or interests of either in relation to the other or to the inhabitants of the other, along the common frontier between the United States and the Dominion of Canada, shall be referred from time to time to the International Joint Commission for examination and report, whenever either the Government of the United States or the Government of the Dominion of Canada shall request that such questions or matters of difference be so referred.

The International Joint Commission is authorized in each case so referred to examine into and report upon the facts and circumstances of the particular questions and matters referred, together with such conclusions and recommendations as may be appropriate, subject, however, to any restrictions or exceptions which may be imposed with respect thereto by the terms of the reference.

Such reports of the Commission shall not be regarded as decisions of the questions or matters so submitted either on the facts or the law, and shall in no way have the character of an arbitral award.

The Commission shall make a joint report to both Governments in all cases in which all or a majority of the Commissioners agree, and in case of disagreement the minority may make a joint report to both Governments, or separate reports to their respective Governments.

In case the Commission is evenly divided upon any question or matter referred to it for report, separate reports shall be made by the Commissioners on each side to their own Government.

ARTICLE X

Any questions or matters of difference arising between the High Contracting Parties involving the rights, obligations, or interests of the United States or of the Dominion of Canada either in relation to each other or to their respective inhabitants, may be referred for decision to the International Joint Commission by the consent of the two Parties, it being understood that on the part of the United States any such action will be by and with the advice and consent of the Senate, and on the part of His Majesty's Government with the consent of the Governor General in Council.

In each case so referred, the said Commission is authorized to examine into and report upon the facts and circumstances of the particular questions and matters referred, together with such conclusions and recommendations as may be appropriate, subject, however, to any restrictions or exceptions which may be imposed with respect thereto by the terms of the reference.

A majority of the said Commission shall have power to render a decision or finding upon any of the questions or matters so referred.

If the said Commission is equally divided or otherwise unable to render a decision or finding as to any questions or matters so referred, it shall be the duty of the Commissioners to make a joint report to both Governments, or separate reports to their respective Governments, showing the different conclusions arrived at with regard to the matters or questions referred, which questions or matters shall thereupon be referred for decision by the High Contracting Parties to an umpire chosen in accordance with the procedure prescribed in the fourth, fifth and sixth paragraphs of Article XLV of the Hague Convention for the pacific settlement of international disputes, dated October 18, 1907. Such umpire shall have power to render a final decision with respect to those matters and questions so referred on which the Commission fail to agree.

ARTICLE XI

A duplicate original of all decisions rendered and joint reports made by the Commission shall be transmitted to and filed with the Secretary of State of the United States and the Governor General of the Dominion of Canada, and to them shall be addressed all communications of the Commission.

ARTICLE XII

The International Joint Commission shall meet and organize at Washington promptly after the members thereof are appointed, and when organized the Commission may fix such times and places for its meetings as may be necessary, subject at all times to special call or direction by the two Governments. Each Commissioner upon the first joint meeting of the Commission after his appointment, shall, before proceeding with the work of the Commission, make and subscribe a solemn declaration in writing that he will faithfully and impartially perform the duties imposed upon him under this treaty, and such declaration shall be entered on the records of the proceedings of the Commission.

The United States and Canadian sections of the Commission may each appoint a secretary, and these shall act as joint secretaries of the Commission at its joint sessions, and the Commission may employ engineers and clerical assistants from time to time as it may deem advisable. The salaries and personal expenses of the Commission and of the secretaries shall be paid by their respective Governments, and all reasonable and necessary joint expenses of the Commission, incurred by it, shall be paid in equal moieties by the High Contracting Parties.

The Commission shall have power to administer oaths to witnesses, and to take evidence on oath whenever deemed necessary in any proceeding, or inquiry, or matter within its jurisdiction under this treaty, and all parties interested therein shall be given convenient opportunity to be heard, and the High Contracting Parties agree to adopt such legislation as may be appropriate and necessary to give the Commission the powers above mentioned on each side of the boundary, and to provide for the issue of subpoenas and for compelling the attendance of witnesses in proceedings before the Commission. The Commission may adopt such rules of procedure as shall be in accordance with justice and equity, and may make such examination in person and through agents or employees as may be deemed advisable.

ARTICLE XIII

In all cases where special agreements between the High Contracting Parties hereto are referred to in the foregoing articles, such agreements are understood and intended to include not only direct agreements between the High Contracting Parties, but also any mutual arrangement between the United States and the Dominion of Canada expressed by concurrent or reciprocal legislation on the part of Congress and the Parliament of the Dominion.

ARTICLE XIV

The present treaty shall be ratified by the President of the United States of America, by and with the advice and consent of the Senate, thereof, and by His Britannic Majesty. The ratifications shall be exchanged at Washington as soon as possible and the treaty shall take effect on the date of the exchange of its ratifications. It shall remain in force for five years, dating from the day of exchange of ratifications, and thereafter until terminated by twelve months' written notice given by either High Contracting Party to the other.

In faith whereof the respective plenipotentiaries have signed this treaty in duplicate and have hereunto affixed their seals.

Done at Washington the 11th day of January, in the year of our Lord one thousand nine hundred and nine.

(Signed) ELIHU ROOT [SEAL]

(Signed) JAMES BRYCE [SEAL]

And WHEREAS the Senate of the United States by their resolution of March 3, 1909, (two-thirds of the Senators present concurring therein) did advise and consent to the ratification of the said Treaty with the following understanding to wit:

Resolved further, (as a part of this ratification), that the United States approves this treaty with the understanding that nothing in this treaty shall be construed as affecting, or changing, any existing territorial or riparian rights in the water, or rights of the owners of lands under, on either side of the international boundary at the rapids of the St. Mary's river at Sault Ste. Marie, in the use of water flowing over such lands, subject to the requirements of navigation in boundary waters and of navigation canals, and without prejudice to the existing right of the United States and Canada, each to use the waters of the St. Mary's river, within its own territory, and further, that nothing in the treaty shall be construed to interfere with the drainage of wet swamp and overflowed lands into streams flowing into boundary waters, and that this interpretation will be mentioned in the ratification of this treaty as conveying the true meaning of the treaty, and will, in effect, form part of the treaty;

AND WHEREAS the said understanding has been accepted by the Government of Great Britain, and the ratifications of the two Governments of the said Treaty were exchanged in the City of Washington, on the 5th day of May, one thousand nine hundred and ten;

NOW THEREFORE, be it known that I, William Howard Taft, President of the United States of America, have caused the said Treaty and the said understanding, as forming a part thereof, to be made public, to the end that the same and every article and clause thereof may be observed and fulfilled with good faith by the United States and the citizens thereof. In testimony whereof, I have hereunto set my hand and caused the seal of the United States to be affixed.

Done at the City of Washington this thirteenth day of May in the year of our Lord one thousand nine hundred and ten, and of the Independence of the United States of America the one hundred and thirty-fourth.

Wm. H. Taft [SEAL]

By the President:

P C Knox

Secretary of State

Protocol of Exchange

On proceeding to the exchange of the ratifications of the treaty signed at Washington on January 11, 1909, between the United States and Great Britain, relating to boundary waters and questions arising along the boundary between the United States and the Dominion of Canada, the undersigned plenipotentiaries, duly authorized thereto by their respective Governments, hereby declare that nothing in this treaty shall be construed as affecting, or changing, any existing territorial, or riparian rights in the water, or rights of the owners of lands under water, on either side of the international boundary at the rapids of St. Mary's River at Sault Ste. Marie, in the use of the waters flowing over such lands, subject to the requirements of navigation in boundary waters and of navigation canals, and without prejudice to the existing right of the United States and Canada, each to use the waters of the St. Mary's River, within its own territory; and further, that nothing in this treaty shall be construed to interfere with the drainage of wet, swamp, and overflowed lands into streams flowing into boundary waters, and also that this declaration shall be deemed to have equal force and effect as the treaty itself and to form an integral part thereto.

The exchange of ratifications then took place in the usual form.

IN WITNESS WHEREOF, they have signed the present Protocol of Exchange and have affixed their seals thereto.

DONE at Washington this 5th day of May, one thousand nine hundred and ten.

PHILANDER C KNOX [SEAL]

JAMES BRYCE [SEAL]

Summary

The treaties between Canada and the United States for the demarcation of the international boundary, and the establishment of a permanent International Boundary Commission, together with the treaties concerning the protection and management of the boundary waters, and the establishment of the International Joint Commission, have greatly contributed to the development of the cordial relationship between Canada and the United States throughout the twentieth century and into the twenty-first century. They can also serve as a model for other countries with respect to the joint management of an international border.

10.

CANADA ABROAD

Introduction

The territorial sovereignty of Canada extends over its entire land mass, atmosphere, and its internal waters, with additional varying sovereign rights applicable to its Territorial Sea, Contiguous Zone, Exclusive Economic Zone, and, potentially, its prolonged continental shelf. Beyond the limits of Canadian territorial sovereignty the Canadian state can also exercise some additional rights under general principles of international law, as well as treaty rights.

Historically, Canada has always resisted proposals that it should acquire non-contiguous sovereign territory. An anti-imperialist ethic has long permeated Canadian relations with foreign states or territories. Nevertheless, extraterritorial rights were obtained through Canada's membership in the British Empire, and by foreign treaties. In addition, historic proposals for the acquisition or control of non-contiguous territories by Canada were made on several occasions since Confederation in 1867.

Extraterritorial Treaty Rights

Under international treaties Canada has obtained several rights in respect of the territories of other countries which it would not otherwise have possessed.

The Great Lakes

Under Article 28 of the Treaty of Washington, 1871, the navigation of Lake Michigan was opened to Canadians as well as Americans, and the right conferred by that treaty was subsequently confirmed by the Boundary Waters Treaty of 1909. Under those treaty provisions Canada has obtained the right for Canadian ships to navigate on Lake Michigan which is the one great lake that lies totally within the territory of the United States. Neither the Jay Treaty of 1794 nor the Webster-Ashburton Treaty of 1842 had provided for Canadian navigation on Lake Michigan. However, the right of Canadian ships to navigate on Lake Michigan is only a conditional right that exists as long as the Boundary Waters Treaty of 1909 remains in force.[1]

The Northwest Rivers

The Treaty of Washington, 1871 provides that: "The navigation of the rivers Yukon, Porcupine, and Stikine, ascending and descending, from, to, and into the sea, shall forever remain free and open for the purposes of commerce to the subjects of her Britannic Majesty and to the citizens of the United States, subject to any laws and regulations of either country within its own territory, not inconsistent with such privilege of free navigation."
Those three rivers cross the international boundary between the Yukon and Alaska or between British Columbia and Alaska and for a considerable distance they traverse American territory. The river navigation rights have continued but they are now of little practical effect and, in the case of the Stikine River, sedimentation of the river, and a change in its course, have rendered it unsuitable for significant commercial shipping, even if a demand for shipping on the Stikine were still present.[2]

World War Memorials

After the trauma of World War One there was an important need to memorialize the sacrifice that Canadians and Newfoundlanders made in the trenches of western Europe and for that purpose the French government made land available to both dominion governments for the purpose of erecting war memorials. The most prominent of those memorials is the memorial at Vimy Ridge, the site of the most famous World War One victory by the Canadian Army. In 1922 the Federal Government entered into an agreement with the Government of France for the acquisition of land for the erection of a monument to Canadian soldiers. The agreement provides for a free gift of the land to Canada by France

Canada-France Vimy Ridge Memorial Agreement (Extracts)[3]

December 5, 1922

Whereas the Government of Canada desire to erect on Vimy Ridge (Pas-de-Calais), in the centre of a park of 100 hectares, which they intend to layout and the maintenance of which they will assume, a monument to the memory of the Canadian soldiers who died on the field of honour in France during the war 1914-1918, the French Government put at their disposal the necessary ground of which the title will remain in the French Government.

Whereas, on the other hand, France desires to associate herself in the tribute which Canada wishes to pay its dead in the great war and as, moreover, the land concerned, comprised in the red zone, is to be acquired by the French Government in conformity with the provisions of Article 46, paragraph 7, of the Act of the 17th April, 1919:

ARTICLE I

The French Government grants, freely and for all time, to the Government of Canada the free use of a parcel of 100 hectares located on Vimy Ridge in the Department of Pas-de-Calais, the boundaries of which are indicated on the plan annexed to this Agreement.

ARTICLE II

The Canadian Government pledge themselves to lay out this land

into a park and to erect thereon a monument to the memory of the Canadian soldiers who died on the field of honour in France during the war 1914-1918.

They moreover pledge themselves to provide for the maintenance of the park and monument, in default of which the French Government would resume the free use of the park, except however the land on which the memorial is to be erected.

ARTICLE III

The land granted to the Government of Canada by this Agreement will be exempt of all taxes and imposts. The French Government will take the responsibility of all difficulties with the borderers, except those arising from damages caused by the personnel or material belong to the Government of Canada and kept in France for the maintenance and protection of the park and monument.

ARTICLE IV

There shall be obligatorily mentioned on the monument all the units of the same class of the Canadian Army having fought on Vimy Ridge during the same period of time.

Importance of the Canada-France Vimy Ridge Memorial Agreement

The Vimy Ridge treaty provides for a gift of land by France to Canada for the purpose of erecting a memorial. In Canada it is sometimes said that the Vimy Memorial, standing within the Vimy Memorial Park, is erected on Canadian soil. For instance, during the ceremonies in 2008 to rededicate the memorial on its 90th anniversary the ceremonial protocol followed for the occasion provided that Queen Elizabeth II, as the Canadian head of state, would arrive after the French Prime Minister to underscore Canadian 'sovereignty' over the memorial, or so it was said by commentators at the event. However, the treaty itself does not cede any part of the sovereign territory of France to Canada.

Rather, France has made a gift of the land to Canada, and exempted Canada from fiscal and legal obligations associated with possession of the land but has not alienated French sovereignty over the land. Thus, there is no Canadian sovereignty over the memorial and the land upon which it stands remains sovereign French territory.

There are a number of other sites in France commemorating the sacrifices made during World War One. Those sites also constitute lands held as sovereign territory by France but were granted to Commonwealth governments for their "free use and enjoyment" for the purposes of erecting war memorials. The other memorials include the Newfoundland Memorial Park at Beaumont Hamel. Those other sites are the subject of a later convention between France and the Commonwealth countries with respect to title; Convention Concerning the Transfer to the French State of the Property in the Sites of British Monuments Commemorative of the war, 1914-1918, signed December 28, 1938.

Embassies and High Commissions

The sites of Canadian embassies and high commissions abroad are also sometimes claimed to be Canadian territory but that is not correct. The land upon which embassies and high commissions are erected in foreign and commonwealth countries remain the sovereign territory of the country in which the embassy or high commission is located. However, under international law, including multilateral treaties (principally the Vienna Convention on Diplomatic Relations of 1961) a large number of privileges are granted to foreign embassies such that they are exempted from the application of local laws that would interfere with their diplomatic status. The land upon which a Canadian embassy or high commission is located may not be trespassed upon by the host state nor may the host state apply its criminal laws against Canadian diplomats without the permission of Canada, as the state to whom the diplomat belongs. Canada likewise grants reciprocal rights to other countries with respect to the foreign embassies and other diplomatic posts located in Canada.

Similar, though lesser, extraterritorial rights apply to consulates and to consuls pursuant to the Vienna Convention on Consular Relations of 1963. Under that convention there is a form of consular immunity although it is not as all-embracing as diplomatic immunity. Despite that, a foreign consulate must remain inviolable, and the representatives of the host state must not trespass upon the premises of a foreign consulate.

Temporary Removal of Sovereignty

Canada provided the world with a unique example of extraterritorial rights when it temporarily divested itself of sovereignty over the maternity ward of an Ottawa hospital in 1943, and provided that the maternity ward would thus become international territory.[4] That declaration was made so that Princess Juliana of the Netherlands, a member of the Dutch Royal Family who had taken refuge in Canada following the German occupation of the Netherlands in World War Two, could give birth to a royal heir that would possess the exclusive citizenship of the Netherlands, and thus would not obtain dual citizenship.[5]

Capitulations

Capitulations are now mainly a subject of only historical interest. However, during the years of European dominance in the international community there was a strong desire by European states to enhance the legal position of their subjects and citizens in non-European states, such as the domains of the Ottoman Empire or the Manchu Empire of China. As described by one writer on the subject, the European states:

> . . . procured the insertion of provisions, usually known as capitulations, giving special protection to their subjects when trading to, or residing in, the Turkish dominions, and securing a special

status for their consuls with an extraterritorial jurisdiction in civil and even criminal matters over the subjects of their nations.[6]

These special rights involved both the application of domestic law within the territory of another state, as well as an immunity for the subjects of the state that acquired the capitulations from the laws of the territorial jurisdiction that would otherwise have applied to them. Capitulations were, and were seen to be, an affront to the sovereignty of the nations which had granted them, and were usually given under duress. Great Britain obtained a number of capitulations from foreign states and Canadians were beneficiaries of those grants in the days of the empire. By the time that Canada obtained its *de jure* independence from Great Britain with the enactment of the *Statute of Westminster, 1931,* the only states where capitulations granted to Great Britain were still applicable to Canada concerned China and Egypt. Under international law Canada succeeded to the treaties entered into by Great Britain when Canada was part of the British Empire and thus Canada inherited capitulation rights in respect of both China and Egypt.

Efforts to abolish the capitulations by Egypt and China were successful in the case of both states, in Egypt pursuant to the Montreux Convention Regarding the Abolition of the Capitulations in Egypt, signed on May 8, 1937, and in respect of China as a decision of the Allied powers during World War Two.[7] In two subsequent treaties Canada agreed to the abolition of the capitulation rights in respect of both countries that it inherited from Great Britain. Canada consented to be bound by the Convention regarding the Abolition of the Capitulations in Egypt; Protocol, by a ratification on September 8, 1938, and in the case of China by the Treaty between Canada and the Republic of China concerning the Relinquishment of Extraterritorial Rights and the Regulation of Related Matters, April 14, 1944 (in force April 5, 1945).

The Svalbard Treaty, 1920

The Svalbard islands (formerly known as the Spitsbergen islands) lie in the Arctic Ocean half the distance between the Kingdom of Norway and the North Pole. The islands were periodically used by neighbouring countries that sought to exploit the natural resources in and around the islands but no country established firm sovereignty over them. Continued exploitation in the twentieth century underscored the necessity of local administration and the disposition of the islands became an issue at the Versailles Peace Conference in 1919. Under the terms of a treaty entered into at that time concerning the sovereignty of the islands, then described as the Spitzbergen Treaty (as the islands were primarily known as the Spitzbergen Islands) but today more commonly referred to as the Svalbard Treaty (after the present name of the archipelago), the overall sovereignty of Norway over Svalbard was confirmed but made subject to a number of restrictions on Norwegian sovereignty in favour of the interests of other countries.

The subjects or citizens of the treaty signatories may establish residency in the islands without visa requirements but must obey Norwegian law. The residents from signatory states may engage in fishing, hunting, industrial, mining, and trading activities, and the Norwegian government must act in a non-discriminatory manner with respect to the application of its laws to the residents of the islands. No state can establish military or naval facilities anywhere within the archipelago.

Canada was an original signatory to the treaty (as a dominion of the British Empire). Subsequently, other states have acceded to the treaty and there are currently 46 countries that have joined in the Svalbard Treaty.

Spitzbergen (Svalbard) Treaty (Extracts)

April 7, 1920 (in force July 29, 1920)

Article 1.

The High Contracting Parties undertake to recognise, subject to the stipulations of the present Treaty, the full and absolute sovereignty of Norway over the Archipelago of Spitsbergen, comprising, with Bear Island or Beeren-Eiland, all the islands situated between 10 ° and 35 ° longitude East of Greenwich and between 74 ° and 81 ° latitude North, especially West Spitsbergen, North-East Land, Barents Island, Edge Island, Wiche Islands, Hope Island or Hopen-Eiland, and Prince Charles Foreland, together with all islands great or small and rocks appertaining thereto (see annexed map).

Article 2.

Ships and nationals of all the High Contracting Parties shall enjoy equally the rights of fishing and hunting in the territories specified in Article 1 and in their territorial waters.

Norway shall be free to maintain, take or decree suitable measures to ensure the preservation and, if necessary, the reconstitution of the fauna and flora of the said regions, and their territorial waters; it being clearly understood that these measures shall always be applicable equally to the nationals of all the High Contracting Parties without any exemption, privilege or favour whatsoever, direct or indirect to the advantage of any one of them.

Occupiers of land whose rights have been recognised in accordance with the terms of Articles 6 and 7 will enjoy the exclusive right of hunting on their own land: (1) in the neighbourhood of their habitations, houses, stores, factories and installations, constructed for the purpose of developing their property, under conditions laid down by the local police regulations; (2) within a radius of 10 kilometres around the headquarters of their place of business or works; and in both cases, subject always to the observance of regulations made by the Norwegian Government in accordance with the conditions laid down in the present Article.

Article 3.

The nationals of all the High Contracting Parties shall have equal liberty of access and entry for any reason or object whatever to the waters, fjords and ports of the territories specified in Article 1; subject to the observance of local laws and regulations, they may carry on there without impediment all maritime, industrial, mining and commercial operations on a footing of absolute equality.

They shall be admitted under the same conditions of equality to the exercice and practice of all maritime, industrial, mining or commercial enterprises both on land and in the territorial waters, and no monopoly shall be established on any account or for any enterprise whatever.

Notwithstanding any rules relating to coasting trade which may be in force in Norway, ships of the High Contracting Parties going to or coming from the territories specified in Article 1 shall have the right to put into Norwegian ports on their outward or homeward voyage for the purpose of taking on board or disembarking passengers or cargo going to or coming from the said territories, or for any other purpose.

It is agreed that in every respect and especially with regard to exports, imports and transit traffic, the nationals of all the High Contracting Parties, their ships and goods shall not be subject to any charges or restrictions whatever which are not borne by the nationals, ships or goods which enjoy in Norway the treatment of the most favoured nation; Norwegian nationals, ships or goods being for this purpose assimilated to those of the other High Contracting Parties, and not treated more favourably in any respect.

No charge or restriction shall be imposed on the exportation of any goods to the territories of any of the Contracting Powers other or more onerous than on the exportation of similar goods to the territory of any other Contracting Power (including Norway) or to any other destination.

Article 4.

All public wireless telegraphy stations established or to be established by, or with the authorisation of, the Norwegian Government within the territories referred to in Article 1 shall always be open on a footing of absolute equality to communications from ships of all flags and from nationals of the High Contracting Parties, under the conditions laid down in the Wireless Telegraphy Convention of July 5, 1912, or in the subsequent International Convention which may be concluded to replace it.

Subject to international obligations arising out of a state of war, owners of landed property shall always be at liberty to establish and use for their own purposes wireless telegraphy installations, which shall be free to communicate on private business with fixed or moving wireless stations, including those on board ships and aircraft.

Article 5.

The High Contracting Parties recognise the utility of establishing an international meteorological station in the territories specified in Article 1, the organisation of which shall form the subject of a subsequent Convention.

Conventions shall also be concluded laying down the conditions under which scientific investigations may be conducted in the said territories.

Article 6.

Subject to the provisions of the present Article, acquired rights of nationals of the High Contracting Parties shall be recognised.

Claims arising from taking possession or from occupation of land before the signature of the present Treaty shall be dealt with in accordance with the Annex hereto, which will have the same force and effect as the present Treaty.

Article 7.

With regard to methods of acquisition, enjoyment and exercise of the right of ownership of property, including mineral rights, in the territories specified in Article 1, Norway undertakes to grant to all nationals of the High Contracting Parties treatment based on complete equality and in conformity with the stipulations of the present Treaty.

Expropriation may be resorted to only on grounds of public utility and on payment of proper compensation.

Article 8.

Norway undertakes to provide for the territories specified in Article 1 mining regulations which, especially from the point of view of imposts, taxes or charges of any kind, and of general or particular labour conditions, shall exclude all privileges, monopolies or favours for the benefit of the State or of the nationals of any one of the High Contracting Parties, including Norway, and shall guarantee to the paid staff of all categories the remuneration and protection necessary for their physical, moral and intellectual welfare.

Taxes, dues and duties levied shall be devoted exclusively to the said territories and shall not exceed what is required for the object in view.

So far, particularly, as the exportation of minerals is concerned, the Norwegian Government shall have the right to levy an export duty which shall not exceed 1 % of the maximum value of the minerals exported up to 100.000 tons, and beyond that quantity the duty will be proportionately diminished. The value shall be fixed at the end of the navigation season by calculating the average free on board price obtained.

Three months before the date fixed for their coming into force, the draft mining regulations shall be communicated by the Norwegian Government to the other Contracting Powers. If during this period one or more of the said Powers propose to modify these regulations before they are applied, such proposals shall be communicated by the Norwegian Government to the other Contracting Powers in order that they may be submitted to examination and the decision of a Commission composed of one representative of each of the said Powers. This Commission shall meet at the invitation of the Norwegian Government and shall come to a decision within a period of three months from the date of its first meeting. Its decisions shall be taken by a majority.

Article 9.

Subject to the rights and duties resulting from the admission of Norway to the League of Nations, Norway undertakes not to create nor to allow the establishment of any naval base in the territories specified in Article 1 and not to construct any fortification in the said territories, which may never be used for warlike purposes.

Importance of the Svalbard Treaty

The Svalbard Treaty dealt with a unique situation in the territory of Europe. As a solution to the overlapping interests and potential sovereignty claims of various states it has proven to be a generally practicable and workable solution to a unique problem of state sovereignty. Canadians have not taken advantage of the rights accruing to Canada under the treaty and, in fact, the only two countries that currently exercise their economic rights under the treaty are Norway and Russia although a number of signatory countries have established arctic research stations within the territory.

The Antarctic Treaty, 1959

During the nineteenth and twentieth centuries a number of European and South American states laid claim to the continent of Antarctica, the only uninhabited continent on the planet. In some cases the claims made to Antarctic territory are overlapping claims, particularly those concerning the claims of Great Britain, Argentina and Chile. While the United States did not claim any part of Antarctica as sovereign territory it had strategic interests on that continent. After World War Two an effort was made, primarily by the United States, to suspend territorial claims within the continent and to maintain it as a scientific preserve open to scientific exploration by all nations. That effort resulted in the Antarctic Treaty of 1959, which suspended national claims to territory on the continent and provided for joint management of the continent by the signatories, as well as a prohibition against militarization of the continent, including the use of the continent to test nuclear weapons, or to dispose of radioactive waste.

Canada was not an original signatory to the treaty because it had no strategic interests in Antarctica, or the Southern Ocean, but in the twenty-first century the country has found it desirable to joint the Antarctic Treaty system in order to promote science and environmental stewardship. Canada therefore ratified the treaty in 1988, and it participates as a non-consultative (i.e., non-voting) state party to the treaty. As a member of the Antarctic Treaty system, Canada has the ability to undertake scientific research in Antarctica. Canada interacts with the Antarctic Treaty System primarily through the Canadian Polar Commission, which liaises with the Scientific Committee on Antarctic Research that is established under the treaty.

External Territories

Canada has never possessed any colonies or overseas territories of any description. That is unsurprising since the country possesses a vast continental empire of its own and has never had any need to acquire an overseas territory. However, there have been a few historical instances when the subject of the acquisition of foreign territory has been publicly raised.

The British Caribbean

In the nineteenth century there were some private initiatives by Canadian businessmen and Caribbean islanders to promote a link between Canada and Britain's Caribbean Sea colonies, principally Jamaica, but also extending to some of the other islands, such as Barbados. However, neither of the ministries of Sir John A. Macdonald, or Sir Wilfrid Laurier evinced any real interest in the possibility, and discussion of the subject soon faded.[8] It was revived again just before the outbreak of World War One and then more seriously during the ministry of Prime Minister Sir Robert Borden during the latter part of World War One. Ultimately, however, Borden concluded that the challenges of geography, economic sustainability, and political issues tolled against any Caribbean expansion, and the subject was dropped by the Federal Government.[9]

The Turks and Caicos Islands

In more recent times there has been speculation in the media about Canada acquiring the British Overseas Territory of the Turks and Caicos Islands, which lie south of the Bahama Islands in the Caribbean Sea. This small British colony first came to the attention of the Canadian public in the mid-1970's when a New Democratic Party Member of Parliament, Max Saltsman, brought forward a private members public bill in the House of Commons to bring about a political union between the Turks and Caicos Islands and Canada. Until then the Turks and Caicos Islands had been a somewhat neglected British colony. It was a dependency of Jamaica until the latter received its independence in 1962, and only thereafter did the Turks and Caicos Islands become a Crown colony in its own right. The population in the mid-1970's was still only six thousand people.

At the time of Saltsman's initiative the subject of a Canadian tropical paradise caught the popular imagination. Many Canadians, facing the wearying prospect of a long cold Canadian winter, could be forgiven for wishing that the country had its very own tropical paradise where the currency and the laws of Canada would apply. However, it is also fair to say that the prospect of Canada acquiring what would have amounted to a foreign colony during an era of decolonization was appalling to the Canadian diplomatic corps and government, and the subject was soon laid to rest. The External Affairs Minister, Mitchell Sharp, tabled a formal government response in Parliament rejecting the proposal on April 10, 1974.[10]

Nevertheless, the subject of political linkage between Canada and the Turks and Caicos Islands has periodically re-emerged. The acquisition of the islands was revived in the 1980's by a Progressive Conservative Member of Parliament, Dan McKenzie, but again the Federal Government demurred at the proposal. The issue was put forward once again in 2003, and then in 2014, by a Conservative Member of Parliament, Peter Goldring, but the Conservative government's Foreign Minister at the time, John Baird, refused any serious consideration of the subject.[11] Although the acquisition of the islands remains an occasional winter seasonal fantasy for the Canadian media, there is no real possibility of the suggestion ever coming to fruition. If the Turks and Caicos Islands do not wish to eventually become an independent state it is much more likely that they would enter into a union with the Bahamas, the neighbouring Commonwealth realm to the north of the Turks and Caicos, with which it shares the Lucayan Archipelago. In the meantime, tourism has helped to economically develop the Turks and Caicos Islands, which at present have a population of approximately 30,000.

Necker Island

In the late nineteenth century an effort was made by Canada to acquire one of the smaller Hawaiian Islands for use as a cable station. Necker Island is a small island lying northwest of the main Hawaiian island chain in the North Pacific and is approximately 45 acres in size. In the 1890's there was no human habitation on the treeless island and it was unclaimed territory, though it had first been discovered by the French explorer La Perouse, in 1786.

Sandford Fleming, the originator of standard time, and an inventor, surveyor, railway promoter, and leading Canadian polymath of the nineteenth century envisioned the construction of a Trans-Pacific cable to connect the antipodean British colonies to London through Canada via the existing Atlantic cable. However the vast distances of the Pacific Ocean required that re-transmitting stations be established at specific points in that ocean. Necker Island, northwest of the Kingdom of Hawaii, was a suitable location and conveniently unclaimed at the time. Although there were alternatives to Necker Island, Necker was the most cost-effective location for the location of a re-transmission station for the proposed Trans-Pacific cable.

In 1893 Fleming persuaded the Federal Government to urge the Imperial Government to secure Necker Island for the purposes of the proposed cable. However, 1893 was a difficult year in Hawaii. In January 1893, a coup d'etat by a group of Hawaiians of American descent, recent American immigrants, and a handful of Europeans, had overthrown the government of Queen Liliuokalani and seized power in the islands by constituting themselves as the Provisional Government of Hawaii for the purpose of advancing a policy of American annexation. American officials actively supported the coup and a formal American protectorate was established over the islands to allow the Provisional Government to consolidate its rule. However, after a change of government in Washington the formal protectorate was terminated in the spring of 1893, without annexation occurring. In light of these developments, the Imperial Government advised the Canadian Government on December 29, 1893 that: "The Secretary of State for Foreign Affairs will defer action, pending the establishment of the government of Hawaii upon a more permanent footing".[12] This was not good enough for Fleming however, and he continued to press for action.

The Canadian High Commissioner in London, Sir Charles Tupper, made further representations to the Foreign Secretary, Lord Rosebery, who replied that nothing should be done due to the unsettled political conditions in the islands.[13] Frustrated, Fleming consulted the Commander-in-Chief of the Imperial forces in Canada, who suggested that a mission should be despatched from Canada to lay claim to Necker Island. Fleming arranged for a retired officer of the Royal Navy, R.E.H. Gardner-Buckner to proceed to Hawaii, charter a vessel, and claim Necker Island.[14] Fleming then reported what he had done to Sir Charles Tupper in London, who reported it to the Imperial Government, to the consternation of the imperial authorities. On May 31, 1894, Fleming was advised, presumably by Sir Charles Tupper, in a cable from London that: "[Foreign Secretary Lord] Rosebery much annoyed at action. Will repudiate. Fears will destroy good prospect of obtaining Necker. Prevent action becoming public if possible".[16]

Meanwhile, in Hawaii, the Provisional Government had gotten wind of what Canada was up to from inquiries about Necker Island that it had received from the British diplomatic representative in Hawaii. The Hawaiian Provisional Government also had knowledge of a pending conference in Canada to discuss the proposed Pacific cable.[15] Gardner-Buckner, now realizing that he might be the focal point of a diplomatic incident wisely decided to drop his mission to Necker Island on May 24, 1893, and on the following day one of the two ships he had chartered for the mission to Necker Island was taken over in charter by the Hawaiian government, which then despatched it to Necker Island. Necker Island was formally claimed on May 27, 1893, for Hawaii by the representatives of the Provisional Government of that country.

Nevertheless, Canada did not entirely end its efforts to acquire Necker Island. The following year, after a colonial conference was held in Ottawa involving Great Britain, Canada, the Australian states, New Zealand, and South Africa, it was decided, in the presence of a representative of the Board of Trade for Honolulu, that a renewed effort should be made to acquire a Hawaiian island as a re-transmission site for the proposed Trans-Pacific Cable.[17] Accordingly, Canada dispatched Fleming to negotiate directly with the government of what was now the Republic of Hawaii.

Apparently, Fleming learned, the Hawaiian government was receptive to being the host for a re-transmission station but it was felt that the Hawaiian Government would be unable to obtain the assent of the United States to any alienation of Hawaiian territory, a restriction on its own sovereignty that the Republic of Hawaii had accepted in order to further its policy of seeking annexation by the United States.[18] Thus, the Canadian effort to obtain Necker Island failed, and the island remained subject to Hawaiian sovereignty. In 1898 the Republic of Hawaii was annexed by the United States. The islands became a US territory in 1900, and an American state in 1959.

However, Sandford Fleming did succeed in helping to create the Trans-Pacific Cable in 1902, although a more costly extension of the line to British-owned Fanning Island, in lieu of Necker Island, was required for the purpose of building a re-transmission station. For his many efforts on behalf of Canada and the empire, and despite his attempted end run around the British Foreign Office concerning Necker Island, Sandford Fleming was knighted by Queen Victoria in 1897.

Greenland and St. Pierre and Miquelon

The two island groups that have continued to be held by European states lying off the coasts of Canada also attracted acquisitive attention in the early years of the twentieth century. During World War One, when the Imperial Government gave some attention to post-war territorial settlements, the potential for a trade of the French islands of St. Pierre and Miquelon in return for territory in Africa was considered by the Imperial Government. Canada was eager to obtain St. Pierre and Miquelon but so, it turned out, was the dominion of Newfoundland, which was geographically much closer to the French islands. Facing competing claims from two dominions, which raised the prospect of an intra-empire conflict, the Imperial Government quietly dropped any consideration of an approach to the Government of France about the islands.[19]

Another island of concern was Greenland, lying northeast of Canada's mainland. In that case Canadian worries about the possibility of the United States acquiring Greenland were spurred by the American purchase of the Danish West Indies in 1917. Fearing that Greenland would be acquired next the Canadian Government approached Denmark through Great Britain to inquire if Canada might acquire Greenland but the Danish Government made it clear that Greenland would not be sold by Denmark.[20] Canada could at least take solace from the Danish refusal that the United States would also not acquire the island.

Wrangel Island

Wrangel Island is a high arctic island lying in the Chukchi Sea of the Arctic Ocean north of Siberia on the 180-degree meridian of longitude. (Scientists believe that it may have been the last refuge of the wooly mammoth before that species became extinct.) In the early years of the twentieth century it was uninhabited and apparently unclaimed. During the Canadian Arctic Expedition of 1913- 1916 headed by a famous Canadian explorer, Vilhjalmur Stefansson, the crew of the Canadian Government Ship *Karluk* became stranded on Wrangel Island when ice carried the ship into the Chukchi Sea and crushed it. Based on the sojourn of some of his expedition personnel on Wrangel, Stefansson thought that Canada should lay claim to the island.

When the Federal Government demurred, Stefansson created a private expedition and dispatched it to Wrangel in 1921 to take possession of Wrangel Island for Canada. Stefansson thought that Wrangel Island would be useful in the future as Arctic air routes opened up. However, the Federal Government thought differently about it, recognizing that Wrangel Island was far outside of the

Canadian Sector of the Arctic at a time when Canada was informally promoting the Sector Theory as a basis for Arctic territorial claims. Furthermore, the Imperial Russian Government had actually claimed the island in 1916, and although the Russian Empire had collapsed the following year the government of the new Union of Soviet Socialist Republics would doubtless seek to inherit the claim made by the former Imperial Government of Russia. Accordingly, Sir Joseph Pope, the Undersecretary of State for External Affairs, advised Prime Minister Arthur Meighen that Stefansson's purported claim to Wrangel Island should be disavowed, which was done.[21] Stefansson then tried unsuccessfully to persuade the US government to claim Wrangel Island. A few years later, in 1924, the Soviet Union formally claimed Wrangel Island and dispatched a warship to raise the Soviet flag. In 1926 the Soviets established effective occupation of the island.[22]

Stefansson's misjudgment concerning the purported Canadian sovereignty claim over Wrangel Island damaged Stefansson's reputation with the Federal Government and he subsequently emigrated to the United States.[23] Wrangel Island remained Soviet territory and became Russian territory following the dissolution of the USSR in 1991.

Armenia

In the final years of the Ottoman Empire the Imperial authorities in Constantinople embarked on a policy of ethnic repression that reached the point of genocide during World War One. It is estimated that 1.5 million Armenians perished in the later stages of that war as a direct result of actions taken by the Ottoman Empire. Both during and after the war there was sympathy and concern for the Armenians in Canada and in other western nations. That sympathy led to calls for the establishment of a League of Nations mandate over a newly-created nation of Armenia, to protect it, and to guide it as it stepped onto the world stage. A League mandate was not, strictly speaking, a territorial possession from the perspective of national sovereignty. As a matter of international law a League mandatory power did not obtain sovereignty over the nation entrusted to it but rather acted as a trustee in possession of the territory until the mandated territory reached a stage of development that allowed it to join the international community as an independent state.

Initially, efforts were made to obtain the assent of the United States to accept the mandate over Armenia, the borders of which were actually drawn by President Woodrow Wilson. However, there was little support for further foreign ventures on the part of the United States after World War One, and the country rejected membership in the League of Nations despite the strong support for the League by President Wilson. When the United States declined to accept the League mandate, the Allied Supreme Council looked for other countries to accept the mandate and considerable discussion about Armenia took place between the Federal Government and the Imperial Government concerning the possibility that Canada would undertake the mandate.

The Supreme Council eventually considered asking Norway, Greece, Brazil, Holland, Sweden, Spain and Canada to consider accepting a mandate for Armenia. British ministers, including Prime Minister David Lloyd George, and Lord Curzon, went so far as to put Canada forward as a potential mandatory power.[24] Canadian officials were not consulted about this however, and it soon became apparent that there was no real desire on the part of Canada, or any other state that was considered for the role, to take on the financial and military burden of a League mandate over Armenia. When the matter was raised in the House of Commons, the Acting Prime Minister, speaking on behalf of the absent Prime Minister Sir Robert Borden, declared that no formal request had been received by the Federal Government concerning a possible Canadian mandate over Armenia.[25] The Leader of the Opposition, William Lyon Mackenzie King opposed any Canadian mandate over Armenia.[26] The Federal Government also refused a subsequent League request to Canada to attempt to mediate a cease-fire between Armenian and Turkish forces.[27]

Canada never expressed any formal interest in assuming a League mandate over Armenia and formally dismissed the suggestion in September 1922.[28] The Armenian state created by the Allied powers after World War One, and whose borders were drawn by President Wilson, was subsequently carved up between Turkey and the USSR and its independence was stillborn. However, an Armenian state subsequently emerged following the dissolution of the USSR in 1991.

Summary

Canada successfully avoided the extra-territorial entanglements that engaged most major nations in the late nineteenth and early twentieth centuries, including many of its Commonwealth partners. Where Canada did inherit extra-territorial rights from Great Britain, such as the capitulations, it subsequently surrendered all such rights.

Canada has benefited in its international relations from its lack of foreign possessions because it has avoided being perceived as an imperialist state in international diplomacy. Today, despite the occasional newspaper editorial decrying the lack of a truly Canadian tropical resort refuge, there is no appetite amongst the government, nor amongst the Canadian people, for any extension of Canadian territorial sovereignty abroad.

ENDNOTES

[1] Piper, *International Law of the Great Lakes*, p. 51.

[2] See *Navigability of Stikine River, Southeast Alaska, Draft*, US Bureau of Land Management, n.d., Anchorage (Alaska), [https://www.blm.gov/sites/blm.gov/files/uploads/

LandsRealty_Alaksa_RDI_StikineRiver_drftnavrpt_08-20-2007.p df] (accessed May 16, 2018)

[3] Translation

[4] Alastair Bonnet, *Unruly Places; Lost Spaces, Secret Cities and Other Inscrutable Geographies*, Viking, Toronto, 2014, , p. 129

[5] *Proclamation, Canada Gazette Part 1*, vol. LXXVI, No. 232, December 26, 1942: "That any place within Canada within which Her Royal Highness the Princess Juliana of the Netherlands may be confined shall, for the period of the lying-in and to the extent of actual occupation for such purpose, be extraterritorial, and for such purpose Her Royal Highness the Princess Juliana and any child that may be born shall be accorded immunity from criminal, civil and military jurisdiction, whether Dominion or Provincial."

[6] Phillimore, *Three Centuries of Peace Treaties*, p. 73

[7] British capitulations in China were terminated pursuant to the *Treaty Between His Majesty in Respect of the United Kingdom and India and His Excellency the President of the National Government of the Republic of China for the Relinquishment of Extra-Territorial Rights in China and the Regulation of Related Matters*, January 11, 1943.

[8] Brian Douglas Tennyson ed., *Canada and the Commonwealth Carribean*, University Press of America, Lanham (Maryland), 1988, p. 14

[9] Ibid, p. 15

[10] Ibid, p. 206

[11] "Baird says no to annexing Turks and Caicos as new province or territory", *Globe and Mail*, Toronto, May 26, 2014

[12] Quoted in John S Ewart, *The Kingdom of Canada, Imperial Federation, The Colonial Conferences, The Alaska Boundary and Other Essays*, Toronto, Morang & Co. 1908, p. 283.

[13] Ibid, 284

[14] David Raymont, "Aloha Canada", in *The Beaver*, Canada's National History Society, Winnipeg (Manitoba) June-July 2003, Vol. 83:3, p. 40

[15] Ibid, p. 42

[16] Ewart, p. 285

[17] Raymont, p. 43

[18] Raymont, p. 43; Ewart, p. 285

[19] P.G. Wigley, "Canada and Imperialism: West Indian Aspirations and the First World War", in Tennyson, *Canada and the Commonwealth Caribbean*, p. 220.

[20] P.G. Wigley, Ibid, p. 221. The United States did attempt to purchase Greenland twice. Once by Secretary of State William Seward in the aftermath of the US Civil War which foundered due to a botched process to acquire the Danish West Indies (later acquired by the US in 1917) and once again in 1946, when the Danes again declined to part with the island.

[21] Grant, p. 219

[22] Grant, p. 223

[23] Grant, p. 224.

[24] Aram Adjemian, *Canada's Moral Mandate for Armenia:*

Sparking Humanitarian and Political Interest, 1880-1923, Masters Thesis, Concordia University, Montreal, 2007, pp. 69-70.

[25] Ibid, p. 72.

[26] Ralph Allen, *Ordeal By Fire*, Canada 1910-1945, Doubleday Canada Limited, Toronto, 1961, p. 241.

[27] Adjemian, p. 81.

[28] Adjemian, p. 88.

SELECT BIBLIOGRAPHY

BOOKS

Ralph Allen, *Ordeal by Fire; Canada 1910-1945*, Doubleday Canada, Toronto, 1961

Pierre Berton, *Klondike*, McClelland and Stewart, Toronto, 1972

Pierre Berton, *The National Dream: The Great Railway 1871-1881*, McClelland and Stewart, Toronto, 1974

Alastair Bonnet, *Unruly Places; Lost Spaces, Secret Cities and Other Inscrutable Geographies*, Viking, Toronto, 2014

Craig Brown, ed. *The Illustrated History of Canada*, Lester and Orpen Dennys, Toronto, 1987

Victor Bulmer-Thomas, *Empire in Retreat; The Past, Present, and Future of the United States*, Yale University Press, New Haven (Conn.), 2018

Michael Byers, *Who Owns the Arctic?; Understanding Sovereignty Disputes in the North*, Douglas & McIntyre, Vancouver, 2009

Michael Byers (with James Baker), *International Law and the Arctic*, Cambridge University Press, Cambridge (UK) 2013

Francis M Caroll, *A Good and Wise Measure, The Search for the Canadian-American boundary, 1783-1842*, University of Toronto Press, Toronto, 2001

Ken Coates, P Whitney Lackenbauer, William R. Morrison and Greg Poelzer, *Arctic Front; Defending Canada in the Far North*, Thomas Allen, Toronto, 2008

Frances Gardiner Davenport, ed., *European Treaties Bearing on the History of the United States and Its Dependencies to 1648*, Carnegie, Washington, 1817

Bailey W. Diffie and George D. Winius, *Foundations of the Portuguese Empire, 1415-1580*, University of Minnesota Press, 1978

Charles Emmerson, *The Future History of the Arctic*, Public Affairs, New York, 2010

John S Ewart, *The Kingdom of Canada, Imperial Federation, The Colonial Conferences, The Alaska Boundary and Other Essays*, Toronto, Morang & Co. 1908

William C. Gilmore, *Newfoundland and Dominion Status; The External Affairs Competence and International Law Status of Newfoundland, 1855-1934*, Carswell, Toronto, 1988

Barry Gough, *Fortune's A River: The Collision of Empires in Northwest America*, Harbour Publications, Madeira Park (British Columbia), 2007

Shelagh D. Grant, *Polar Imperative; A History of Arctic Sovereignty in North America*, Douglas & McIntyre, Vancouver, 2010

Amy S. Greenberg, *Manifest Destiny and American Territorial Expansion; A Brief History with Documents*, Bedford/St. Martins, Boston, 2012

Norman Hill, *Claims to Territory in International Law and Relations*, Oxford University Press, New York, 1945

Charles Jenkinson, Earl of Liverpool, *A Collection of All the Treaties of Peace, Alliance, and Commerce, Between Great Britain and Other Powers*, London, Debrett, 1772

D.G.G. Kerr, *A Historical Atlas of Canada*, Thomas Nelson & Sons, Don Mills (Ont.) 1966

Richard Kluger, *Seizing Destiny: How America Grew from Sea to Shining Sea*, Alfred A. Knopf, New York, 2007

T. J. Lawrence, *The Principles of International Law*, D.C. Heath, Boston, 1910

Lord Lloyd of Hampstead, *Introduction to Jurisprudence, 3rd ed.*, Stevens and Sons, London, 1972

Walter A McDougall, *Let the Sea Make a Noise, A History of the North Pacific from Magellan to MacArthur*, Harper Collins (Basic Books) New York, 1993

Peter W. Noonan, *Peace on the Lakes, Canada and the Rush-Bagot Agreement*, Magistralis, Ottawa, 2016

Sir Walter George Frank Phillimore, *Three Centuries of Treaties of Peace, and their Teaching*, John Murray, London, 1917

Don Courtney Piper, *The International Law of the Great Lakes, A Study of Canadian-United States Co-operation*, Duke University Press, Durham (N.C.), 1967

Richard Sale & Eugene Potapov, *The Scramble for the Arctic; Ownership, Exploitation and Conflict in the Far North*, Frances Lincoln, London, 2010

Admiral (ret.) James Stavridis, *Sea Power, The History and Geoplitics of the World's Oceans*, Penguin Press, New York, 2017

Reginald C. Stuart, *United States Expansionism and British North America, 1775-1871*, University of North Carolina Press, Chapel Hill, 1988

Brian Douglas Tennyson ed., *Canada and the Commonwealth Caribbean*, University Press of America, Lanham (Maryland), 1988

GOVERNMENT TREATY SERIES

Canada Treaty Series, Department of Global Affairs Canada, Ottawa, Canada

UK Treaties Online, Foreign and Commonwealth Office, London, England

United States Treaties and International Agreements: 1776-1949, Library of Congress, Washington DC

NEWSPAPERS AND MAGAZINES

"Baird says no to annexing Turks and Caicos as new province or territory", *Globe and Mail*, Toronto, May 26, 2014

David Raymont, "Aloha Canada" in *The Beaver Magazine*, June/July, 2003, Canada's National History Society, Winnipeg (Man.) 2003.

GENERAL REFERENCES

Canada Gazette Part 1, vol. LXXVI, No. 232, December 26, 1942

The Canadian Encyclopaedia, http://www.thecanadianencyclopedia.ca/en

WikiSource https://en.wikisource.org/wiki/Main_Page

The Avalon Project, Documents in Law, History and Diplomacy, Lillian Goldman Law Library, Yale University, New Haven (Conn.)

ARTICLES AND PAPERS

John Adams, *First Annual Message of John Adams,* Philadelphia, November 22, 1797, from the Avalon Project, Yale University

Aram Adjemian, *Canada's Moral Mandate for Armenia: Sparking Humanitarian and Political Interest, 1880-1923,* Masters Thesis, Concordia University, Montreal, 2007

Samuel Edward Dawson, *The Lines of Demarcation of Pope Alexander VI and the Treaty of Tordesillas A.D. 1493 and 1494,* in From the Transactions of the Royal Society of Canada, Second Series – 1899-1900, Vol. V, Section II, page 465

William Cullen Dennis, *Compromise–The Great Defect of Arbitration,* Columbia Law Review, Vol. 11, No. 6 (Jun., 1911), p. 493

J.K. Hiller, *The French Treaty Shore,* Heritage Newfoundland and Labrador, (http://www.heritage.nf.ca/articles/exploration/french-shore.php) (Accessed April 27, 2018)

James C Kraska, *The Law of the Sea Convention and the Northwest Passage* in *Defence Requirements for Canada's Arctic,* Vimy Paper 2007, Brian MacDonald, ed., The Conference of Defence Associations Institute, Ottawa, 2007, pp. 36

Michael F. Scheuer, *From the St. Lawrence to Lake Superior: The Anglo-American Joint Commission of 1816-1822 and the Charting of the Canadian – American Boundary,* Masters Thesis, Carleton University, 1982

US Bureau of Land Management, *Navigability of Stikine River, Southeast Alaska, Draft,* n.d., Anchorage (Alaska), [https://www.blm.gov/sites/blm.gov/files/uploads/LandsRealty_Alaksa_RDI_StikineRiver_drftnavrpt_08-20-2007.pdf] (accessed May 16, 2018)

George Washington, *Eighth Annual Message of George Washington*, Philadelphia, December 7, 1796, from the Avalon Project, Yale University

ABOUT THE AUTHOR

Peter William Noonan was born in Windsor, Ontario, and attended Marlborough Public School, Belle River District High School, Wilfrid Laurier University, and the University of Windsor, graduating with degrees in history and in law. Afterwards, he joined the Public Service of Canada where he practiced public law before his retirement from the Government of Canada. He was a sessional instructor in law at the University of Calgary and he occasionally lectured and coached students in the dispute resolution program at the University of Ottawa. He has previously written on the subjects of Canadian constitutional law, and on the Rush-Bagot Agreement.

www.ingramcontent.com/pod-product-compliance
Lightning Source LLC
Chambersburg PA
CBHW031532260326
41914CB00026B/1663